Black Sash

To

"Hasher" Seth

from " Sasher"

Elinor

x-mas 93

BLACK SASH

The Beginning of a Bridge in South Africa

KATHRYN SPINK

With a Foreword by
ARCHBISHOP DESMOND TUTU

Methuen

First published in Great Britain 1991
by Methuen London
Michelin House, 81 Fulham Road, London SW3 6RB

Copyright © 1991

A CIP catalogue record for this book
is available from the British Library

ISBN 0 413 62380 7

Printed in Great Britain
by St Edmundsbury Press, Bury St Edmunds, Suffolk

Contents

List of illustrations   vii
Acknowledgements   ix
Foreword   xi
Preface   xiii
Map of South Africa   xv

Chapter One *Walking briefly in a troubled land*   1
Chapter Two *Warriors for justice*   24
Chapter Three *The right to move freely*   50
Chapter Four *New home – old story*   81
Chapter Five *'Voluntary removals'*   103
Chapter Six *A watchdog not a lapdog*   129
Chapter Seven *Mothers of the struggle*   161
Chapter Eight *The violence debate*   186
Chapter Nine *Alignment*   209
Chapter Ten *Women organise*   241
Chapter Eleven *Striking a rock*   260
Chapter Twelve *Where to now?*   292

Appendix 1 *The Freedom Charter*   319
Appendix 2 *The Iceberg Principle*   323
Appendix 3 *Glossary*   324
Index   325

Illustrations

1a Protesting against the Senate Bill, 28–9 June 1955.
1b A vigil in Bloemfontein, November 1955.
2a An early haunting.
2b The East London convoy joining the great protest trek to Cape Town, February 1956.
3a In mourning for the Constitution, February 1956.
3b Protesting against the General Law Amendment Bill, 1964.
4a A Black Sash advice office.
4b Waiting for advice.
5a Sheena Duncan helping with a pass-book problem.
5b A Black Sash member with women in the Driefontein community.
6a Noël Robb.
6b Damage caused to the Port Elizabeth advice office, October 1989.
7a Jean Sinclair.
7b Protesting against the death sentence imposed on the Sharpeville Six.
8a A march by Crossroads residents.
8b Black Sash members sit in a 'shack'.
8c The vigil held at Mogopa, November 1983.
9a A former Mogopa resident in Bethanie, March 1984.
9b A Black Sash member with a woman from Mathopiestad.
10a Molly Blackburn at a funeral in the Eastern Cape, July 1985.
10b The funeral of Molly Blackburn, January 1986.
11a Black Sash delegates with Oliver Tambo in Lusaka, June 1989.
11b Mary Burton and Di Bishop.
12a Illegal multiple stand, Cape Town, August 1989.
12b A Black Sash stand in Cape Town, February 1990.

The photographs in this book are reproduced by kind permission of the following:

The Star, Johannesburg: 1a; Historical Papers, William Cullen Library, University of Witwatersrand, Johannesburg: 1b, 2a, 2b; Black Sash Archives: 3a, 6a, 6b, 7b, 8a, 12b; Popperfoto: 3b, 10a. Orde Eliason/LINK ©: 4a, 5a; Afrapix: 4b, 5b, 7a, 8b, 8c, 9a, 9b, 11b, 12a; Colin Urquhart: 10b; *Urye Weekblad* (Elsabe Wessels): 11a.

Acknowledgements

First and foremost I would like to express my particular thanks to Cherry Fisher, without whose encouragement, research and great love for South Africa this book would never have been completed. A special debt of gratitude is also acknowledged to Mary Burton, who took a stranger very much on trust and gave of her time to answer questions and read the manuscript, and to Rosemary Meny-Gibert, whose kindness and assistance in locating sources of information has been invaluable.

A sincere thank you also to the South African Police, especially to General Herman Stadler, General Nolly Hulme, Colonel Stefan Grobler and Steve Russell Brett; and to the International Police Association, in particular to Brigadier Gijsbers, for all the hospitality and help received.

In Johannesburg, I would further like to thank Andrew and Kathy Duncan, and Steve and Margaret Chart. To Jill Wentzel of the South African Institute of Race Relations and to Joe Seremane of the South African Council of Churches I am also greatly indebted. A word of appreciation, too, for the staff of the William Cullen Library at the University of the Witwatersrand for the access they provided to the Black Sash archives. To Aninka Claassens, Sheena Duncan, Joyce Harris and Judith Hawarden, who made themselves available for interview, I am also very grateful.

In Durban, a special thank you is due to Archbishop Denis Hurley, who gave so readily of his time and his extensive experience. To Wendy Annecke, Zilla and 'Scotty' Harries Baird and Jill Nicholson, also my warmest gratitude.

I am especially grateful to Sharlene Crage and Marietjie Myburgh in East London, and to Sue Power who so generously introduced me to the area, its people and its problems. Thank you also to Leo Mtatsi of the Kwelerha Residents Association and to Vuyani Qwati of Detainees Support.

My gratitude is also due to Rosemary Van Wyk Smith, Bronwyn

Brady, Betty Davenport and Priscilla Hall for making my brief visit to Grahamstown a rich and interesting one.

Similar thanks are due to Judy Chalmers, Janet Cherry, Isobel Douglas Jones and Mr Mackay in Port Elizabeth, and to the people of Cradock, especially Gertrude Adams, Alex Goniwe, Dorris Magraza, Arthur Thulani Mzila, Julius Ngesi and Gille Skweyiya, whose spirit remains an inspiration.

I am particularly indebted to Archbishop Desmond Tutu, who found the space amongst other more pressing commitments to share his insights and to give encouragement. Among others in Cape Town, I am also greatly indebted to Di Bishop, Ros Bush, Muriel Crewe, Wendy Douglas, Joan Grover, Tish Haynes, Sue Joynt, Annemarie Hendrikz, Mary Livingstone, Candy Malherbe, Sue van de Merwe, Margaret Nash, Sue Philcox, Noël Robb, Janet Small, Jenny De Tolly and Helen Zille, who in many and various ways gave of their experience, their knowledge and their practical help. To Beva and Dunstan Runciman, my special thanks for the warmth of their welcome and the scope of the information they provided.

I would also like to express my appreciation to David Viti and Nomaphlubi Nabe, to the staff of the South African Institute of Race Relations in Cape Town, to Barbara Versfeld of Dependents' Conference, to Amy Thornton of the Cape Democrats, to Jane Raphaely of *Cosmo* magazine, and to Lettie Malindi. I am additionally grateful to the staff of the African Studies Department at the University of Cape Town for the use of the Black Sash records there.

My thanks to Ann King Hall who opened many doors; to Pauline Clough and Pat Atkinson, who provided documentation; to Miranda Thompson, who, in her Sunbury nursing home, shared the memories of her early Black Sash membership; to Linda Birkovitz for her knowledge of East London and her reading of the manuscript; to Ray and Diane Sutton, who facilitated the task of relaying and checking information; and to Eleanor Lewin of the South African Research Trust, whose 'addresses' stimulated a different vision.

I would further like to express my thanks to the many others whose reports, speeches and articles provided a wealth of information, and to the substantial number of contributors to this book who remain unnamed. They will know who they are and their collaboration has been deeply appreciated. Last but by no means least, my heartfelt thanks go to my friend Lex Alport, who tolerated my comings and goings in Cape Town with such generosity of heart, to my mother for her work on the manuscript and to my husband who was a companion for much of my journey.

Foreword

Our country, South Africa, is truly remarkable. It is a country filled to the brim with paradox. This is not only the usual kind of paradox of extraordinary affluence existing cheek by jowl with abject poverty; and there is a great deal of that ghastly contrast, as for instance exemplified by Alexandra Township to the north of Johannesburg – a black township which has known deprivation and squalor of the worst type, although now there is amelioration as new housing goes up, electric lights illuminate what for long used to be known in the black community as the Dark City, and waterborne sewage is replacing the primitive bucket system to remove night soil, the buckets full of human waste which used to line the streets even during the daytime. The Alexandra Township ghetto is just a stone's throw away from Sandton, the most affluent of Johannesburg's rich white suburbs.

It is not just that sort of paradox we see in South Africa, nor paradoxes such as a country which has been a net exporter of food tolerating thousands of its children suffering and dying from malnutrition, kwashiorkor and other easily preventable deficiency diseases. Nor is it the even more bizarre paradox of a country which has led the world in pioneering sophisticated medical technology, as in the matter of heart transplantation, still having to deal with outbreaks of cholera just because politics made it impossible to provide many black rural communities with something cheap and easily procurable, a supply of clean water. Nor is it that of a country that boasts over fifteen education departments and yet is facing the most serious education crisis in our history,

a time-bomb in a highly volatile situation, when one department closes teacher-training colleges because there are too
many white teachers and too few white pupils, when there is
a desperate shortage in black schools of competent and
adequately trained teachers.

It is not one of these and many more that I could adduce.
No, the paradox in South Africa is that after all these years of
white racism, oppression and injustice there is hardly any
anti-white feeling.

To illustrate my thesis I am going to refer to funerals, not
because I am morbid, but because what have come to be
called political funerals have become an important social
phenomenon in modern-day South Africa, as they have provided platforms for the expression of viewpoints and feelings
that had few other outlets. This was the case in the pre-
F. W. De Klerk days.

At a massive funeral in Cradock for Matthew Goniwe and
his comrades, whose car was found mysteriously burned out
(most people believed that the 'system' was responsible for
this nefarious act), the predominantly black mourners carried
Dr Allan Boesak shoulder-high after one of his typically
rousing addresses. That was to be expected and it was not
surprising. What was certainly very surprising, given the
anger in the black community at yet another example of the
evil of apartheid perpetrated by whites against blacks, was
that they lifted shoulder-high another cleric – this time a
white man and at that an Afrikaner, Beyers Naude. Our
people were saying by this act that we were not anti-white.
We were anti-injustice, anti-oppression, anti-apartheid.

Any white person who showed that he or she was equally
committed to our struggle against these evils was honoured
as an upright person. Equally, if a black person was thought
to be a collaborator with the system he was rejected and often
paid the horrible price, which we roundly condemned, of
being 'necklaced' or otherwise executed.

I attended a funeral in Uitenhage where over twenty people
were killed by the police during a peaceful demonstration on
21 March 1985 – a horrendous commemoration of Sharpeville,

on 21 March 1960, when peaceful anti-pass law demon-
strators were killed. I was sitting on the platform next to
Allan Boesak. There were two young women sitting on the
grass in front of the rows of coffins. They were hugging each
other. I said to Allan, 'That is the South Africa we are
preparing for.' One was black and the other white. The
women were out of earshot, but it was as if they could hear
me, for they hugged each other even more tightly. And among
that funeral crowd of nearly 100,000 people, tense and angry,
there was a young white couple. It might have been foolhardy
for whites to come at all, but this couple had gone one step
further. They had brought their two children with them.
Nothing could have been crazier. The older of the two
children could not have been more than four years old. This
was a tightly packed audience, but when the couple wanted
to move to another part of the stadium the crowd opened a
way through for them, almost as if it were Moses parting the
Red Sea, and as they passed people smiled and patted and
touched the children. What an extraordinary sight; what a
country!

When a white doctor who had been working with black
trade unions died in detention as mysteriously as others
before him, thousands turned out for his funeral in St Mary's
Cathedral in Johannesburg. Young black radical activists gave
this white man, Neil Aggett, a hero's funeral such as very
few blacks will have – because what was important about
him was not that he was white, but that he was a person who
recognised others as human beings and treated them as
persons. The same happened when Molly Blackburn was
buried.

I have no doubt that the relative lack of anti-white feeling
has been due in part to the work of the remarkable women
who are the heroines of Kathryn Spink's balanced and well-
written account. Starting with their outrage at the rape of the
Constitution by a race-obsessed Nationalist government,
they have carried out a sterling job of work in a network of
advice offices dotted all over the Republic of South Africa.
Helping many distressed blacks, who were the harassed,
confused and perplexed victims of a plethora of laws and

regulations applying only to blacks in the urban areas, these women demonstrated that they cared. Blacks realised then that not all whites were the same.

The Black Sash were vigilant in watching out for erosions of already minimal black rights. They protested and demonstrated against forced population removals; they collated information about a whole range of subjects relating to justice, apartheid and oppression and helped our opposition to be just that bit sharper for being buttressed with the right facts. They helped to look after the ever-growing number of dependants of political prisoners. Most of these splendid women performed what was a thankless task, running the gauntlet of taunts, assaults and worse; they did this, most of them, voluntarily. They were and are truly remarkable, for in a sense they need not have done it.

But our country would be in a worse situation had it not been for the outstanding work of these women. Kathryn Spink has done us a great service, for hers is not a hagiography. She has tried to be objective. I want to salute the Black Sash. Whatever your motives, you have served our country well and your names must appear on a roll of honour when our country's real history is written.

Archbishop Desmond Tutu
February 1991

Preface

It was a newspaper article relating to the death of one of the most celebrated members of the Black Sash which in 1985 first drew my attention to the existence of a human rights organisation seeking by peaceful means to promote justice in South Africa. Drawn by the vision which the report of 20,000 blacks attending the funeral of a white woman in Port Elizabeth offered of the relationship which could and sometimes manifestly already did exist between the different race groups, I went first to Cape Town in October 1988. This book is based upon research undertaken and interviews conducted during that visit, during a subsequent period spent in the Transvaal, Natal and Cape Province in 1989, and on information gathered in England over the last three years.

As a writer whose previous books had dealt largely with the lives of some of the great spiritual leaders of our time and the special relationship they have to the poor, my concern for the plight of the suffering and underprivileged was a long-standing one. As a former police officer, I was not unsympathetic to the overriding requirements made of the law-enforcement agencies to maintain public order or to such considerations as the almost intolerable degree of responsibility imposed on individual police officers in situations of potential conflict. I went to South Africa with no particular political axe to grind. Indeed, I hope that I was guilty of the kind of openness sadly frequently dismissed as political naivety: the readiness to listen to people of all colours, creeds, castes and political convictions.

Much has already changed in South Africa since the months I spent there. 1990 was a year in which political events in South Africa unfolded at an unprecedentedly rapid rate. With the unbanning of the major liberation movements, the release of political prisoners and their leaders from jail and the lifting of the State of Emergency, some aspects of the political process in South Africa were normalised. 1991 should see the removal of three great pillars of apartheid – the Group Areas Act, the Land Act and the Population Registration Act. This will effectively purge the South African statute book of discriminatory and segregationist laws. At the same time F. W. De Klerk's 'new era' has been marked by the spread of violence to many parts of the country.

For many organisations to the left of the government this has been a difficult period, as some roles which they had previously assumed have been rightly taken over by the now unbanned groupings. For the Black Sash, which was enjoined during the period of most rigid repression and the State of Emergency to use its 'space' as a legal organisation on behalf of others whose voices had been silenced, some roles have fallen away. It has been called upon to reassess its identity and activity in the light of a changed and still changing political environment, and perhaps even to question its own relevance.

The quest for human rights, however, is an eternal one. The emphases and focuses of the Black Sash as a service and political organisation committed to working for human rights may change, as they have already changed since its foundation in 1955, but it is doubtful whether the need for such an organisation will ever be entirely eliminated. Indeed, the requirement to shape a new and just South Africa in which human rights are established and maintained poses a particular challenge. From the history of the Black Sash as recorded in the pages that follow the reader may judge how well equipped it is to rise to that challenge.

Kathryn Spink
February 1991

South Africa

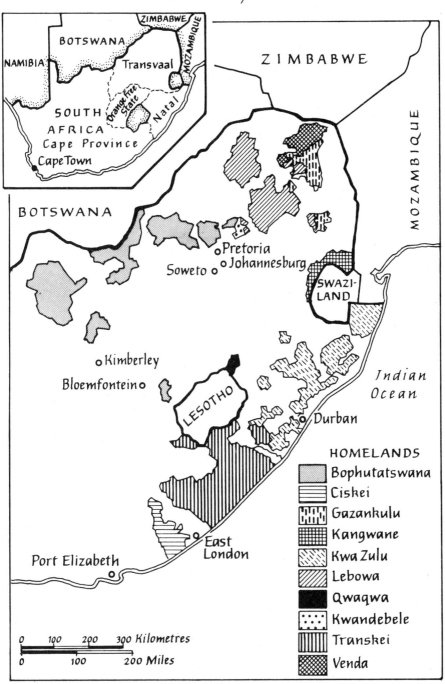

ZIMBABWE
BOTSWANA
NAMIBIA
Transvaal
MOZAMBIQUE
SOUTH
AFRICA
Cape Province
Orange Free State
Natal
Cape Town

ZIMBABWE

MOZAMBIQUE

BOTSWANA

Pretoria
Johannesburg
Soweto

SWAZI-
LAND

Kimberley

Bloemfontein

LESOTHO

Indian
Ocean

Durban

Port Elizabeth

East
London

HOMELANDS
Bophutatswana
Ciskei
Gazankulu
Kangwane
Kwa Zulu
Lebowa
Qwaqwa
Kwandebele
Transkei
Venda

0 100 200 300 Kilometres
0   100   200 Miles

Chapter One

Walking briefly in a troubled land

'Lady, lady, can you tell me how I can avoid becoming political?' His name was Wilfred Tshegane. He lived in the black township of Guguletu outside Cape Town with his widowed aunt, who brewed large paraffin drums of beer into which he had obviously been dipping. His eyes were red with rough alcohol and the hopeless emotion of a thousand others of his kind. He had been in and out of prison since the age of twelve on various convictions of theft. 'But a thief is not me, lady. I steal to live.' Some fifteen years previously his father had left his mother in the Transkei and made his way to Cape Town to find work. For a while the letters and the money had come regularly to their home village but then, quite suddenly, they had stopped. After several months had elapsed his mother left his two younger sisters with his grandmother and set off with Wilfred for the city in search of her man. She never found him. Instead she died of tuberculosis and Wilfred was taken in by an aunt who made her living brewing beer.

He had no official employment until a taxi service, the product of a recent black enterprise initiative, was set up in the form of a fleet of combination vehicles (minibuses) to transport the township residents to the city of Cape Town. Then he found work in one of those 'combis', collecting the fares and sliding open the doors and relaying passengers' requests to the driver to stop. Now, however, another fleet of taxis was contesting the right of his 'combi' to wait at the spot in Guguletu where for months it had been collecting its passengers. The rival taxis were undercutting the already minimal fare. The man who owned them was powerful in

Guguletu. Three of his employees had come to Wilfred's
aunt's two-roomed house one night and told him that he had
a choice, but he had known that there was more at stake
then the choice between working for different taxi companies, that he must decide between different political factions, and that really there was no choice. Now, in his mid-
twenties, he was once again without means of earning a
living. 'Can you tell me, lady,' came the disconcertingly
repeated appeal for advice, 'how to stay out of politics?'

Wilfred Tshegane had chosen to unburden himself of his
story to a total stranger invested in his eyes, it seemed, with
a certain authority and capacity to resolve problems simply
by virtue of the whiteness of my skin. It was during my first
visit to South Africa in October 1988. Our chance encounter
had occurred a few yards from the modest single-storey
building which the Black Sash advice office shared with the
South African Institute of Race Relations. It nestled in a
shabby corner of the white suburb of Mowbray, convenient
for the railway station, the bus terminus and a gathering
point for the abundance of 'black' taxis used, at least in
relatively liberal Cape Town, by people of all colours, and
more popularly known as 'Zola Budds' because of the break-
neck speed with which they negotiated their way through
the unpredictable South African traffic. I knew little then
other than what I had discovered through the British media
of the struggle for power in the black townships, of 'cooperation', coercion, boycott and the constant call in South Africa
to 'take a political stand', but I was beginning to discover the
enormous reality of suffering which lay beyond the South
African media reports of rhinoceros-horn smuggling, wild-life
preservation, Springbok rugby and Mother Teresa's visit.

I had spent several hours in the advice office run by the
Black Sash to which I referred Wilfred Tshegane with a
confused mixture of guilt, compassion and relief. To that
same advice office there flowed each weekday a steady trickle
of, for the most part, black people from all over Cape Town
and its townships to queue for long hours, sometimes with
extraordinary good humour, sometimes in mute sorrow, for

advice and assistance through the Kafkaesque web of regulations that enmeshed virtually every aspect of their lives. There I had sat in on a succession of interviews, patiently conducted beneath posters proclaiming that this was an apartheid-free zone, wishing Nelson Mandela a happy birthday and asserting with Gandhi that: 'Non-violence is the most active force in the world. It is a tool not for cowards but for the strongest and the bravest.'

There were people in those queues showing signs of mental illness, people who had never before owned property needing help with the pitfalls of purchasing houses, people who had agreed to pay a monthly bond repayment based on the joint income of husband and wife and who had found their house unexpectedly repossessed by the bond-holder when one of the earners lost his or her job. A woman had come to the advice office needing maintenance for her three children. Hers had been a tribal-custom marriage and her application did not fall within the jurisdiction of the established courts. There had been problems with the inefficient and sometimes obstructive bureaucracy responsible for administering old-age pensions and disability grants, and there had been a succession of queries relating to labour issues, many of them involving unfair dismissal or exploitation in some form. Some were referred to advice offices elsewhere; some were dealt with in Mowbray. Often such cases, it was explained, were the result of misunderstandings between employer and employee and were resolved when a Black Sash intermediary took the time to listen and facilitate communication.

For thirty-four years Noël Robb had been listening and advising and interceding. The wife of a highly respected pillar of Cape Town's business community, she had first come to South Africa from England to teach science and mathematics. Long years of voluntary service to the Black Sash, however, had turned her into an expert on African law as it relates to the everyday lives of the most vulnerable. Unsentimental but resolute when the opportunity arose to rectify an injustice, at seventy-four she listened still with infinite patience as a Xhosa interpreter slowly unravelled the distress stories of otherwise resourceless people. Laboriously the relevant details – name, date of birth (approximate, if known at all), marital status, number of children, etc. – were established. 'It can be very boring taking all these details, but I can't tell you how often it comes in useful.' It took just under an hour for the salient facts of the dismissal of a domestic servant without notice or payment in lieu of notice to emerge. 'It's hopeless,' Mrs Robb confided. 'If they work for a firm then we can send them to Manpower with a letter explaining their grievance, but there's no proper legislation governing the working arrangements of domestic servants.' Nevertheless she picked up the telephone and spoke persuasively to the woman's former employer; on this occasion to no avail. The Indian lady in question had failed to respond to Mrs Robb's polite enquiry from the Black Sash office as to whether she realised that if she dismissed someone she was supposed to give either a week's notice or a week's pay.

The advice office in Mowbray, one of eight Black Sash offices currently providing a para-legal service run by lay people, was actually coordinated by the wife of a Democratic Party MP, who as a paid employee was one of a more recent school of Black Sash members. A gulf of years and approach separated these two women and yet they, like the other dozen volunteers who gave what time they could during the week, were bound by a shared commitment to an organisation founded in 1955 which was, according to its constitution, non-party-political and interdenominational, and which sought by non-violent and peaceful means to 'promote justice and the principles of parliamentary democracy in South Africa'. As Black Sash members, they were also committed to seeking 'constitutional recognition and protection by law of human rights and liberties for all', to promoting 'the political education and enlightenment of South African citizens and others' and to 'undertaking whatever other activities may further the objectives of the organisation'. They were bound also, as I would subsequently discover, by the fact that, white and socially and educationally privileged as they for the most part were, they too, albeit from a very different perspective, had asked themselves the question which so preoccupied Wilfred Tshegane.

For many of them there had come a point where they could no longer accept the existing and often unquestioned conditions and parameters of white lives, the lack of access to information, the political inertia of the English-speaking community in general and the toothlessness of the widely accepted female role in South African society. There had come a point where they could no longer not respond to a sense of heightened tension and consciousness about political issues in South Africa.

There is an Afrikaans expression which maintains that *die gewente maak die gewoonte* – habit becomes second nature. The first habit instilled in South African childhood is, arguably, that of not asking questions. It is a criticism frequently laid at the door of Afrikaners raised upon a political and religious vision of separate racial development as necessary for white supremacy and for the survival of the Afrikaner race. According to the 1985 national census the total population of South Africa (excluding the homelands of the Transkei, Bophutatswana, Venda and the Ciskei) was 23,385,645, of which 12.1 percent were coloured or mixed race, 3.5 per cent were Asian and 19.5 per cent were white (both English- and Afrikaans-speaking). The remainder were black. By 1988 Afrikaners constituted no more than 8 per cent of the population. Hence the very specific need to meet the perceived challenge of the blacks. The long-standing belief that apartheid was the only way of avoiding friction between those whom God had created differently was not, however, intended to be a policy of suppression. Rather it was held in the conviction that it was a nation's Christian duty to defend its identity and honour its history, and with the assurance that the white man had been called by God to civilise southern Africa. Under his paternalistic guidance the black races would achieve political fulfilment, but on a basis separate from that of whites. Until recently, although the Afrikaner community had produced liberal leaders like Dr Frederik van Zyl Slabbert, former leader of the Progressive Federal Party, and even radicals like the Reverend Beyers Naude, at one time a member of the Broederbond (a secret Afrikaner brotherhood) but later banned for his anti-apartheid

activites, that conviction had remained for the most part
unchallenged from within the Afrikaner community.

But what of the even smaller English-speaking white community from which the vast majority of Black Sash members
were drawn? Bearing in mind the limitations of such ethnic
generalisations, most of South Africa's liberal traditions came
from English-speaking whites and their institutions – their
newspapers, churches and universities. At the same time, as
Helen Zille, a former political journalist and Black Sash
member, would point out, as many English-speaking people
as Afrikaners supported the National Party and 'for much
less thought-through reasons'. The Afrikaners might tend to
be more conservative in their politics but they at least
thought about political issues. Furthermore, their need for
morality, as reflected in their rationalisation of apartheid into
a 'moral' system in accordance with the tenets of their faith,
gave cause for hope. The real analysis of apartheid, the facing-
up to its consequences, tended to result in the conclusion
that the only alternative was a fundamentally different
system, and even those on the far right who wished to
maintain apartheid had begun to try and give it a more sound
moral content. By 1988 an increasing number of people on
the extreme right were acknowledging that the manner in
which apartheid had been formulated was unacceptable, that
if whites wished to have a separate state they must take a
small piece of land, move into it and start from scratch. For
some commentators there was more hope to be derived from
this kind of realistic reasoning – which recognised the existence of two alternatives, partition or majority rule, and which
opted for partition on the grounds that majority rule was
unacceptable – than in the vague feeling of moral superiority
manifested by many English-speaking whites from the vantage point of their affluent unthreatened suburbs. Beyond the
righteous mantle of the English-speakers' moral condemnation of apartheid there lurked all too often the less noble
fear of having the boat rocked.

South Africa is not a country where racial hatred is an
obvious aspect of daily life. Many of those in favour of
maintaining the apartheid state do not actively hate their

black compatriots. Rather, they are conscious of the inter-tribal violence that erupted in many black African states when the whites surrendered power and are afraid that in South Africa's multi-tribal society 'one man, one vote' in a unitary state could conceivably produce similar violence and chaos. There is undoubtedly a fear also of the vengeful victim of apartheid, of the ultimate white South African nightmare: a black man who comes in the night to stalk the prosperous houses in the small towns of the Eastern Cape or the suburbs of the big cities, bent upon violence and destruction. As divisive as hatred, however, is the ignorance that bears witness to the effectiveness, on one level, of the policy of 'separate development'. Few whites have cause to be particularly conscious of the black townships other than as places from and to which their servants or workforce travel at the beginning and end of the day, or as the settings for 'black on black violence'. Each Christmas, Black Sash members take a much-needed two or three weeks of respite from the 'struggle'. In the course of that brief interlude, Rosemary Meny-Gibert, the organisation's national administrative secretary, would indicate, it became apparent how swiftly it was possible to become 'totally out of it', how easy it was, as members of the white South African public, to be completely ignorant of the events that shaped black lives.

The full significance of the encounters across the tables in the advice office could not properly be appreciated without some understanding of the broader context which made such meetings, and the readiness of white women in comfortable circumstances to become politically aware and actually to act upon that awareness, exceptional. In the autumn of 1989 I returned to South Africa, spurred on by the memory of an article in *The Times* which in January 1985 had first attracted my attention to the existence of the Black Sash. It was a report of how some 20,000 blacks had attended the funeral of one of the organisation's most celebrated members, Molly Blackburn. This display of black affection for the white middle-class wife of a Port Elizabeth doctor had so unnerved the South African authorities that they had banned the memorial service due to be held a week or so later on the

grounds that it posed a danger to public peace. Yet Molly
Blackburn had apparently reached across the racial divide and
received a welcoming response.

I travelled through South Africa, an outsider in a land
understandably loved for its beauty and equally understandably defended against potential judges of its rigidities and its
anomalies, not least of these the curious coexistence of
dictatorial powers with the tolerance of certain forms of
questioning and opposition. Beyond the generous readiness
to answer queries and inform, a patient indulgence was
discernible towards a victim of misinformation by the foreign
media which chose, as the media invariably did, to focus
upon the violence and injustice and to overlook the many
attractions of South Africa. Yes, South Africa had its problems, was the frequent message, but then so too did most
countries. Nobody shouted in quite the same way about
colour discrimination in the United States or imprisonment
without trial in El Salvador. Whites in parts of Britain chose
very deliberately not to live next door to Indians or Pakis-
tanis. It was time the outside world stopped standing in
judgement and gave support to the State President's recent
declaration that the Nationalist goal was 'a totally new South
Africa free of oppression and domination'.

I hope that I passed through a beautiful and troubled land
not in a spirit of condemnation but in the real desire to
discover the full significance of what took place on the day
of Molly Blackburn's funeral and what was still occurring in
the daily encounters between the white women of the Black
Sash and South Africa's dispossessed majority. Certainly I
went without having previously taken 'a political stand'. My
own concern for poverty, injustice and suffering had never
found political expression. South Africa showed me many
things. There was the white ignorance, both real and culti-
vated, which formed the basis of a mythology of 'the black
man'. Over breakfast one morning in the Eastern Transvaal I
found myself inveigled into one of the political conversations
which I had come to discover was the almost invariable
outcome of even the most chance and fleeting encounter.

With amazing frequency, the bottom line of such exchanges was: 'You do not understand the mentality of the black man.'

On this particular occasion the reproach came from a builder who had emigrated to South Africa from England some twenty years previously. He had established a business in South Africa and was now enjoying a level of affluence and a lifestyle which he cheerfully acknowledged he could never have achieved in Britain. President Frederik De Klerk had just released eight key long-term political prisoners and speculation with regard to the imminent release of Nelson Mandela was rife. Nelson Mandela was, in the view of my breakfast companion, nothing but a power-seeker acting in his own personal interests. My bemused attempt to suggest that I found it hard to see how twenty-six years of imprisonment could be in anyone's personal interest, that there must be some collective purpose behind Mandela's refusal to accept release before the unbanning of the ANC, met with the unhesitating response: 'You've got to understand the black man. The black man is better off in prison than he would be outside.'

This was an extreme example. Nevertheless, it gradually became apparent how precious and vital to the existence of many whites was the insistence on 'the black man's' totally different mentality, what an essential contribution it made to attitudes which could view the garden boy and the nanny almost as goods and chattels to be looked after, which could allow them the run of white houses and entrust to them the care of white children, but which could simultaneously condemn them as 'cruel', 'fiercely tribal', 'dishonest', 'dirty' and 'stupid'. The examples of the people's courts and the necklacings were always to hand, as were the filth and the rubbish that littered the mud alleyways and roads of the townships, the manner in which blacks defecated on the beaches when Durban allowed them on to stretches of flawless sand hitherto reserved for whites, the high incidence of AIDS and other sexually transmitted diseases among the black population and the failure of schemes to teach blacks essentially Western modern farming methods. For one year 'they' had managed to produce a good crop but then because they had enough to eat for two or three years, they did not plant for the next: 'The black man cannot think beyond his immediate needs.'

Much of the gulf of understanding which exists between white South Africans and their black countrymen was crystallised for me when, in the course of a stay in the Eastern Cape, I joined in a mass march that took place on 4 November 1989. The route of the march was from Lingelihle township to Cradock police headquarters. Its purpose was to deliver a petition calling for the lifting of the State of Emergency, the scrapping of the Labour Relations Amendment Act,* the unbanning of all banned and restricted organisations, the release of all political prisoners and the repeal of capital punishment. Cradock and its environs were a politically highly sensitive area. Lingelihle, which had a strong tradition of organised black activism, was the home of Matthew Goniwe, Fort Calata, Sparrow Mkhonto and Sicelo Mlauli, the four United Democratic Front activists who disappeared while driving home from a political meeting in Port Elizabeth in June 1985, and a place where the work of Molly Blackburn and other Black Sash members had attracted much attention. The granting of permission for the march to take place gave the inhabitants of the township their first opportunity for five years publicly to express their political feelings.

The press estimated the number of blacks who gathered in the township stadium and then marched the several kilometres to white Cradock at between 30,000 and 40,000. Buses and cars bearing members of a wide range of activist

---

* Among other provisions, the amendments to the Labour Relations Act of 1956 made 'sympathy' or 'secondary' strikes illegal. It also designated as unfair labour practices: 'The incitement to, support of, participation in or furtherance of any boycott of any product or service by any Trade Union, federation, office bearer or official of such Trade Union or federation.' Another controversial clause stated that in the event of dismissals followed by some re-instatements, an employer could re-employ 'selectively' according to fair criteria (efficiency, etc) but not on the ground of an employee's trade-union activities. In spite of this important qualification, the concession was regarded with mistrust. Many trade unionists insisted that length of service, the 'last in first out' policy, was the only fair criterion, and in general the Amendment Act was perceived as an attempt to curb hard-won trade-union achievements. The establishment of a special labour court for labour litigation was also felt to have clogged up the institutional channels for resolving industrial conflict.

organisations from elsewhere arrived to don the T-shirts that displayed their political allegiances and to show their solidarity. Every single resident of Lingelihle turned out to squat upon the scorched turf of the vast but completely unshaded stadium and listen attentively to a succession of speakers, among them Dr Allan Boesak, then president of the World Alliance of Reformed Churches. This march was just one of a series of marches being held all over South Africa, Dr Boesak reminded his audience. Previous marches had shown the international community that 'we are a disciplined and peaceful people'. He urged them to do nothing that day to alter that impression. As he spoke, a South African Police helicopter passed low over the crowd. It circled and returned. When it passed overhead for a third time, drowning the speaker's words, a flicker of tension and hostility ran through the assembly. The pilot then withdrew and the only evidence of police presence was the glint of attendant yellow *casspirs* (armed vehicles) on a distant hillside.

I had gone to Lingelihle in the company of a Black Sash member who had on more than one occasion been detained for her political activism and whose mere presence there was in defiance of a restriction order. No doubt she ensured the warmth of the welcome on our arrival, but as the carefully marshalled march organised itself into rows and made its way out of the stadium on to the dusty road to Cradock, we were separated. I saw only two other white faces in the remainder of the vast crowd, but the kindness I was shown in the course of that orderly procession was overwhelming. Somewhere amongst the singing and the toyitoying (a sort of rhymthic dancing) I was adopted by a young Zulu. Thulani steered me carefully to the outer edge of the procession, where the hot dust churned up by thousands of dancing feet was less intense: 'My people are sweating. They have no money to buy deodorants. I am thinking you must find them smelly. Look how she is sweating.' It was true that perspiration was pouring down the face, neck and back of the girl next to me, but she linked her arm through mine and insisted on holding an umbrella over my head throughout the entire march. A succession of small acts of consideration came from all around me. Thulani was deeply concerned that I should not be afraid, firstly of his people: 'There was a time when the Pan-African Congress said we would drive the white people into the sea, but people do not feel that way any more. We know we need the white man economically, and anyway we do not want to do to them what they have done to us. Many of them were born here. South Africa is for all of us regardless of colour or creed, isn't it?' Then, as we approached the edges of the white town and the road was lined with police carrying their customary firearms, his anxiety was that I should not be afraid of them. I do not think that he would have understood that it had not occurred to me to be.

We entered Cradock at a run to the accompaniment of two words repeated over and over in a rhythmic chant. They meant only 'let's run', a relatively innocuous phrase even if the implied context was undoubtedly that of the black liberation struggle, but the sound and sight of over 30,000 black people running down the main street was manifestly a terrifying one for the white residents of Cradock. They could not know the warmth with which I had been received by people exultant at this long-awaited opportunity to express themselves. And so they looked out in fear and apprehension from behind closed doors and half-open windows, and the few feet that separated them from their black neighbours was the physical expression of an immeasurable divide.

One advantage an outsider does have in a land which the South African Tourist Board advertises for very sound geographical reasons as a 'world within one country' is the freedom to move about within that world, or rather between the country's different worlds, in a way that few South Africans either can or choose to do. Perhaps by virtue of the fact that I had spent three years in the Metropolitan Police in London and was married to a senior British police officer, perhaps because as a consequence of the same wind of change that had induced the South African Police to create a new Public Relations Department the opportunity to offer a different perspective on the Black Sash and the human rights issues the organisation had taken up over the years was welcomed, the South African Police in Pretoria were very hospitable. As a prelude to a *braai*, a South African barbecue, due to be held by members of the International Police Association in the black township of Soweto – so named because it lies south-west of Johannesburg – I was to be introduced to the township.

Soweto today sprawls over an area of some sixty square miles of red earth and Transvaal boulders. Its air is often heavy with the smoke of thousands of fires lit morning and evening as a traditional sign that the 'householder' is at home and guests are welcome. Its recorded population is 2.5 million and its recreation facilities include stadia, swimming pools, rugby fields, athletic tracks, netball fields, basketball fields and a golf course. It was on Soweto's golf course that the *braai* was to be held. A tent was in the process of being erected by black policemen armed with the guns they carried at all times. Preceded by a bright yellow police vehicle, I was taken in a 'combi' on a conducted tour of the township intended to show both 'the best' and 'the worst' of it.

Our convoy drove first through row upon tightly packed row of shanties, corrugated tin and cardboard shacks, between which ran mud tracks submerged in litter and effluence. 'As fast as we move them, others appear,' Brigadier Gijsbers, my guide explained. 'We don't know where they come from. The shanty town is not something we are proud of but it is part of the Third World scene and we are doing our best.' The taxpayers of South Africa, however, predominantly white because so few blacks earn an annual income that would make them eligible for income tax, (by 1990, R20,000 per annum), were growing impatient with the burden of financing development schemes for the black townships. 'What has the black man actually done to help himself or his environment?' was another recurring refrain. The Brigadier pointed to a pathetic-looking shack with two shining Mercedes cars parked outside. I was shown schools that had been built and burnt down, rebuilt and burnt down and finally not rebuilt. The street lighting on those roads which were lit at night was set at an extraordinary height, a necessary precaution to prevent the continual theft of the lamps.

The Brigadier was a tough veteran police officer facing the demands of very real crime problems. He had previously been in charge of riot control but for him the average black man was 'not a bad fellow'. It was in crowd situations when the singing and the dancing began and individuals worked themselves into a frenzy that the problems arose. Brigadier Gijsbers was a man whose love for his country seemed to generate an inveterate optimism. There had been no serious unrest in Soweto for the last eighteen months, he pointed out when I talked to him at the end of 1989. In any case, there was very little premeditated murder and *pro rata* the crime rate for South Africa's various population groups was the same. As to the question of over-aggressive policing, there were some 3,600 police in Soweto – 2,000 SAP and approximately 1,600 municipal police drawn from the black community itself to police a population of 2½ million. The principle of minimum violence was stressed at the training centre. Officers resorting to undue force were severely punished. In the previous year four policemen had actually been sentenced to death.

Baragwanath Hospital, (the largest general hospital in the southern hemisphere), a university with places for 884 students currently under construction, eighteen centres for adult education, a transport system of trains, buses and eleven taxi associations enabling 400,000 Sowetans to commute to Johannesburg daily, 625 miles of underground cable installed since electrification was first started at the end of 1979, 52,000 telephones – these were the elements the foreign media invariably failed to convey. Life in Soweto, he said, was not all shacks, poverty and violence. Soweto had its own relatively prosperous black middle-class, who lived in carefully maintained houses pervaded by an atmosphere of unruffled suburban respectability. 'We are not a zoo for tourists' was scrawled in bold letters across a long brick wall. For R70 a head, tourists could take coach tours from Johannesburg to inspect the disadvantaged of Soweto, but such tours also featured the Soweto house used by Archbishop Desmond Tutu when he was in Johannesburg, Winnie Mandela's home marked by a fluttering African National Congress flag, and her lavish unfinished new house. An estimated quarter of a million Rand had been spent on this building, it was pointed out, before inquiries into the misuse of ANC funds had interrupted its construction. 'Some of these houses I wouldn't even mind owning myself' came the telling remark. Compared with most of Africa's shanty towns, Soweto could be very much worse.

The black people wishing to enter South Africa from other African countries posed a continuing problem for the South African authorities for this very reason. The black residents of Soweto, however, like those of South Africa's other townships, had not for the most part been to other African countries. They drew their comparisons from the rich white suburbs of South Africa, in which under the apartheid system they were permitted to mow the lawns and clean the swimming pools, but not to live. Like many of his colleagues, Brigadier Gijsbers was a man reconciled to inevitable change. His hope for the future rested with the fact that 80 per cent of the population of South Africa were Christian, and that gave everyone something on which to build. He did not say how readily he would be reconciled to change if the day ever came when the blacks of Soweto did not have to make their home in the township.

Beyond the apparent acceptance on the part of many whites of the necessity for black servants or labourers to start their day with a two-hour journey from some distant and frequently squalid township to provide a satellite workforce to support white cities and their businesses lay the guilt that crept as insidiously into conversations with Black Sash members and whites who to a greater or lesser extent identified with the black liberation struggle, as it lurked behind others' heated defence of fixed ideas about 'the black man'. There was the white guilt that was the burden of many English-speaking liberals and socialists there as elsewhere: guilt born of the recognition that the people of Europe had dominated the modern world and thereby attained standards of living out of reach of the people of Asia, Africa and Latin America, and exacerbated by the belief that it was by some special virtue of the white-skinned that people in Europe were so powerful, prosperous and technologically advanced.

As Eleanor Lewin, an historian and socialist who emigrated to England with a broken heart in the sixties, but who knew the Black Sash well during its early years, would point out:

> Because these ideas were believed and, worse, acted upon, by the German Nazis in ways so ruthless that they horrified the world, caring white-skinned people in the UK and USA, as well as South Africa, have gone to great lengths to prove to themselves and to all dark-skinned people, in every way that they can, that they reject beliefs in the inherent superiority of white-skinned people, and the inherent inferiority of brown- or black-skinned people.

Such guilt feelings prevented them from asking the question: if European superior technology or wealth was not due to inherent racial superiority, to what was it due? One answer was to deny European superiority. Another was to attribute it to the inherent greed and lust for power of Europeans, as reflected in the emotive words 'imperialism' and 'neo-colonialism'. The rational answer was to recognise that at this point in world history European technology and wealth was predominant, that it had not always been so and that its modern predominance was due to accidents of geography and history – to the fact, for example, that the dark peoples of Africa had found themselves on the wrong side of the Sahara desert thousands of years ago – and not to inherent genetic superiority.

The guilt I encountered was not rational. It was, none the less, real and complex. It was not always as obvious as the straightforward unease of one who has much confronted with those who have so little. The woman who cleaned my hotel room in Johannesburg left Soweto at 5.30 a.m. seven days a week and did not arrive home until 6 p.m. She had five children. The youngest, aged six, spent all day at a township crèche. The eldest was a teacher and the next was studying to be a lawyer. 'Perhaps they will not have to live in Soweto,'

I tried to encourage her. 'Oh please God,' she pressed her hands together in supplication. 'How can I explain to you? There is so much burglary. The people have no work.' Day after day she greeted me with fresh tea and coffee bags and a luminous smile, and I thought of the journey she had had to make, of the family life she could not really have, and I insisted that I could make my own bed. But then I felt good about this tiny token gesture, and there was the guilt. So should I avoid even such small acts of compassion and solidarity because they gave me a satisfaction the real nature of which was dubious? It was a question not without bearing on Black Sash membership.

Given such factors, how far could the campaigning for human rights of an organisation made up of white and mainly middle-class women really be identified with the liberation struggle? 'How far can they really be committed to the cause of poor blacks,' a police spokesman challenged, 'when they come for the most part from the higher echelons of, particularly, the English community?' In Johannesburg they lived in the most luxurious suburbs. I should ask them what they paid their servants. How far could any white person really understand the suffering of non-whites under the apartheid system? All the wisdom and eloquence in the world could not really enable one person to know another's pain. 'You can never know,' a coloured teacher reasoned, 'what apartheid is for me.' In the course of accompanying Black Sash members to meetings with other political organisations I watched as often, although these days by no means always, well-heeled white women stood alongside their black comrades singing *Nkosi Sikelei iAfrika*, the African nationalist anthem, with their right fists held aloft in the ANC salute. Afterwards they would climb into their private cars and their black 'comrades' would climb into the dusty rattling buses that would transport them back to the townships. How easily, I wondered, did the title 'comrade' sit upon the shoulders of those who under most other circumstances would more readily be regarded as capitalists? Was there something irretrievably contrived about their attempt to span the racial divides? And why as it approached its thirty-fifth anniversary was the Black Sash still almost exclusively white?

Its full membership was also still exclusively female. On the whole the between two and three thousand women's organisations in South Africa today fall into two schools of thought on the issue of gender in terms of power relations in the country. One holds that the struggle for women's rights should be left out of the present phase and attended to after liberation, urging women to throw in their lot with the common struggle. The second emphasises that freedom is indivisible and insists that the liberation struggle must integrate all the issues that impede a just society, including not only race and class but also gender. What then was Black Sash policy in relation to women's issues?

It was in pursuit of answers to questions such as these that I moved in a very privileged way from the black townships to government representatives, from Church leaders to those for whom religion was very much the opium of the people, from detainees and those constrained by restriction orders to the law-enforcement agencies, from black to coloured to white communities and from Afrikaans-speaking to English-speaking whites. I spent time with Black Sash members in Johannesburg, Durban, East London, Grahamstown, Port Elizabeth and Cape Town. I travelled in the overloaded 'black taxis', interestingly enough to the surprise of some Black Sash members, but often to the accompaniment of gospel-singing and cheery good humour and courteous choruses of 'Thank you, driver'. I discovered that sometimes black South Africans would also speak to a potential bearer of 'truth' to the world beyond South Africa in a way in which they might not confide in their white compatriots. I saw the change of attitude when even some Black Sash backs were turned. Well-intentioned though she manifestly was, Mrs X became just X, for she was white and her heart was white and it always would be. The anguish of her options would be luxuries for most black mothers and their children. Such moments gave substance to the suspicion, discernible though frequently unvoiced in white South Africans, that there was a secret behind even the impassive, subservient and smiling attitude of their black compatriots, a secret which they would never completely fathom. I learned, too, a little about the full spectrum of white commitment to the struggle for human rights, ranging from the kind of liberal attitudes which involved simply treating one's servants well to the readiness to sacrifice career, friends and possibly one's own freedom in the cause of a just society for all.

A bucket of sand in the corner of the advice office in Mowbray served as a poignant reminder of the possible consequences of Black Sash membership. Only weeks before my visit, the Black Sash advice office in Port Elizabeth had been set on fire. It was the actions of right-wing extremists that the organisation feared, but there was manifestly a perception of the police not as an independent law-enforcement agency and the protectors of people's rights but as an extension of the Nationalist government, not always as eager as they might be to establish the guilt of those responsible for the illegal and sometimes violent harassment of anti-apartheid organisations. My own police connections were clearly at times a source of certain reservations among some, although not many, members of the Black Sash, and perhaps I was inclined to be more sympathetic to individual policemen struggling to do their duty under difficult circumstances than I might otherwise have been. My own years in the Metropolitan Police, which I had joined with the loftiest aspirations of implementing the law with honesty and fairness to all, had given me glimpses of what it was like to be hated simply for the uniform I wore, even before I opened my mouth, and although I understood that the bitterness I sometimes encountered was by no means always without foundation, much to my horror I had felt my own attitude changing. I did not find such bitterness in the black people of South Africa but I knew enough about the escalation of resentment and misunderstanding not to be too quick to stand in judgement.

The South African Police Force for its part made no secret of its interest in the Black Sash. 'The reason we monitor the Black Sash,' Major General Herman Stadler, newly appointed head of the Public Relations Department in Pretoria but

previously one of South Africa's most senior intelligence
chiefs, volunteered unprompted, 'is because wittingly or
unwittingly – it's not to say they always know what they are
doing – the fact is that they are working with certain radical
groups. And the ultimate goal of these radicals, the African
National Congress and the South African Communist Party,
is the overthrow of the present system.' The goal of the ANC
was the implementation of the Freedom Charter, (see Appendix) he said. The SACP for its part saw the implementation
of the Freedom Charter as paving the way for a socialist and,
eventually, a communist order in the Republic of South
Africa. On the face of it the Freedom Charter appeared a very
innocent document, 'although perhaps Utopian'. It was not
so much the goal as the method of achieving it which
concerned the SAP. The ANC, because it was an illegal
organisation working from outside South Africa's borders,
had to make use of the 'internal dimension' – i.e. certain
organisations and individuals inside the country. Its 'people's
war' revolutionary strategy was based on four pillars: firstly,
the activities of the ANC as vanguard organisation, including
those of the 'Democratic Movement' and its underground
structures; secondly, united mass action (this pillar included
the drive to unite and arm the masses); thirdly, the activities
of Umkhonto we Sizwe, the ANC military wing engaged in
'acts of terrorism'; and fourthly the foreign dimension which
entailed the isolation of South Africa from the international
community and the drive from within other countries to
muster material and financial support because, as an organisation banned within South Africa, it was also obliged to
gather its resources overseas.

The SAP's interest in the Black Sash must be understood,
the General elaborated, within the context of the underground structures of the 'internal dimension' of this four-
pillared revolutionary onslaught against South Africa by the
ANC and SACP alliance. The United States government had
appointed a group of academics and military experts to
conduct research into revolutionary tactics, particularly in
relation to Vietnam, but their findings applied to the revolutionary process in general. In General Stadler's experience

the 'iceberg principle' (see Appendix) revealed by this research fitted the South African situation like a glove. Under this principle the greater part of the process of establishing revolutionary cadres, the preparation of the masses for revolution and the setting up of parallel hierarchies for taking over government positions went on underground. Only the final stages happened overtly. Preparation for the revolution began with the exploitation of genuine grievances. The realities of contemporary South Africa were undeniably rich in them: 'At the moment in South Africa we have a Third World – First World situation. Today a black person is working in the First World. Tonight he goes back to the Third World.' This situation rendered him particularly open to exploitation by those whose objective was initially to aggravate dissatisfaction with existing political, economic, social and administrative conditions, to discredit the government, police and military authorities, increase agitation, expand front organisations and ultimately overthrow the government by violent means.

The General was emphatic that everyone in South Africa wanted change. Apartheid had manifestly not worked, but it was imperative that such change was brought about not by revolutionary but by evolutionary means. He was not denying that much of what the Black Sash did to assist people as a human rights organisation was commendable, but unfortunately it had 'politicised the situation', blaming the government for all that was wrong. The Black Sash tended not to listen to both sides. It did not recognise the realities of policing problems, the need to create a stable atmosphere in which change could take place. Many of the leading figures in the Black Sash were, in his view, politically inclined. 'Perhaps it is difficult to stay out of politics in South Africa,' he conceded, and he was sure that some Black Sash members were apolitical. 'But they are being used and that is the point. We are interested in individuals who are part and parcel of the revolutionary onslaught and these people, most of them I believe unwittingly, are being used to further the aims and objectives of radicals.'

He showed me a video of the victims of township necklacings, the charred remains of people who had had tyres filled
with petrol rammed over their shoulders and set alight. With
their arms tightly trapped such victims had no chance of
freeing themselves. They burned alive while the scalding
rubber seared into their flesh and their attackers looked on.
The camera had closed in on black township youngsters
kicking what was left of one such victim. Some of what was
shown was, as the General himself was quick to point out,
obviously staged for the film crew, but there was no denying
the fundamental horror of such actions. How then, he asked,
could the Black Sash ladies, for all their otherwise laudable
work, align themselves with people who perpetrated acts of
this nature?

Violence – its presence made itself constantly felt in
affidavits taken in the advice offices, in the silence kept at
the beginning of Black Sash meetings for those who had died
in detention, in the scars both physical and emotional that it
had clearly left on so many South Africans that I met – most
tangibly in the deafness resulting from the introduction of
sharp instruments into one man's ear, less so in the suspicion
that crept into even the most everyday relationships. In
Johannesburg, I listened with horror to Joe Seremane, Director of Justice and Reconciliation in the South African Council
of Churches, as he spoke of how in the course of interrogation
he had been gagged, blindfolded and manacled, then tortured
with electricity, until his mind had gone blank and he no
longer felt the pain and he had believed he was on the point
of death.

'Forward to the 1990s' was the title of a conference I
attended at the University of the Western Cape in November
1989. Even that event opened with the announcement of the
death of Anton Franz, a self-professed member of Umkhonto
we Sizwe who had been killed during the previous night,
having reportedly resisted sustained gunfire for six hours.
That same conference included an open telephone call to
Pallo Jordan, media officer for the ANC in Lusaka. The lines
of communication with the ANC leadership in Lusaka were
overtly opening. People were marching, not only in Cradock

but all over South Africa, and President De Klerk was facing the awesome challenge of balancing his Nationalist party's conservatism with the requirement that South Africa must adapt or die.

In such a climate the role of the Black Sash as bridge-builders could well assume a new relevance, but the question must then inevitably arise as to whether Black Sash sympathy for the suffering victims of injustice, of the 'structural-ised violence' of the apartheid state, had so entrenched it in a position of opposition to the Nationalist government that a less confrontational role for the future would not be feasible. The Black Sash had a long tradition of *fighting* for human rights. 'A warrior for justice' was how Sheena Duncan, the then Black Sash national president, had described Molly Blackburn in a memorial tribute in 1985: 'A warrior for justice had walked briefly in a troubled land, seeded the minds of men and women with new visions of themselves and changed the course of history.' Molly Blackburn herself had maintained that the reaching out of a hand in friendship was the beginning of a bridge. And so, as February 1990 brought the release of Nelson Mandela, the unbanning and unrestricting of organisations and individuals, the amendment of the State of Emergency and the suspension of executions, perhaps the most pertinent question of all was whether it was warriors or peacemakers that were most needed, and how well an organisation of just over 2,000 women qualified for either role.

Chapter Two

Warriors for justice

It was moral outrage that on 19 May 1955 brought six Johannesburg housewives together for afternoon tea. The focus of their outrage was a Bill devised by the Nationalist government to remove the 'coloured' or mixed-race voters of the Cape from the common roll. These voting rights were entrenched in the constitution, protected by it, and could not be changed except by a two-thirds majority of members of South Africa's two parliamentary houses, the House of Assembly and the Senate, in a joint sitting. Overruled twice by the Supreme Court in their previous tactics to circumvent the entrenchment, the government now proposed to change the constitution itself by packing the Senate or Upper House with its own supporters. Significantly, the preoccupation of the ladies who gathered in a comfortable suburban Johannesburg home that day, and of the public outcry that would ensue, was not so much with the assault on the voting rights of a group of non-white South Africans as with the manipulation or 'rape', as it was emotively described, of the constitution. The issue that would give rise to the extraordinary mobilisation of angry women and the formation of the organisation which grew out of that small tea party, initially called the Women's Defence of the Constitution League, was thus not so much a racial one as one of constitutionality.

The passion felt by a section of the public not usually unduly preoccupied with the machinery of government could not be dissociated from the historic struggle between Briton and Boer, and a constitutional struggle dating back to the drafting of the Act of Union, the South Africa Act. The South Africa Act passed by the British parliament in 1910, eight years after the end of the Boer War, established a Union embracing the two former Boer republics of the Transvaal, the Orange River colony and the two British colonies, Natal and the Cape. The document was drawn up at a national convention at which former opponents from the Boer and British camps endeavoured to shape a future for their country. As a result of it South Africa would become a self-governing dominion within the British Empire. The delegates from the four former parliaments spent months preparing a draft constitution, during the course of which it was recognised that certain guarantees would need to be built in to the agreement in order to ensure a rather shaky unity. Some of these guarantees were to stand for a limited time as safeguards for the transition period only. Others, the entrenched clauses 137 and 35, the first of which concerned the Transvaal language rights giving equality to both English and Afrikaans and the other concerning the franchise rights of the coloured voters in the Cape, were to stand for an indefinite period and be altered only under very specific conditions.

Prior to 1910 coloureds (those of mixed race) living in the Cape could obtain the franchise and be elected to parliament subject to certain property and wage qualifications. Blacks, too, had enjoyed the franchise in the Cape since 1853. In Natal a small number of blacks had similarly secured voting rights. No such arrangement existed, however, in the Boer republics of the Transvaal and the Orange Free State. The end result of the compromise reached at the national convention was that suffrage was restricted to whites in the provinces of the Transvaal and the Orange Free State, while nonwhite voters in the Cape kept their franchise but gave up the right to stand for actual election to parliament. The nonwhite franchise rights were secured on paper but never implemented in Natal. The Cape insisted, however, that the franchise rights of its coloureds and relatively small number of blacks were entrenched in the constitution with a view to protecting them in the event of the conservative Boer republics ever gaining a position from which they could outvote the more liberal former British colonies. Although the opposition of the English-speaking community to the Afrikaners' more forthright belief in white supremacy was ambivalent, the compromise failed really to satisfy either the English-speaking liberals who were committed to a non-racial franchise for the new Union or the Afrikaner Nationalists who looked upon the Union constitution as an imposed settlement and an inadequate compensation for the ignominy to which they had been subjected as a result of the 1899–1902 Boer War.

There were some moderate voices among the Nationalists but the programme of the National Party, founded in 1914, came to reflect the progressive erosion of all economic, social and political rights of non-whites. The establishment of an Afrikaner Republic and the removal of non-white voters were the party's two historic goals. In 1925 the first Nationalist government enacted colour-bar and wage acts, restricting the economic advancement of non-whites. In 1930 again a Nationalist government restricted the enfranchisement of women to European women only, reducing whatever effectiveness the Cape coloured voters enjoyed. Prime Minister James Barry Munnik Hertzog, although a moderate by temperament, led a ten-year struggle to enact the Native Representation Act of 1936, which struck the African voters in the Cape from the common roll. He was able to do so without strong opposition. The rallying cry of 'Black peril' had struck a chord of recognition in whites, both English-speaking and Afrikaner, who were instinctively afraid of blacks. Dissident views within the United Party did bring about certain modifications to the proposed legislation: Africans in the Cape Province were for example given the right to elect three white members to the House of Assembly. Nevertheless, General Jan Christiaan Smuts, unable politically to overlook the prevailing fears of the electorate, had shown himself willing to purchase white unity at the expense of supporting the move to remove the black voters in the Cape from the common roll.

Following the National Party's electoral victory in 1948, the entrenched clause relating to the Cape coloured voters became a thorn in the flesh of the newly elected government.

The knowledge that they could only be removed by a two-thirds majority which the Nationalists, in the ordinary course of events, could never hope to achieve, rankled with the dominant strain of Nationalists who favoured the objective of Afrikaner supremacy. The removal of the entrenched clauses became synonymous in the minds of many Afrikaners with the achievement of long-awaited sovereignty. The Union parliament could not, it was maintained by Johannes Strijdom, leader of the National Party, be a sovereign parliament while it remained bound by the terms of a 'British' constitution forced upon South Africa at Union.

In 1951, the Nationalist government, encouraged by its previous successful removal of the African voters in the Cape from the common roll, tried at first simply to bypass the entrenched clause in the constitution. It submitted the Separate Representation of Voters Bill, which undertook to do the same to the Cape coloureds, separately to each of South Africa's two Houses of Parliament. Having secured simple majorities in each, it then declared the Bill to be law. This time, however, outraged by such flagrant disdain for the constitution and spurred on by anti-Nationalist feeling in the country, the opposition in the form of the United Party instigated a case to test the validity of the legislation before the nation's Court of Appeal. The Nationalists turned the case into a test of the 'sovereignty' of South Africa's parliament, threatening also to reverse the decision of the court if the case went against them.

Undeterred, the court's judgement was none the less that the passing of the Separate Representation of Voters Bill was invalid and that: 'The Union is an autonomous state in no way subordinate to any other country in the world. To say that the Union is not a Sovereign State because its parliament, functioning bi-camerally, has not the power to amend certain sections of the South Africa Act, is to state a manifest absurdity.' The judgement went on to point out that the sections in question could be amended by parliament sitting uni-camerally. The Union was therefore, through its own legislature, able to pass any law it pleased. Stung by this failure to demonstrate the South African parliament's lack of 'sovereignty', Strijdom and his government next set about finding a way round the jurisdiction of the Appeal Court by introducing the High Court of Parliament Bill in the 1952 parliamentary session. The High Court of Parliament Bill made provision for a body, to be known as the High Court of Parliament and to be made up of members of the Union Parliament, to have the power to repeal any judgement of the Appeal Court which invalidated any act. United Party members refused to participate in this legislation. Thus the newly appointed High Court of Parliament, which countermanded the Appeal Court's pronouncement of the Separate Representation of Voters Act as invalid, and declared the law in force, was made up exclusively of Nationalist MPs.

The constitutional battle was further intensified when the Cape Supreme Court, meeting simultaneously with the High Court of Parliament, pronounced the act invalid. Its decision was upheld by the Appellate Division. Thwarted in this direction, but encouraged by the fact that the 1953 general election had returned the Nationalist government for the first time in its history as a majority party, the government now turned its attention away from the judiciary and attempted to pass the Separate Representation of Voters Bill by the means actually laid down in the constitution. Despite its newly won electoral strength, however, it still failed to achieve the necessary two-thirds majority in joint session. The final manoeuvre, therefore, was to pack the two institutions blocking the passage of the bill: the Appeal Court which had declared it invalid, and the Senate. It was the Senate Bill, duly validated by an Appellate Division newly constituted for the occasion, which licensed the enlargement of the Senate from 48 members to 89, 77 of whom were government supporters, which finally outraged and ignited popular reaction.

The six who met for tea on the morning of Sunday, 19 May 1955 – Ruth Foley, Jean Sinclair, Jean Bosazza, Helen Newton Thompson, Tercia Pybus and Elizabeth Maclaren – regarded this cynical manipulation of the constitution as the last straw. As Noël Robb, who joined the Black Sash not long afterwards, put it: 'Even to simple apolitical housewives it

was obvious that if you cannot defeat the Lions with fifteen
players it is quite unacceptable to double the size of the
rugby side.'

'We can't sit still and do nothing – I don't know what we
can do, but we must do it. We must act,' announced Ruth
Foley at the time. 'There must be thousands like us and we
must get together.' Within the hour those six friends had
telephoned six more, who in turn telephoned six others.
Within twenty-four hours a large group had assembled ready
for action. Jean Sinclair, a United Party City Councillor,
explained to this gathering that the machinery of civic
government made provision for a petition to be addressed by
responsible citizens to their mayor, calling on him to hold a
public meeting. A petition was swiftly drawn up and delivered to the Mayor of Johannesburg, George Beckett.

The women were by no means alone in their outrage. They
were giving voice to the attitude of many others. As early as
1951 the War Veterans' Torch Commando, an organisation
of ex-servicemen determined to stand up for the values for
which they had fought during the Second World War, had
marched together in protest at the government's proposal to
place the coloured voters on a separate roll. The implications
of the Senate Bill had already alarmed foreign investors.
Within twenty-four hours of the tea party, thirty-one profes-
sors at Rhodes University had also issued a protest statement.
In response to requisitions received from more than five
hundred citizens the mayor of Johannesburg did call a public
meeting, to be held on 25 May 1955 in front of the Johannesburg City Hall. By 23 May the press had announced that
Witwatersrand women would march through Johannesburg
as a separate body, to take part in the Senate Bill protest.
Participants in the march would include housewives, shop
assistants and women from all walks of life. Their action was
billed as 'the first move in a sustained campaign by women
of the Rand against the Senate Bill'. Despite the self-professed
uncertainty on the part of the women concerned as to the
exact lines along which the organisation would develop,
the Women's Defence of the Constitution League, a pressure group of political good faith committed to making the

government aware that there was strong opposition to the
destruction of the constitution, had been born. The new
organisation's committee drew up and publicised a manifesto calling upon all women to unite in defence of the
constitution:

> The time has come for the Government to listen to the
> voice of the women of this country.
>   We are the ones who have borne the children of today
> who are the South Africans of tomorrow, and who will
> have to bear the brunt of the sins of their fathers.
>   We cannot stand by doing nothing. This Government
> has stated that it will listen to no protests. As mothers
> and grandmothers, as wives and sweethearts, career-
> women and professional women, as young women
> looking forward to a peaceful South Africa we are
> uniting to take common action.
>   As women we intend to bring this Government to its
> senses. We therefore call on all women, English or
> Afrikaans-speaking, to join us in this march. Let all
> women who value liberty and freedom heed this call to
> action.

When Wednesday 25 May came, 2,000 women gathered at
the memorial to the soldiers of the Transvaal Scottish who
had fallen in the war, and marched to the City Hall, preceded
by a drummer beating out the rhythm with a muffled drum
and bearing banners with such slogans as 'Women defend
your children's future' written large in both English and
Afrikaans. A further 18,000 Johannesburg citizens joined in
the meeting outside the City Hall to ratify the resolution:
'Withdraw the Senate Act.'
The League's constitution opened membership to all
women who were citizens of South Africa and thus entitled
to vote. By virtue of the fact that a few Afrikaner intellectuals
had criticised the Senate Act, the leaders of the Women's
Defence of the Constitution League, whose social contacts
with the Afrikaner community in those days were minimal,
assumed considerable potential support from that quarter.

The organisation's appeal was thus extended to Afrikaners as well as English-speakers. Women were welcomed regardless of their political affiliations, provided that they subscribed to 'the aims of the League, and objected to the methods used by the Nationalist government to attain their ends, feeling that thereby democratic government, government by consent of the people, was being destroyed and confidence and trust in the rules of government shattered'.

Members flocked in, and the cell system that had first brought the League into being was swiftly expanded to apply to branches. All over the country meetings were held of new branches, the movement developed almost spontaneously and a period of frenetic activity followed. Encouraged by the immediate success of their first petition to the Mayor of Johannesburg, the women then decided that two further petitions should be drawn up, one to the Prime Minister calling on him either to repeal the legislation or to resign, the other to the Governor General asking him to withhold his assent from the Act. The petitions were to be signed by women only.

Time was of the essence. The Senate Bill was being debated in parliament and the newly formed League had at best two weeks in which to collect their signatures. The preamble to the petition to the Governor General, pronounced by committee members to be 'a fine piece of prose and reasoned argument', was printed by 4 June, and women working in continuous shifts over the weekend of 4, 5 and 6 June dispatched petition forms to 290 towns throughout the country. More than 100,000 women signed the two petitions within the next ten days. Despite threats on the telephone to canvassers, mysterious postal delays, taunts, insults and even the loss in the post of certain parcels of signed forms which could not be included in the final count, the petition to the Governor General was handed to his secretary with 94,680 signatures. Ruth Foley visited the main centres of the Union. Pretoria too was mobilised and almost overnight the League became 'news'. The Afrikaner press ridiculed and criticised them but the English-speaking press showed its support, likening the women to suffragettes and identifying with the League's fundamental tenet that the prelude to and the purpose of the Senate Bill were very much more sinister than the mere alteration of the composition of the Senate.

> They have shown [wrote one leader-writer in an article entitled 'The Women'] that they can act quickly and effectively when a matter that touches the future of the country is at issue. Women have seldom intervened directly in public affairs, except as ordinary members of political parties, but their intervention has sometimes been dramatic.
> The suffragette movement in Britain in the early part of the century demonstrated how formidable such action could be.
> In the present situation in South Africa much more than the composition of the Senate is at stake. It is clear that if spurious majorities can be created for particular policies and occasions, democratic procedures have gone by the board and no rights can be regarded as safe.

Despite such feeling the Governor General, Dr Jansen, assented on behalf of the Queen to the Senate Act. The Bill was signed and parliament rose. The League was inevitably disappointed but it remained staunchly resolved not to give up the fight. Even if it were not possible to stop the government's actions, the Nationalists must not be allowed to represent what they were doing as the *volkswil*, the will of the people. They must be shown that their behaviour was neither accepted nor forgotten. The women would continue to collect signatures for the petition calling upon Strijdom to resign. The Prime Minister let it be known that he was not prepared to meet a delegation from the League in person, but on 28 June a procession of over a thousand women representing dozens of cities, towns and villages all over South Africa marched, once again to the sound of a muffled drum, from the centre of Pretoria to the Union Buildings to hand over the petition to the Prime Minister's representative. The petition calling for Prime Minister Strijdom's resignation was received on his behalf by Ben Schoeman, Minister of Transport. Eighty women took turns to stand in silent vigil for forty-eight hours outside the Union Buildings. It was the first of many heroic 'stands' to come. They slept out in bitterly cold weather with little apart from groundsheets and army blankets for protection. The suffragette movement was not all that distant a memory for some of the individuals involved, nor were the war years in Nazi Germany: 'I saw years of hell in Germany. I have seen before, all that is happening now,' one protester gave as her reason for marching. 'I do not want ever to live in a country where arrogance and the *Herrenvolk* ideal can suppress the freedom and honesty of any group of people.'

A substantial crowd welcomed the convoy of twenty-five cars bringing the women back to Johannesburg after the first of what was to become a long succession of vigils. The day after the forty-eight hour protest at the Union Buildings, it was decided that ministers should be made constantly aware of the women's stand against unconstitutional measures by their continued presence at the seat of government in Pretoria. On 18 July four women, representatives of the four corners of the Union, accordingly took up their stance just inside the entrance used by the ministers. They waited in silence, wearing the black shoulder sash of mourning for the death of South Africa's constitution. This vigil would be maintained on every working day until parliament sat again in January. Ministers going about their daily business were forced to run the gauntlet of the women's reproachful presence. Soon the scope of the vigils was extended to include attendance on ministers wherever they went. The women did not speak. They simply stood in a dignified manner in their hats and gloves and sashes wherever they felt their presence would be an effective symbolic protest. A large reserve of such protestors was established throughout the Union, who could be called upon to 'haunt' ministers when they arrived in a particular town, attended functions, emerged from the House of Assembly or generally went about their ministerial duties. Older members of the Black

Sash still hold vivid memories today of the coded messages that were sent all over the country as ministers left Jan Smuts airport in Johannesburg for various parts of South Africa. One member of the League ran a flower shop in Johannesburg. An order for carnations in Port Elizabeth meant that a particular minister was on his way there. Roses, proteas and a whole range of floribunda represented other ministers, whose arrival at the order's fictitious destination would then be greeted with a row of grimly silent women in black sashes.

Throughout the months that followed, white women in black sashes seemed to be everywhere South Africa's Nationalist ministers tried to turn. They even on one occasion invaded Skukuza, a camp in the Kruger National Park some sixty miles from any town or village, where P. Sauer, the Minister of Lands, was due to open a conference. Slowly, disconcerted by the women's blank stares, government officials resorted to defensive measures. During a visit to East London in his capacity as Minister of Bantu Affairs, Dr Hendrik Verwoerd, the architect of apartheid, was reduced to coming through the non-European entrance at the aerodrome in order to escape the Black Sash reception at the entrance he should have used. At a ceremonial opening of a police barracks, the Minister of Justice, C.R. Swart, was reported to have scrambled over a fence to avoid running the Black Sashers' gauntlet. Such scenes had great publicity potential. Cartoonists such as Bob Connolly of the *Rand Daily Mail* made the most of the comic possibilities, showing the rear end of Mr Swart disappearing over a wall in an undignified scramble to escape Black Sash women. Ridiculous figures were seen desperately cutting additional back doors at airports for the convenience of ministers. Eric Louw, Minister of Finance, who had tried to conceal his discomfort on being met at Jan Smuts airport by twenty-seven women in black sashes by remarking jocularly, 'What is this, the Housewives' League?' and again, on being met in Cape Town by members of the Cape Town League, by inspecting their shoes and commenting that they were 'quite clean', found himself depicted as a clown clutching a large book entitled, 'How to cover up embarrassment by witty remarks.'

Even the international press took up the story. In September 1955 *Time* magazine reported how:

> Ministers took to concealing their movements, ducking
> through side doors, arriving at parties or weddings
> without warning, buying theatre tickets under false
> names, asking meeting organisers not to announce
> scheduled speeches. Nothing helped. The women were
> always waiting. The Government was goaded into
> irritable complaint. 'Weeping Winnies', one Minister
> called them; and Prime Minister Strijdom himself jibed
> nervously at 'these foolish virgins'.

In that same month, twenty-five Black Sashers formed a double line outside the Bloemfontein City Hall, where the Nationalist party was due to have its annual conference in the Orange Free State. Shortly before the arrival of the Prime Minister, one hundred muscular members of the Nasionale Jeugbond, the Nationalist youth group, pushed the women to one side and formed their own defensive line between League members and the area where Strijdom would have to pass. After he had made his entrance, the Jeugbond turned on several of the women, tore off their black sashes and ripped up their posters, bearing the by now familiar words, *Erbiedig ons Grondwet* (Honour our constitution). Fists were shaken and threats made at the silently protesting women. Inside the hall, Justice Minister Swart gave vent to his frustration: 'This ridiculous action by these people will only make us more determined to put Cape Coloureds on a separate roll.' Undeterred by this and other similar incidents, the League's headquarters in Johannesburg sent ten cars and two aeroplanes full of reinforcement Black Sashers to the aid of their embattled Bloemfontein sisters, one of whom professed not to be above carrying an extra long hatpin and using it to jab someone if necessary.

Despite the hazards involved – the heckling, taunting, and bombardment with eggs, toilet rolls and even stink bombs to which members were sometimes subjected – more and more women, including some Afrikaans-speakers, a proportion of whom were themselves Nationalists, came forward to join and be a reproach to the men dishonouring the Convenant of Union. The organisation grew and spread. 'Black Sashing' was only the outward symbol of the League's work. Public lectures to open women's eyes to their civic rights, drawing-room meetings, the formation of branches in different parts of the country – all were designed to inform the public and awaken South Africa to the death of democracy. Encouraged by its own swelling membership, the League set about creating an equivalent organisation for men. An appeal was made to brothers, husbands and sons to join in the battle against the destruction of parliamentary government. A convenant was adopted, calling upon all South Africans to work for a national convention to agree upon rules for governing the country. While the League women grew in number and public acclaim, however, their male counterparts, the Covenanters, organised to a large extent by former members of the Torch Commando, never really got off the ground. Perhaps because women had more time to engage in the activities of steady harassment and continuing symbolic reminders to the government than men, perhaps because such activities were felt to be better suited to the female than the male temperament, vigils for men were unsuccessful. For a time, however, the Covenanters did continue to support the League's protests, primarily in their individual capacity.

Demonstrations were planned for all important political occasions. On 10 August 1955, at the nomination of the new Nationalist Party senators, women in black sashes had taken their stand at the Raadsaal in Pretoria and on 12 November, following the dissolution of the Senate, widespread demonstrations took place in thirty-five South African cities and towns. In Johannesburg, thousands of women once more marched through the city streets, this time bearing a vast book draped with a black sash, symbolising the constitution. Throughout that day they kept their vigil over it. In Cape Town, Port Elizabeth, Durban, Bloemfontein, East London, Pretoria and many country towns women showed their protest in a similar fashion. After a crowd of over 5,000 assembled outside the City Hall in Johannesburg had pledged themselves aloud to 'uphold the ideals by which our Union was inspired', Ruth Foley pointed out to a silently attentive audience the appropriateness of the coincidence of their mourning for the dissolution of the Senate with the week in which South Africans wore the red poppy symbolising the life blood of those who had made the supreme sacrifice in order that South Africans today might live in freedom. Both occasions, she claimed, were part of the age-old struggle for freedom:

> The tragic question fills our minds: 'Was it for this our comrades, our husbands, sons and brothers died? Did they make their sacrifice in vain?' And we are here to answer 'No'.
>
> We are here to testify we will not let their sacrifice be made in vain. We have come to dedicate ourselves to serve our country, to carry on the struggle and make our stand for freedom.
>
> We, the people, are here to demonstrate to the junta of the Party in power that South Africa will never accept the Senate Act. For we are democrats and will not submit to dictatorship.

Fifty thousand pamphlets had been distributed throughout South Africa with mourning crêpe attached and bearing the organisation's dedication:

> In pride and humbleness we declare our devotion to the land of South Africa, we dedicate ourselves to the service of our country, we reaffirm our loyalty to the contract of Union which brought us together. We pledge ourselves to uphold the ideals by which our Union was inspired, of mutual trust and forbearance, of sanctity of word, of courage for the future, and of peace and justice for all persons and peoples. We pledge ourselves to resist any diminishment of these, confident that this duty is required of us, and that history and our children will defend us.
>
> So help us God, in Whose strength we trust.

A dedication service followed Mrs Foley's speech. All but the most pro-Nationalist press reported how the November skies were rent that day with thousands of voices singing not only 'God Save the Queen' but also *'Die Stem van Suid-Afrika'* (The voice of South Africa), which in 1938 Prime Minister Hertzog had declared the official national anthem. From 12 November 1955 onwards public support for the ladies of the Womens' Defence of the Constitution League and the dignity and the orderliness of the strange funereal pattern of their protest seems to have mounted. Membership rose to something in the region of 10,000, although the Black Sash claims never really to have counted very precisely. In London, the *Economist* likened the League to Gandhi's passive resistance movement in an editorial entitled 'Satyagraha in a Black Sash' (19 November 1955). The national and international press continued to give respectful coverage to the women's protest as on 25 November, the day of the election of the new Senate, the League held vigils outside the Raadsaals and their equivalents in the four provincial capitals where the elections were being conducted, while other silent vigils were held throughout the country. A few days later, on 29 and 30 November, the organisation held its first national conference in Port Elizabeth. This was followed by the election of an interim National Executive to organise and correlate the whole of the nationwide activity of the League, with Ruth Foley as president and Jean Sinclair as national chairman.

With the opening of parliament on 13 January 1956, the Black Sash ladies once again demonstrated their protest against the Senate Act. Four women maintained a daily vigil outside Parliament in Cape Town from 8.45 a.m. to 5.15 p.m., and every half-hour they slow-marched down Parliament Street and into Government Avenue. In the meantime plans were being laid for the largest demonstration yet made against the government's packing of the Senate. As soon as the date was announced on which the new Senate would fulfil its function of meeting in joint session with the House of Assembly to pass a Bill attacking the entrenched clauses of the constitution, thousands of women in more than 140 cities, towns and country dorps would be ready to travel in convoys from north, south, east and west to converge on Cape Town and carry their protest to parliament itself.

The convoy from the north would be the first to leave Pietersberg and move south to join the largest contingent from Johannesburg led by Jean Sinclair. It would then travel down to meet groups from the Free State, Durban and Port Elizabeth at various points along the route. At Stellenbosch cars from Cape Town would join them to complete the convoy. The cars would cover only 300 miles a day because it was planned to distribute information along the way. Vigils would be held when the travellers stopped for the night and speakers would be ready to inform everyone prepared to listen of the reasons for the protest.

The great trek to Cape Town along the more than 1,000 miles of arterial road that leads across the semi-desert expanses of the Karoo was to prove a masterpiece of behind-the-scenes planning. Provisions were made in detail for children to be looked after in their mothers' absence. Detailed directives were issued concerning babies, bottles, napkins and homework. Iron rations for the journey were recommended. The most explicit instructions were also sent to drivers of vehicles. Each car-owner, a letter from Jean Sinclair directed, must have her insurance policy endorsed for carrying passengers for the duration of the convoy. On no account must the fact that car-owners were not paying all travelling expenses be mentioned to anyone. There were doubts about the advisability of carrying petrol, owing to the fact that it might affect the insurance policies. It was decided, therefore, that no one would be asked to carry petrol. Soap and elastoplast, it was pointed out, would mend a hole in the petrol tank, and a siphon tube might well be useful.

The dusty heat of the Karoo was intense. Ample water for the radiators should therefore be carried. A canvas water bag was advised. Any puncture must be mended at the first garage reached. The only two men to take part in the convoy would be two mechanics who travelled at the rear. Cars were to be neatly emblazoned with signboards inscribed with the words *Erbiedig ons Grondwet* and pennants denoting the area they represented. Participants were to wear dresses, not 'slacks', and their black sashes were to be pinned with the League's badge. The exact date of departure was kept a closely guarded secret to deter organised interference *en route*.

The first sixty cars in fact assembled at dawn outside Johannesburg on 9 February and, after a hazardous journey made at the speed of the slowest vehicle in the procession, a convoy of 150 cars led by a small green Morris Minor with the symbolic gold book of the constitution on its roof finally drove through the centre of Cape Town on 13 February, the first day of the joint sitting of both Houses of Parliament. The crowds had turned out in force to greet them. A ticker-tape welcome awaited them along one of Cape Town's main streets. The *Cape Times* reported next day how thousands of onlookers had cheered, clapped and shouted words of encouragement as the convoy passed:

> Adderley Street, which is about half a mile long, was lined solidly on either side and along the islands in its centre by people of all ages and races, and hundreds more saw the procession from balconies and windows.
>
> There were moving scenes as the seemingly endless convoy, carrying nearly 600 women from cities and villages all over South Africa, passed by.
>
> Some men stood silently with bared heads, while others gave the wartime 'V sign', and many people, in and out of the convoy, were in tears.

Letters from Johannesburg City Council to the central executive of the Black Sash had already revealed that the women's protests would only be tolerated provided they were made up exclusively of Europeans. The convoy parade was followed, therefore, not by a march because it was feared that the coloured people of Cape Town would join in and trouble might ensue, but by a forty-eight-hour protest vigil. Ninety women stood throughout the night outside parliament, to be relieved next morning by others who would stand all through that day and a second night. On the morning of 14 February, shortly after Prime Minister Johannes Strijdom had asked leave to introduce the South Africa (Amendment) Bill, which sought to remove the last non-white voters from the common roll by amending section 35 of the South Africa Act, there were extraordinary scenes in the public gallery.

Fourteen representatives of the League who had entered without their sashes suddenly produced them from their handbags and put them on. A parliamentary messenger duly confiscated them, whereupon the women proceeded to pin black roses to their dresses. When they were required to remove these also, at a signal from Ruth Foley and Jean Sinclair, the women left the bay to the accompaniment of cries of 'Police State' from the floor of the Chamber. Outside the public gallery, the Sergeant at Arms gave instructions that they should be given back their roses but that they must not wear their sashes. The women duly pinned on their roses, returned to their seats in the gallery and watched in silence as the debate proceeded. While League women in other towns throughout South Africa took up their stand outside post offices and other public buildings, the tense, watchful presence of the women in and outside parliament added to the drama of the joint sitting, and undoubtedly also to the discomfort and embarrassment of Nationalist members. 'Thank goodness they're on our side,' one opposition MP was heard to remark with evident relief.

On 24 February, the day of the second reading of the Bill, four members of the League took advantage of a chance encounter with Johannes Strijdom to make yet another of their repeatedly abortive requests to see him. 'I know your viewpoint,' was the Prime Minister's response, 'and there is nothing more to discuss.' The women's next move was to appeal to ten men of honour who would put honour and principle before party: 'We ask ten Nationalists, particularly in the joint sitting, to vote against the South Africa Act (Amendment) Bill, or at least to abstain from voting.' The appeal failed to evoke any response, however, and the third reading of the Bill was announced. To mark this reading two hundred women stood with bowed heads on the City Hall steps in Johannesburg. They stood in ranks flanking a banner with large black roses at its corners and the inscription: '*Die Grondwet Vernietig*', 'The Constitution Destroyed'.

On the night of the final all-night sitting on the South Africa Act (Amendment) Bill, 27–28 February, thousands of South Africans joined in a mass vigil all over the country. Nevertheless, the Bill passed the third reading with eight votes more than the necessary two-thirds majority. 'There is nothing now,' responded a member of the League's Johannesburg regional committee, 'to give the people of South Africa any guarantee that, slowly, each civil liberty may not be similarly undermined; until our nation is completely at the mercy of despots – ruling in the name of an idealism which has already become translated into a mockery through the use of the term *volkswil*.'

The battle waged in the name of all that was good and honourable and just had been lost. It was a battle which was not entirely above criticism precisely from the point of view of the high moral cause it purported to represent. 'Moral outrage' had brought the organisation into existence. The tone of its pronouncements and of its magazine, which had come into being in January 1956, was that of the righteous conducting a crusade. 'The League is a pressure group to be used for the restoration and encouragement of political morality and the preservation of a constitutional government,' explained the opening pages of the first issue of *The Black Sash*. The campaign was waged against the 'lowering of the standard of political morality'. The country's honour was being besmirched. Christian principles were being flouted. Appeals to the nation were rich in biblical quotations and calls to prayer, to a point where the confrontation between good and evil, as many members of the Black Sash were then inclined to see it, took the form of a kind of pious one-upmanship.

When the Pretoria chairman of the League, as the position was referred to in the days before sexist language had become an issue in the Black Sash, sent the Nationalist Minister of Finance and External Affairs, Eric Louw, a copy of a prayer used at a gathering at the Union Buildings, his response was to refer her to the sixth chapter of St Matthew's Gospel, with which, he had deduced, members of the League must be unfamiliar. It reads, 'And when thou prayest thou shalt not be as the hyprocrites are. For they love to pray standing on the corners of streets that they may be seen by men. Verily I say unto you they have their reward.' Alternatively, Mr Louw suggested, the League might like to take a look at chapter 23, verse 27 of the same Gospel: 'Woe unto you scribes and Pharisees, hypocrites! For you are like unto whited sepulchres.' In her reply, the Pretoria chairman maintained that the prayer was a 'simple supplication to God for His guidance in our troublous times'.

Yet it is arguable that the *status quo* which the League fought to defend in such exalted tones was not quite the bastion of democratic rights and liberties that it was set up to be. At the time of the South Africa Act few if any English-speaking whites had been outraged at the idea of bargaining away the rights of non-whites for the supposed greater good of a united white South Africa. It had been left very much to blacks to communicate their own discontent with the franchise arrangements adopted at Union and with early post-Union discriminatory legislation. In fact it had been precisely as an expression of accumulated black resentment and the feeling that blacks must pursue their own interests on a national basis that in 1912 prominent black people from all over South Africa met in Bloemfontein and established the South African Native National Congress, renamed the African National Congress in 1925. Among the organisation's primary objectives were black unity, the extension of political rights and the economic and social advancement of blacks.

Whites, meanwhile, had remained for the most part unconcerned by the lack of black rights and prospects. There had been no furore when the 1936 Native Representation Act had struck the African voters in the Cape from the common roll. Even though it too had affected one of the entrenched clauses, there had been little reaction then among English-speakers. The League did include some Afrikaans-speaking women who were undoubtedly as concerned as their English-speaking counterparts for the future of their children. One of its avowed aims was furthermore to encourage 'bi-lingualism'. Nevertheless it was instigated and led by English speakers and the possibility exists that a stronger factor in the rather sudden expression of moral outrage on the part of the League was the awareness that the Nationalist government could use methods to remove English as an official language similar to those it was using to remove the coloured voters in the Cape from the common roll.

Hitherto the attitude of the English-speaking community had been characterised largely by complacency. As a young housewife at the time of the enactment of the Native Representation Act, Jean Sinclair would later recall her own relative indifference to politics, an attitude which she shared with a substantial proportion of the English-speaking community. The English-speakers were not uncomfortable with the country's allegiance to the British Crown – far from it. They therefore felt no indignation at the idea of the constitution having been laid before the British parliament for ratification, and largely ignored the Nationalist dissatisfaction with the supposed limitation on South African sovereignty. Furthermore, women in particular were not for the most part concerned with politics. As one long-standing member of the Black Sash later put it: 'We were for the most part complacent in our ignorance, particularly as women. We had the vote but we voted as our husbands voted and did not really think too closely about our own personal political principles.'

The ridicule to which some Nationalist supporters subjected the 'Housewives' League', the kind of humorous indulgence which depicted one obviously well-heeled lady directing another over the telephone – 'Don't give me your special recipe over the phone, dear – I'm sure it's tapped' – was not entirely without foundation, for most of the early membership were prepared to admit that they had not hitherto been particularly politically aware, let alone active. Noël Robb would recall being so apolitical at the time of the Senate Act that she did not even know what the ultimate motive for packing the Senate was. Her own Damascus experience occurred when, after a relatively brief period in

South America where she 'got used to white taxi drivers jumping out and opening doors for black mammas', she returned to Cape Town. 'I was taking the kids to the circus and joined in the queue; this was multi-racial, which didn't strike me as odd after South America. Suddenly the hatch opened and somebody said, "All coloureds out of the queue." Having been well back in the line, I suddenly found myself at the front. It just hit me between the eyes. Prior to that queue it had never entered my head to notice that such things were happening.' She remembered attending the first official meeting of League members from different parts of the country and being nicknamed Madame Lafarge because she knitted throughout proceedings.

Even after the spontaneous flare-up of indignation, the emotion that was finally aroused by the government's lack of fair play, the League's pronouncements and its actions reflected a combination of high moral attitudes and homely domesticated common sense in which the ladies themselves could discern the humour. One article included in *The Black Sash* magazine in 1956 detailed protesters' thoughts as they took part in haunts and vigils in a way which highlighted, albeit in a humorous way, the tension between lofty commitment to political principle and more mundane duties:

Many, as we know, pray. This indeed is a sound
approach and should be a habit with all of us, even if our
prayer is just a matter of moments.

Others work out problems, simple or complex
according to their natures. A school teacher I know told
me that she used up the silent minutes by making sure
that she knew all her tables. This did not, however,
involve a simple recitation of these mysteries up to
twelve times twelve. No, this doughty soul began at
thirteen times thirteen and carried on into some
frightful mathematical complexity that makes me come
over cold even to think of it.

I do not believe that many feel actively angry or
militant because, although our cause is just and so
many of the things that are happening in our country

today are deserving of the deepest anger, it is hard to be consistently angry when one's attention is concentrated on how best to shift the weight from one foot to the other. The most common reaction, probably, is just a delightful hotchpotch of diverse thoughts and feeling: a human and homely blend of the serious and the frivolous, the sublime and the commonplace.

The writer went on to relay the notes of her own particular 'hotchpotch' of thoughts made after one stand:

Here am I, standing in this rather curious attitude when I really ought to be at home attending to my household chores, because I genuinely believe that my rights as a citizen are at stake; because I know that unless someone does something about it my children's future in this country is imperilled. I am going to stand here for a long time so I might as well get down to it properly, and do some intelligent thinking on the whole subject, but before I begin I wish I could remember if I put the potatoes on for lunch.

I then, perhaps, get through a few minutes of concentrated thought on constitutional as opposed to arbitrary government, democracy versus totalitarianism, when I become aware of a pair of legs that are standing close to me. In our part of the country we take our vigils very literally and stand with downcast eyes, and so I cannot find out what the legs are attached to higher up, and because I cannot do so, I want to very much. I want to know, for instance, why this particular person wears shiny black shoes with white shorts. I feel that if I can get a glimpse of his face I shall find out the answer. As I struggle with myself, he moves on, and I return to higher thought.

I consider the National Convention, the great men of the past who made Union; I think of the liberty of the individual, the freedom of thought, the freedom of speech, the need for tolerance, of government by consent. I am really warming to my subject and losing

myself and the consciousness of my surroundings, when
I suddenly become aware that a fly has settled on the
end of my nose. There is no reason, of course, why I
should not just brush it off, but another pair of legs has
just moved up close to me and for the honour of the
branch I feel I must wait until he has moved on again.

The writer's thoughts roam on via parliament, Bills passed,
South Africa and eventually back to the potatoes and the
recollection that it is Monday – washing day: 'I have forgotten to separate my nylons from the general wash and even
now Annie is probably scrubbing them on a stone.'
Despite their concern with such homely considerations as
cabbages and nappies, despite their general lack of political
knowledge and despite the fact that it is arguable that many
of the women had joined the protest on unrealistic grounds,
their position was none the less unquestionably courageous
and significant. It was the first time that women in South
Africa had taken such action, action which included, as one
black ANC member pointed out, a form of demonstration
more readily associated with the black culture: protest-
marching. Of those who did not recognise the significance of
their stands at the time, many would come to regard them
with respect. The Roman Catholic Archbishop of Durban,
Denis Hurley, himself now an honorary member of the Black
Sash, would recall considering the ladies with their black
sashes something of a curiosity.

We didn't think there was much sense in just parading
and holding demonstrations and protest stands. We
didn't think it was a very efficient way to oppose
legislation. We hadn't thought of it, I suppose. We didn't
see its symbolic meaning. It took courage to do what
they were doing. Demonstrations always demand
courage, but the women persevered and they grew
through that, and those of us who were cynical of the
value of what they were doing came to admire them
very much.

It should be stressed that the League's committees were made up of women who were teachers, lawyers, social economists, historians, civic office-holders and business executives. The leadership included women who held qualifications and degrees at a time when university education was not so readily accessible to women. They immediately recognised the necessity to educate their membership, and that process of education inevitably opened the women's eyes to other examples of diminished rights and opportunities.

Following the passing of the South Africa (Amendment) Act and the Senate Act which had permitted the amendment to go through parliament, J. G. N. Strauss, leader of the United Party, the official opposition, announced his intention of testing the Act in the courts and the matter had consequently to be regarded as *sub judice*. The women's haunts and vigils in relation to that particular issue ceased accordingly. The Appeal Court in any case later endorsed the Nationalist victory. The failure of the women's initial protest and the ensuing sense of anti-climax might have induced the organisation to disband. Instead it caused the leadership to widen the focus of the League's attention. At an Extraordinary General Meeting of the Johannesburg region, Jean Sinclair spotlighted three further pieces of legislation soon to be debated in parliament: the Deportation Bill, giving power to deport a South African citizen not born in the Union without recourse to any trial or appeal to any court; the Prohibition of Interdicts Bill, which would take away the right of an 'African' to appeal to the courts against eviction from a place of business or dwelling, whether or not such eviction was with good cause; and the Cape Coloured Voters Bill, which would take away the right of the Cape coloured voter to sit on the Cape Provincial Council. 'The League considers these and many other actions of the government to be undemocratic,' announced Mrs Sinclair. 'There is only one standard of political morality – a thing is either right or wrong. Whenever a section of our population is threatened with discrimination, injustice or loss of liberty, we shall protest.'

At the national conference held in Bloemfontein in April

1956 the nickname originally given to the League by the press, 'The Black Sash', was adopted as the organisation's official name. Thereafter the women in their black sashes would renew their campaign of protest against 'those through whom political morality has reached its nadir', against any legislation they considered to be immoral, and against the removal of anyone's rights. They objected to the Suppression of Communism Act, which could take away a person's civil rights if the Minister merely chose to think that person was communistically inclined; to the Criminal Law Amendment Act, which made it an offence either to break a law in order to protest against it or to persuade anyone else to do so; to the introduction of Christian National Education in white schools, which called for separate schools for English- and Afrikaans-speaking children and which taught all race groups Afrikaner Nationalist views of history, geography and government — as well as the religious views of the Dutch Reformed Church, which were Calvinist and fundamentalist and banished even widely accepted scientific theories such as Darwin's theory of evolution from the curriculum whenever they conflicted with fundamentalist ideas. Black Sash women also protested in their distinctive style against the Bantu Education Act of 1953, which brought all schools for Africans under the direct control of the central government and which subjected black children to an educational process based on the assumption that there was no place for them in the European community above the level of certain forms of labour, and in general they turned their attention to the legislation that supported the system of apartheid.

Chapter Three

The right to move freely

'Nobody lost his job, went hungry or lay awake sobbing all night over the Coloured Vote. But that is what is going to happen over the Group Areas Act,' predicted *The Black Sash* magazine in June 1957. It had started to look at some of the great pillars of apartheid in detail, and was becoming ever more acutely aware of the suffering they caused. Passed in 1950 to legislate for the complete residential separation not only of whites and blacks but also of coloureds and Indians, the Group Areas Act gave power to prescribe to within a few yards where every race must live, and to move families, streets and whole communities from places where they had been living sometimes for two generations or more. Under it a white area could be turned into a black area; a black area into a white. A township could be prohibited or abolished. Municipalities could be told where to put their parks, suburbs, swimming baths or recreation grounds. The Indians of Johannesburg, some of whom had trading rights of over fifty years standing, could be scheduled for upheaval without any consultation. So too could the Cape coloureds who had lived peacefully in Cape Town with their white neighbours for over a century. And all this could be ethically justified on the grounds that, since the Group Areas Act applied to all races in South Africa, its application could not involve prejudice to any one race.

The strong core of Black Sash members, awakened and set upon continuing the fight, was outraged by such 'hypocrisy', as it was by the whole system of 'influx control'. Having instigated a programme of 'apartness', having racially classified the population, forbidden it (under the Immorality

Amendment Act and others) to cross the colour line in the most intimate areas, having introduced the Separate Amenities Act and created separate facilities for different races in those situations where they inevitably came together, the government had then taken steps to regulate the number of blacks allowed to live on the outskirts of the white cities. As early as the 1920s, at a time when 'poor whites' had become a pressing political issue, attempts had been made to control the flow of Africans from the tribal areas to the cities in order to protect white labour from black competition and the 'white man's land' from black invasion. This and subsequent attempts to control influx by means of the Native (Urban Areas) Act of 1923 and the Native Laws Amendment Act of 1937 had proved largely ineffective. South Africa's large cities, with their alluring promise of wealth and employment, had inevitably continued to represent a form of Eldorado to rural blacks from the Bantustans. Furthermore, employers faced with the offer of cheap labour and the constrictions of a wartime economy had frequently been prepared to ignore regulations relating to the employment of blacks. So it was that in a further attempt to tighten up these laws, in 1945 the Bantu (Urban Areas) Consolidation Act had been introduced, followed in 1952 by the misleadingly named Abolition of Passes and Coordination of Documents Act.

The effect of this latter legislation was essentially to stipulate that no African could remain for more than seventy-two hours in an urban or proclaimed area under Section 10(1) of the Bantu (Urban Areas) Consolidation Act unless he or she:

(a) had resided there continuously since birth.
(b) had worked there for one employer continuously for ten years; or had been there continuously and lawfully for fifteen years and while in the area had not left it for more than a year or been sentenced to a fine exceeding one hundred Rand or to imprisonment for a period exceeding six months.
(c) was the wife, unmarried daughter or son under eighteen years of the African falling into clases (a) or (b).

(d) had been granted a permit to remain by an
employment officer in the case of a workseeker or by
the local authority.

Permission to work or reside in a proclaimed area, an
African's service contract, together with his tax receipts,
citizenship, name, photograph and tribal affiliation, were all
contained in a 'reference book', which under the Abolition of
Passes and Coordination of Documents Act all Africans over
the age of sixteen and born in the Union were required to
carry at all times and produce whenever called upon to do so
by an authorised person. The pass system 'abolished' by this
Act had obliged African men for decades constantly to carry
on their persons an assortment of documents, permitting
them to work or simply to 'walk abroad', providing evidence
that they had some European's permission to return from
church on Sunday nights or that they had paid their tax,
curtailing their freedom to go from one place to another and
laying them open more than any other set of laws to encounter with the police, casual demand, organised check and raids
at any time of night or day.

Prior to 1952 a few men had been able to earn release from
this system. Men such as life-long employers, clergy of
recognised churches or school teachers had been required
only to carry their 'exemptions'. In reality, far from abolish-
ing this old-style system, the 1952 Act simply gathered the
previous assortment of papers between the covers of a single
reference book and extended and intensified it. The men were
worse off than they used to be. There were no more 'exemptions'; no man could earn his release. The Act did nothing to
reduce the revenue gained from pass-offence fines or the
frequency with which the system led to the rigours of police
attention. In fact the number of officials entitled to demand
the book was increased, while to move a yard without it, to
leave it by mistake in the pocket of another jacket, invited
criminal prosecution. African women had seen what the
obligation to carry passes had meant to their men. Men had
had to stand in long, wearisome queues in order to acquire
the requisite pieces of paper. They had had their meagre

earnings diminished by fines imposed for a signature missing, an inexplicable word wrong, or an unheard-of document not obtained. The women had been involved in this suffering through their men, but until the Abolition of Passes and Coordination of Documents Act came into force they themselves had been exempt from pass laws. They had to a large extent been left alone. They had borne and reared the children; they had planted and reaped the crops. They had provided domestic labour for city, town and farm. They had trained as nurses, worked in factories, taught in schools – all without permit or pass – but the 1951 Act made provision for the gradual introduction of registration books for women, books in which permissions would have to be entered: permission to travel in order to seek work required at both ends of the journey, permission to be in a stated place for longer than seventy-two hours, permission to return.

It was doubtful whether a large proportion of the African women, particularly in rural areas, who by 1956 were actually being asked to purchase these reference books fully appreciated the reason why they were being issued. They may not have understood that the books would serve the purpose of controlling movement, controlling labour, preventing labour shortages and so keeping down the price that could be asked for labour. They might not have realised that they would serve also to make African labour more migrant than ever, since the reference books were to be used gradually to evacuate from town and city all non-European 'undesirable elements'. They did, however, know intimately what the pass laws had meant to their menfolk. As for the men, they submitted reluctantly for a while at least to their own 'abolished' passes, but the extension of the pass-law requirements to African women aroused strong reactions. They knew that the system invited abuse. For them it was one thing; for their wives and daughters and sisters it was quite another. Nor were the government's attempts to persuade Africans that their reference books were no different from the identity cards which Europeans would be required to carry altogether convincing. No summary arrest would follow on a European's inability to produce his document to a policemen on demand. For a European there would be no demand. The Africans strongly resented the latest move in the control of influx and one section of the white community at least shared in their resentment.

On 9 August 1956, at the instigation of the Federation of South African Women (an organisation founded in 1954 because the need had been felt for a body which embraced all women of South Africa irrespective of race), thousands of women, predominantly black, assembled at the Union Buildings in Pretoria in the largest mass gathering of women in South African history. They were there to protest against the pass laws. The fact that it was the lives and liberty of women that were now being affected touched a chord of particular recognition in the Black Sash. The inferred message from the failure of the Torch Commando – which, having at one stage reached a membership figure of more than a quarter of a million, had died when it did not achieve its main objective, the ousting of the Nationalist government in the 1953 election – and from the failure of the Covenanters had been the endorsement of a sense of an almost mystical potency of women who prevailed even when their menfolk fell by the wayside. That sense was seriously called into question when the Senate Act was passed despite all the Black Sashers' valiant efforts. Nevertheless, the Black Sash remained conscious of its particular identity as an organisation of women. At a time when married Black Sash women were not required to have careers or support families financially there was a feeling that women were freer to act from principle than men. They were not required to be as pragmatic as men and could therefore follow their consciences in greater liberty.

As an organisation concerned with human rights and made up of women, the Black Sash applauded the action of the thousands of African women and a small number of whites who marched to the Union Buildings to present a protest to the Prime Minister about the introduction of reference books for African women. The deputation was not even received by a Cabinet minister, but perhaps, the Black Sash pointed out, members of the white population in general did not care

about the treatment the women received because they considered themselves unaffected by the legislation at issue.
'Apathy Ann' became a target of fierce criticism by the Black
Sash: 'It may be that you can only think in terms of colour
and as the people directly concerned are not white you think
these things do not matter, but please make note of this. You
may be as white as the driven snow, but that fact will not
necessarily protect your liberty.'

For a substantial proportion of the population, and for a
similar proportion of the Black Sash membership, the broad-
ening of the campaign to defend civil rights in the context of
apartheid, especially those of South Africa's disenfranchised
black majority, was too much. Being *for* something was quite
different from being *against* something. It had been easy to
work up indignation for a relatively short period about an
action which looked and was as totally immoral as the Senate
Act, but to take on a long-term battle was a very different
proposition. The Black Sash had, if it was going to continue
as an organisation, to decide what it actually stood for, and
people were afraid. Husbands were afraid for their wives,
afraid for their own positions in the business world. Quite
apart from racial considerations, for most Black Sash women
close identification with the black cause would involve the
spanning of social barriers not previously challenged. Black
Sash members in those days were unquestionably ladies,
seldom parted from their hats and gloves and the social
niceties which went with them. Zilla Harries Baird, who
joined the Black Sash in Durban as soon as it was initiated
and who by 1989 still undertook to take part in legal protests,
dressed impeccably in hat and gloves, would admit with self-
denigrating humour to a certain nostalgia for the days when
meetings were held not, as now, in Durban's ecumenical
centre but in Miss Tilly Campbell's elegant garden, and coffee
was drunk out of bone china. Eleanor Lewin, who went to
school with Jean Sinclair and taught her daughter, Sheena
Duncan, history, remembers the Black Sash ladies in those
days as 'socially prosperous people with whom I felt ill at
ease because I was socially unskilled'.

Many were the kind of characters not easily thrown,

women like the large-bosomed lady who when it came to her turn to be questioned by an importunate member of the public working his way along a line of silent Black Sash protesters, enquiring of each one what she was waiting for, pulled herself up to her full height and replied unhesitatingly and solemnly: 'Justice.' Nevertheless, for many, commitment to the anti-apartheid cause was too great and overturning of a hitherto largely unquestioned way of life. Noël Robb would recall having thought the pass laws rather 'neat and tidy and practical' until she went to a meeting held by the National Council of Women and heard a black woman speak. The woman in question delivered her lecture with her baby on her back. 'You must be wondering why I have brought the baby,' she addressed her audience, then went on to explain that the likelihood of her being arrested for being in an area illegally was considerable, and that if she was arrested a baby left at home and requiring breast-feeding might die. For the white women of the Black Sash, most of whom were accustomed to a life-style of servants and all the support systems that their influential husbands could provide, this explanation for why black women kept their babies constantly with them was a revelation. From then onwards a number of them worked very hard to induce the Sash to put its energy into opposing the pass laws, but the response would frequently prove to be far from positive: 'My husband says that if we do that, we'll be flooded out with Africans.' At the first truly multi-racial meeting organized by CATAPAW (the Cape Association to Abolish Passes for Women) Mrs Robb's mother, an English woman visiting from Britain, found herself sitting next to a large black woman breast-feeding her baby, and listening to black women 'shrieking down the microphone as they always do, instead of talking in measured Black Sash tones'. She found the experience quite difficult to swallow, as did others present.

When, furthermore, the Federation of South African Women, encouraged by the moral support given to its protest, made overtures to the Black Sash, the Black Sash carefully kept its distance, wary of too close an association with the Congress Alliance, initiated in June 1955 to unite all the chief organisations fighting apartheid, which constituted the Federation's major affiliates at the time. Helen Joseph, white secretary of the Federation of South African Women, had camped out at the Union Buildings beside the League women, as a token representative of South Africa's non-white women, who formed the main constituents of her organisation, but she was regarded by the Black Sash in those days as an extremist for identifying herself with the non-white liberation movement. Other issues raised within the organisation touched upon areas of long standing sensitivity for whites, and the response from some members was not always unambiguously non-racial. South Africa, it was discovered, had not signed the Universal Declaration of Human Rights, which had been drawn up in December 1948 by the United Nations Organisation and to which some forty-eight other nations were signatories. Several leading members of the Black Sash gave talks to the various branches with regard to this omission, but for many Sash ladies there was one major obstacle to subscription to the Declaration of Human Rights, namely mixed marriages. 'Nobody is saying that you have to make mixed marriages,' it had to be pointed out. 'All they're saying is that people should have the right to choose and that if they wish to make one they should have the right to do so.' Gradually, acceptance of the right to choose prevailed, but several annual conferences went by before the motion was carried. 'It took us a couple of conferences to get the Sash to accept the Declaration of Human Rights,' Noël Robb acknowledged, 'and in those days we accepted it as something to aim for, not something to do tomorrow because of the mixed-marriage question, which was of course illegal.'

It would also take three annual conferences for the Black Sash to open its membership to all races. The initiative for it to do so came from East London, a tiny region which was repeatedly defeated in its proposal, not on the grounds of colour but on the grounds that the Black Sash was a voters' organisation. There were many who felt that the prevailing conditions in the country were the result of the way in which whites had voted, and that it was therefore the responsibility of white women to rectify it. The inclusion among its members of people who had no vote would, it was also felt, weaken its potency as a pressure group. 'We felt responsible,' said Noël Robb. 'We had the vote as white women, although we had not had it for so long, and people must listen to us, but if we filled our ranks with coloureds and blacks who had no vote, we would lose our strength.'

There were many who sincerely believed that they would have a better chance of righting wrongs brought about by the arbitrarily enfranchised whites if they remained the conscience of the white electorate, a voice of protest from within. They felt that as a group of privileged white women obviously seeking no material advantage for themselves in their work for justice, they would have greater strength than as a mixed group in which many women would be fighting to establish their own rights. Black women would also be so much more vulnerable to possible punishment from the authorities for commitment to such an organisation. By the time, after much soul-searching, that in October 1963 the Black Sash did open its doors in principle to all women residents of the Republic of South Africa, in a sense the damage was done. Even if, as one member would point out, black women had wanted to find the money to join the Black Sash – for although membership fees were probably never so high as to exclude black members, they have never been cheap – by then it had been perceived as an essentially white organisation. As Noël Robb said, 'It was too late. Very few non-whites joined but the fact that the possibility was there did mean that in time younger people joined us. They would not have joined us if we had not been non-racial.'

Support for universal franchise was yet another contentious issue which would arise early in the history of the Black Sash. Again, it is arguable that the objections raised to it were not based on racial prejudice but on the conviction that it was inappropriate for the organisation to have a particular political policy. It had been stressed since the organisation's inception that it was open to people of all political parties, yet here members were being called upon to support an objective which people of certain political persuasions would be unable to pursue. Many were eventually won over by the realisation that the disenfranchised would have no time for the Black Sash until its members appreciated that those without the vote would not receive fair treatment until they were enfranchised. Others, particularly members of the Progressive Party newly formed in 1959, who subscribed to a qualified franchise and some kind of devolved legislative structure to ensure that one race group did not dominate another, would resign.

These were testing times for the Black Sash. The re-election of the Nationalist Party in 1958 had brought home to the organisation how little of what it stood for had been taken into account. In the run-up to that election all members, irrespective of their party allegiance, had been encouraged to work within their own party organisations for the same ideal that had moved them to join the Black Sash in the first place – the defence of the constitution. A vigil had been maintained in Pretoria without lapse since July 1955, and the government had been constantly reminded that its actions incurred the strong disapproval of the Black Sash women. Nevertheless, so much of the organisation's work of 'enlightenment' seemed to have gone for nothing. The days of the high-profile protests in the form of mass marches came to an end during the 1960s. The 'haunting' of ministers was discontinued because it was felt that, quite unintentionally, it was giving the impression that the Black Sash was anti-Afrikaner. 'We black sash the minister, not the occasion', proclaimed banners carried by the Black Sash when they haunted the Voortrekker Monument in Pretoria, the shrine of Afrikaner Nationalism. There was, none the less, a feeling among members that an impression was being given that their disapproval was directed against the Afrikaner people collectively, and although with hindsight Jean Sinclair felt that the haunts had been such good publicity that it was probably a mistake to abandon them, the practice was relinquished.

The haunts had boosted the morale of the League, however, and older members of the Black Sash have a tendency to look back on the early days of protest as a halcyon period when hope had not yet been abandoned. It was in a more sober and perhaps more penetrating fashion that the Black Sash endeavoured to go on examining all legislation and judging it according to whether it was immoral or an infringement of anyone's rights. Stands continued to be made, but by August 1958 police objections had twice caused the cancellation of Black Sash public protest meetings. With the Black Sash's growing concern for the plight of black and coloured South Africans, its members were increasingly looked at askance by their friends and even their own husbands. Not only were they now laughed at for being hopelessly visionary, dismissed as a silly band of crusading women who should be devoting their time and attention to their homes and children and not meddling in politics, but they were even accused of being communists. Despite, and in some instances because of, its determination to educate its membership and attempt to change the thinking of the country through open meetings, symposia, brains trusts and conferences, all but the most committed fell away.

The Afrikaans-speaking membership, such as it had been, dwindled. In the days before South Africa became a republic and left the Commonwealth the Afrikaner community was a much more narrow, closely linked body than today. Those who stepped out of the scope of accepted attitudes within the Afrikaner community had even greater hardships to contend with from their own people, friends and families. The few who joined the Black Sash had to be exceptionally courageous. For a while *The Black Sash* magazine continued to be published in both Afrikaans and English, but the implicit message of its pages was one of a nostalgic bias in favour of things British. 'The most precious thing the English brought to South Africa,' it exclaimed, 'was a belief in the dignity of the individual human being.' Criticism of the interference of the Nationalists with the judicial system found its expression in an apposite quotation from *Alice's Adventures in Wonderland*:

> *'I'll be judge, I'll be jury,'*
> *Said cunning old Fury.*

'I'll try the whole case
And condemn you to death!'

The South African policeman was compared unfavourably with the London 'bobby', who was traditionally calm, imperturbable, stolid, friendly and firm as a rock when under fire. He directed traffic, broke up demonstrations, tackled thieves and murderers, all with the same good-humoured efficiency. By contrast, his South African counterpart was tense and unsmiling in the performance of unpleasant duties. But then of course he was living in a violent land, enforcing laws which were unpopular with the majority, and when the 'bobby' was white and the people among whom he was operating were black the situation was likely to be explosive.

The Black Sash did not protest against the formation of the Republic in 1961, for this in itself could not be regarded as a deprivation of rights. Rather, it confined its objections to protesting against the fact that only whites took part in the referendum to decide whether South Africa should become a Republic. The news of South Africa's withdrawal from the Commonwealth, however, was received by members with a sense of shock and disbelief. Rose-tinted references to the British culture and way of life were in ready supply. If this was a reflection of the general tenor of the organisation at the time, it is not hard to imagine that even if many Afrikaans-speaking women had been prepared to stand up unambivalently in favour of justice for black people against the majority of their friends and associates, they still might not have felt too readily at home in the Black Sash.

Among the approximately 1100 women who remained in the organisation the commitment to fighting legalised injustice was uncompromising. Protest from the Africans, to which they gave their support, did produce a slight concession as far as the Abolition of Passes and Consolidation of Documents Act was concerned. Once again implying some sort of parity of Africans' reference books with European identity cards, the government agreed to suspend the implementation of the extension of reference books to women until such time as the other population groups were compelled to carry identity cards. In most of the country the regulations would not come into effect until February 1963. In the Western Cape, however, officials began demanding that women produce reference books or permits to be in the area, before the fixed date, using the system to carry out a plan first drawn up in 1955 by W. H. Eiselen, the then Secretary of Native Affairs, under which the Western Cape was to be a white and coloured preferential area from which all Africans were ultimately to be removed. Under this Coloured Labour Preference Policy, all blacks west of an imaginery border line running roughly north to south through the Cape Province, and known as the Eiselen line, were to be moved. The government had ordained that the Western Cape was to remain the 'natural home' of the coloured people, who would be given job preference and employment protection.

Already in 1958 African women in the Western Cape whose reference books or permits were not in order were being arrested and summarily imprisoned. Its involvement with CATAPAW alerted the Black Sash to the real implications of the pass laws in the Western Cape. State photographers were coming round to photograph black women for their new 'reference books'. African women were required to appear at Rondebosch Town Hall and other similar centres in front of a cameraman equipped with a large old-fashioned camera with a stick attached to it, indicating the exact distance the subject must stand from the device. Amy Thornton, who attended such occasions to protest as a member of the ANC, later recalled how the women were made to stand against a wall and the stick was pushed up against their breasts for the picture to be taken. 'I've never forgotten this, it was such a revolting sight.' She recalled too, being asked by one of the early Black Sash members to take some of the African women from the townships to meet the white ladies in one of their homes.

> In those days there was no contact. Very few whites
> were actively involved with Congress organisation. The
> Black Sash was this group of rather prim and proper

upper-middle-class ladies with their gloves and their
sashes. Everybody took it for granted that the blacks
carried passes, and sometimes there was a raid and the
police came and knocked your 'boy' up to ask him for
his pass, but of course nobody knew that in the
townships the police would come knocking people up at
3 or 4 a.m., breaking doors down and asking for their
passes. They didn't know that when the authorities
were short of money they would have a raid on passes
and reap in the fines. They didn't know what those bits
of paper really meant.

There had actually been a case in Cape Town where a
shack caught fire and the occupant, realising his pass was in
his jacket inside, ran back to get it and was burnt to death.
Such was the importance of one small piece of paper. The
African women spoke at length of what pass laws meant in
their lives and the Black Sash ladies were 'totally horrified'.
Together with the Anglican Church Mothers' Union, the
National Council of Women, the Society of Friends, the
Federation of South African Women and the ANC Women's
League, the Black Sash directed considerable energy into
highlighting the consequences of the coloured Labour Preference Policy in the Western Cape. The commitment to this
cause of a number of Black Sash individuals became so well
known that a queue of Africans regularly formed in their
backyards seeking assistance and advice. Long-suffering
Black Sash husbands, some of whom had already undergone
the embarrassment of their wives using their social standing
to attend functions and then producing their sashes of protest
at opportune moments, and many of whom had become
adepts with a tin-opener, did not greet these strings of needy
people with unmitigated delight. Fortunately, the need to
save certain Black Sash marriages coincided with the availability of people more experienced in the application of the
apartheid laws than Black Sash members then were.
Prior to the banning of the African National Congress in
1960, the ANC's Women's League conducted various campaigns to try and show the government what suffering the

pass laws were causing African women, and to help those arrested with their court cases. Mrs Lettie Malindi, an executive member of the Athlone branch of the ANC Women's League and wife of Zoli Malindi, a leading Cape Town member of the ANC and subsequent executive member of the UDF, was among the African women who saw cases in the evenings after she had done her day's work and referred them to volunteer lawyers, all of whom would subsequently have to go into exile. Some time before the banning of the ANC, she would point out, the writing was on the wall.

> Before we were banned, we knew we were going to be, so the Black Sash decided to open an advice office in the place where we used to work in the evening in Athlone. The Black Sash was not very much in touch with the African laws in those days, so they asked us, the ANC's Women's League, to send volunteers to open their office. I and five others who were very much involved with the laws went. We had memorised them and we knew where to plead and where not to plead when the lawyers were not there.

The establishment of the first Advice Office, or Bail Fund Office as it was then called, in Athlone, Cape Town in 1958 in order to assist the victims of apartheid's laws, was a major milestone in the development of the Black Sash. It would open up a second dimension to what was fundamentally a political pressure group, a 'service' aspect. The white women were resolved to undertake practical work among Africans deprived of their civil rights and liberties. The African volunteers sent to work alongside them to translate from Xhosa what the people coming into the office were saying, and explain under which section of the pass laws a particular case came, were not at first, however, unduly impressed. 'At that time it was terrible. I had to explain three times one thing. They were not sure I knew what I was talking about.' For white women whose only previous relationship with blacks had been with their servants, taking advice from the Africans who worked with them did not come easily. Mrs Malindi was shrewd enough to discern the reason for their failure to accept her credibility.

> When a new person comes in she thinks, 'Hey, this
> domestic servant doesn't know what she's talking
> about', because in our country the majority of our
> people are domestic servants. She asks me, 'Who must I
> talk to?' and I must tell her who to talk to and then I
> must tell her the right way of tackling this case. Then
> she asks me again and I tell her. Then she goes and asks
> another white person. But I have no ill feelings and I
> couldn't do otherwise. I had to tolerate this like my
> plates or my stove or whatever. There have been a few –
> we had to stand breast to breast – but after that they
> understood, 'These African people know what they're
> talking about. They know these laws, they know what
> they want and what they are saying in God's truth.' I
> kept on saying, 'We can't tell you what hasn't happened,
> what isn't right, because it's going to be tested legally.'

Initially, Mrs Malindi and the other black people who came to help in the Athlone advice office were regarded by their own people as 'selling them to the white people'. She was accused by the less 'enlightened' of having abandoned the black anti-apartheid organisations to run around with white women. The more 'enlightened' recognised, however, that they 'needed the next hand to help us', and after three years or so they would come to understand that there was nowhere else to turn to: 'They had to bring their troubles somewhere and they trusted the Black Sash because one of their own was there.' To be fair to the white women in the advice office also, there were times when they felt very much at the mercy of their interpreters, times when they sensed that the information they were being relayed was incomplete and that friction was arising between the translators and the applicant for help, over which they had absolutely no control. Gradually, despite their initial inexperience, the advice office workers would win the confidence of a number of Africans.

At first the prime focus of attention was on the predicament of women arrested under the pass laws who had no money for bail and whose families frequently suffered in their enforced absence. Many of the women who appeared in court had had no alternative but to spend the whole night in the cells, leaving their small children in the care of neighbours. They had been arrested because they had left their passes inside their house while hanging up the washing or borrowing a cup of milk from a neighbour. The Black Sash was told that even if these women pleaded with the police to allow them to fetch their passes from the house, they were not allowed to do so and were jailed until the next session of court began. The organisation invited people to lend it money interest-free to form a bail fund. When a woman was arrested for a pass-law offence she would then be able to contact the Black Sash, who would send someone to the police station or the magistrates' court to lend her the bail money. When she appeared in court to face the charges against her, the bail money would be returned to her and she could then give it back to the Black Sash. If she was guilty and had no good cause to plead otherwise, she would be found guilty and sentenced.

In the years prior to 1961 when South Africa became a republic, the sentence was usually a fine of anything between £1 and £5, with imprisonment or transport to the reserves as an alternative, and usually the accused would have been able to raise the money for the fine in the meantime. Often it would not occur to Africans, confused by the whole legal process conducted in a language they were frequently unable to understand, to enter a 'not guilty' plea in the event of their having a good excuse or being wrongly charged. They were totally at the mercy of an interpreter who, though he too was black, was usually as smooth-tongued as he was well dressed and who frequently left no doubt as to where his personal interests lay. The need for legal support and advice became strikingly apparent. The Black Sash managed to persuade a number of young lawyers and advocates, often those still completing their articles with local law firms, to appear *pro amico*. The Chairman of the Law Society was then contacted and his permission was given for the *pro amico* rules of the Society to apply. The magistrate in each case was informed of the existence of the bail fund and the Black Sash's intention 'to keep good women out of jail'. The Chief Native Commissioner was next informed that the Black Sash had drawn up a questionnaire to show that the existing pass laws could not be administered without the greatest hardship, injustice and disruption of family life, and that the bail fund was an endeavour to help Africans to their civil right to bail.

Then began the slow process of making Africans believe the unbelievable fact that white women earnestly wished to help them for no financial or political gain, of contacting African organisations and societies to inform them of the availability of the bail fund and ask them to contact the Black Sash if any of their women members needed bail for pass-law offences. These societies were also asked to hand out Black Sash questionnaires with a view to having them completed by 'reliable' people. 'We have found,' reported one Black Sash memorandum on the bail fund, 'that when unknown white people approach Africans for their 'story' they often hedge and/or lie, but that when their own elected leaders approach them our questionnaire is reliably filled in.'

The experience of collecting this information and, above all, of encountering at first hand the suffering of black South Africans under the many different aspects of influx control was invaluable. As one early advice office worker would reflect, 'It is only when you help the victims of unjust laws that you become entirely convinced that they are not only unjust but cruel and inhuman.' The predicament of the coloured people of South Africa was by no means an easy one. They too suffered from the sheer fact of being non-white and, additionally, from being a hybrid group. Many blacks did not care for the so-called coloureds, regarding them, because they had been granted privileges denied to blacks, as part and parcel of the machinery of oppression. Yet, as one coloured person would put it, 'A dog is a dog irrespective of what breed he happens to be. We are all dogs and the fact that I'm a dog with ten fleas and you are one with fifty doesn't make any difference.' Nevertheless, it was primarily blacks who turned

to the Black Sash advice offices over the years and who
became the organisation's primary focus of concern, for
coloureds would have their own municipal advice bureaux,
and in any case it was not they who suffered most under
influx control.

By the end of the 'fifties, black protest with regard to the
inhumanity of influx control was mounting. In 1959 young
leaders of the African National Congress broke away from
the organisation to form the Pan-African Congress, members
of which considered themselves to be first and foremost
Africanists and were deeply suspicious of the role played by
white radicals in the freedom struggle. Sporadic protests in
1959 developed during the early months of 1960 into a larger-
scale campaign of resistance to the enforced carrying of
reference books. The campaign involved Africans going to
the nearest police station and inviting arrest for not carrying
their passes. It was as part of that campaign of passive
resistance that on 21 March 1960 a crowd gathered outside
the police station at Sharpeville. Police gunned down 69
people and wounded 186 others, including women and children. On the same day, at Langa, a black township near Cape
Town, more lives were lost and soon afterwards 30,000
Africans from Langa and other neighbouring black townships
marched in protest towards Cape Town, although the march
was subsequently peaceably dispersed. The government's
response was to ban both the PAC and the ANC and impose
a State of Emergency. Over 1,500 people were arrested and
detained without trial.

At a time when, as far as the Black Sash was concerned,
the rule of law had been suspended and it was left to senior
officers of the Special Branch to decide whether an action
was dangerous to the state or not, Black Sash women set
about helping those who were suffering as a result of having
protested against laws which both they and the Black Sash
believed to be unjust. After detainees had been charged and
served a sentence or had been found not guilty or simply
discharged, some found their way quite naturally to the
advice office. In the small room at the back of the Athlone
advice office, workers began to have dealings with members
of the African Resistance movement. 'They were nearly all

banned people who were not allowed to talk to more than one person at a time so they couldn't be in a room with a whole lot of other people wanting advice.' Together with an interpreter, Noël Robb would interview one person at a time, hoping no one would notice. On one occasion Special Branch officers did turn up and remove all the African Resistance files. They kept them for a while but then returned the papers without further intervention.

The Black Sash publicly condemned the resort to violence in resisting apartheid, but it also protested against the banning of a large number of ANC leaders. It further protested against the banishment of people like Elizabeth Mafeking, a mother of eleven children, who the Black Sash believed was sentenced to an unknown period of exile in a remote and desolate part of the country away from her husband and family, primarily because her trade-union work to secure better wages for Africans and against the extension of the pass laws to women had made her a discomfort to the government. Government supporters held the Black Sash partly responsible for some of the outbreaks of violence that had occurred. The cause of the disturbance, according to the Nationalists, was not to be found in what the government was doing but in the activities of the 'enemies of South Africa', who included the English press, 'liberalists' and the Black Sash.

In the advice office, the Black Sash carefully explained to those seeking assistance that no attempt would be made to evade the law, but that every effort would be made to establish their rights within the framework of what was lawful. A simple filing system was instigated to record each case that came in. It became a catalogue of the human tragedies suffered by individuals seeking passes, permission to work, permission to remain in the area, and people 'endorsed out', ordered to leave the area under the Coloured Labour Preference Policy and return to 'homelands' – the bantustans which the government maintained conformed to areas where the various black tribes of South Africa traditionally lived, and which under the apartheid system originally conceived by the National Party in 1948 were eventually to become the home of all of South Africa's blacks, except those whose labour was required in white areas.

The people who came to the advice office often had no means of proving that they satisfied the criteria which determined whether they could stay. They could not prove that they had resided in the area since birth because they frequently had no birth certificate. Many of them did not even know exactly how old they were. Often they knew nothing about the legalities of work permits; only that they had worked. They did not understand why it was suddenly illegal for them to live in an area where, although they had no documentation to prove it, they had lived all their lives. Sometimes they had left the area for just a little more than twelve months and found only on their return that this meant they no longer had the right to be there. A wife who had the right to live with a husband in an urban area could lose this right if she left the area for any length of time. If, for example, she went to nurse a dying mother in the country, her husband could be required to move into bachelor quarters and when she returned she could find herself endorsed out.

If a man who was born in an area and had lived there continuously wished to marry a woman from elsewhere, he had to apply for permission for her to enter the area in order to marry her. This might be granted, but permission for the bride to remain was usually refused on the grounds that there was no suitable accommodation available. There were troubled women who came for advice on how or whether to divorce their husbands who had been endorsed out of the urban area. These were women who qualified in their own right, by reason of birth, long residence or length of employment, to remain. As married women they lost these rights and must leave with their husbands, but by obtaining a divorce they regained their own rights of residence. They were faced, therefore, with the heart-rending choice between deserting their husbands and retaining their own rights and those of their children, or following their husbands into exile, to areas where there might be no houses, no schools, possibly not even the means of making an adequate living. Other women found themselves told to leave the township where they lived within days of being widowed because their right to remain there had depended on their husband's right to live there under Section 10 (1) of the Bantu (Urban Areas) Consolidation Act as amended by the Abolition of Passes and Coordination of Documents Act. Not only had they lost their husbands and the family breadwinners, but by the same stroke of tragic misfortune they had lost their home and the right to work to support their children. The children would have to leave their school and their home and go to a new 'home' in the Transkei which they might never have seen before and where the chances of ever earning a living were, at the very least, remote.

What they were hearing in the advice office induced Black Sash women to take a closer look at the hardships suffered by evicted Africans, by men like Kleinbooi Sikade who swept the roads of Wellington, some forty miles from Cape Town, wearing an old army greatcoat several sizes too large and a khaki woollen cap. He lived in a tin shack in Sakkieskamp with his wife Pauline, whom he had brought back as his bride after his last visit to the reserves. The authorities said he had done this illegally, but he knew nothing about that. He also had two children, aged five and one, of whom he was very proud. Then came the 'troubles', triggered off by Sharpeville. Kleinbooi and many others put their reference books in a drum supplied by the municipality because some Africans were beating up those who had not burnt their passes. When all was quiet again, Kleinbooi went to fetch his pass. It took some time for the officials to find it and he was away from work for two days. When he returned it was only to find that a coloured labourer had taken his place. Like many of his friends, he was endorsed out of the area. Suddenly he found himself arrested. For the first time in his life he found himself in jail, for not having left the area as ordered. At home his wife, Pauline, was sick. She was tubercular and utterly dependent on Kleinbooi, and they had never before been parted since their marriage.

After Kleinbooi was released the Black Sash applied for a railway warrant so that the family might go to Lady Frere, Kleinbooi's birthplace, to which he was entitled to return. By then, however, all his savings had gone. The family could not afford to pay for their tickets plus all the expenses of moving. Months went by during which their house was broken into by police on a routine raid for pass offenders, but Kleinbooi and his wife escaped. They spent the night in hiding with friends. The day came, however, when Pauline was arrested. The authorities only released her when the Black Sash explained who Pauline was and that the family had been ready to go to Lady Frere for some time. Next Kleinbooi developed acute asthma and the children also fell ill. There was still no news of the railway warrant, nor had they received the necessary confirmation from the Native Commissioner that there was a place for them in Lady Frere. Such letters of authority frequently took months. Neither warrant nor permission arrived for Kleinbooi and Pauline, yet they must get out of Wellington somehow.

The Black Sash decided to take them to Lady Frere. It might be helpful to the work to see what difficulties such families encountered. A reply-paid telegram was sent to the Commissioner in Lady Frere, a special compartment was reserved on the train, a lorry was hired to take them to the station, and a cramped and difficult journey began. In the end they were given a not very warm reception by the assistant magistrate in Lady Frere. It was discovered that Kleinbooi had a stepmother with a piece of land about twenty-five miles away, and the magistrate immediately assumed that their home would be with her. The two Black Sash women were simply informed that relatives were always pleased to receive members of the family even if they brought no money or food and stayed for ever. Work was always available in the mines and on the road. When it was pointed out that in view of Kleinbooi's asthma such work was hardly suitable, the magistrate responded that if he registered at the labour bureau when his turn came he would be offered a job. The next Black Sash task was to arrange for treatment for Pauline. The assistant magistrate informed them that Pauline would have to walk twenty-five miles to Lady Frere and twenty-five miles back again twice a week to receive treatment. A hundred miles a week for a TB patient to receive treatment seemed a little unrealistic. 'It may be unrealistic but thousands do it,' was the reply. The experience of Kleinbooi's family was no worse than that of a multitude of others the Black Sash ladies would come to know.

In the meantime they were also concerning themselves with academic freedom, freedom of the press, the South African Broadcasting Company's propaganda and with how they could cooperate with other organisations in protest against such issues. By 1961 there was a fear that the organisation's activities were becoming so diffuse that its energy and identity might be lost. There had also been a certain lack of continuity in the early leadership. Following the national conference of 1959, the headquarters of the Black Sash had moved from Johannesburg to Cape Town and the need for a Capetonian national president had been felt. Ruth Foley had thus been succeeded by Cape Town's Molly Petersen and, a year later, by Eulalie Stott. In 1961, however, the headquarters returned to Johannesburg, and at the national conference that year Jean Sinclair was elected to the presidency.

Mrs Sinclair is Scottish, full of guts and tenacious. Together with Helen Suzman, another dedicated opposition figure, she had belonged to the so-called liberal wing of the Witwatersrand Women's Council of the United Party. Also with Helen Suzman, she was a founder member of the Progressive Party and very nearly became its first elected representative when she stood for the city council of Johannesburg as a Progressive Party candidate and lost by the narrow margin of ninety-nine votes. For the fourteen years of her national presidency of the Black Sash she kept the organisation going, to a large extent by sheer force of character. Jean Sinclair was at that time an innately shy person who overcame her dislike of public-speaking to commit herself uncompromisingly to the fight. Many years later, on the occasion of the twentieth anniversary of the founding of the Black Sash, Helen Suzman would describe how her fellow campaigner for the improvement of the lot of the black people of South Africa had been 'mostly in a state of burning indignation – only her sense of humour saved her from being

a chronic ulcer sufferer'. In the view of Jean Sinclair's daughter, Sheena Duncan, an equally resolute personality who in
March 1975 would succeed her mother as national president,
if it had not been for the industry and energy of this 'very
thoughtful and very determined sort of woman', and a handful of other original members, the organisation might have
foundered during the 'sixties, 'those years when it was
difficult even for the Black Sash to get anything into the
press'.

Instead, other advice offices were opened – in Johannesburg
in 1963 and subsequently in Durban, Pietermaritzburg, East
London, Port Elizabeth, Grahamstown and Pretoria. The
organisation would ultimately operate in seven regions. In
different regions the people who came seeking the advice
these offices gave free of any charge would reflect different
local concerns, problems and deficiencies. Regional differences would arise out of the politics that informed or directed
the region's policy. Natal, for example, proved to differ from
other areas in its need to contend with the complex politics
of an area closely involved with Kwa Zulu and Chief Gatsha
Buthelezi's Inkatha.

For years, however, the battle against the pass laws would
constitute the primary focus of the Black Sash advice offices
in general, although by 1966 the Department of Bantu
Administration and Development was still responding that
the 'pass laws' had disappeared in 1950 and that a reference
book was not a pass but 'an identity card and a holder for
important documents'. Unimpressed, the Black Sash produced a carefully researched brochure against the pass laws,
citing thirty-two cases dealt with in the advice offices and
claiming that for every non-European who came into the
offices there were thousands with the same problem. This
the government dismissed as being a misrepresentation based
on exaggerated examples:

They say that these restrictions lead to the break-up of
family life, unemployment, poverty, malnutrition,
uncertainty and hopelessness. Anyone who has the
most elementary knowledge of these controls knows

that this is not so – otherwise why should the Bantu make use of all means, legal or otherwise, to land themselves into this cursed network of controls by coming into the city? If conditions are so hopeless why is it so difficult today to keep the foreign Bantu out of the country? Far from being oppressive, these measures are a method of protecting the Bantu against unemployment and exploitation, squatting and slum conditions. Take away these labour regulations as the Black Sash asks, and every clear-thinking person can see that conditions will be created over night in South Africa, in which communism would flourish.

In its statement, the government enquired what these 'Advice Bureaux' were in which the Black Sash was so actively giving advice. 'The organisation makes no secret of it, that it pleads for integration, also in white South Africa. All its thinking is dominated by this. The tragedy is that in its excessive zeal to propagate its philosophy it only confuses the Bantu, and our officials and the local authorities are brought into disrepute.'

As far as the Black Sash was concerned, the philosophy behind the advice offices was to enable people to understand what the law was, to enable them to make choices about how they wished to act and to support them in their chosen action. That support did not take the form of financial assistance, although people could be referred to other organisations offering such help. Where it was a matter of officials being unduly slow to provide documents, white persuasive powers could be brought to bear. Legal loopholes could be found. Appeals could be made against some orders. Test cases were taken to court by *pro amico* lawyers and occasionally won. Precedents were set, as in the case of Elizabeth Pikashe.

The handwritten notes in the advice office files in Mowbray, Cape Town, record that she had first come to the office in April 1971 wanting a pass. She had no birth certificate. Her father was dead. Her mother had disappeared. She had been brought up by an uncle and aunt. She had gone to school first in Athlone, then in Langa and then at a boarding school in the Transkei. By 1971 she was living with another aunt in the black township of Guguletu outside Cape Town and working as a domestic. She had not registered at any time. Her uncle was cross with her for not giving him money from her wages and now she was attempting to register. He was maintaining that she had left Cape Town at the age of five and gone to live with her mother in Lady Frere. Her aunt was prepared to state otherwise. A later entry in the same file registered the fact that on 23 January 1973 she had been arrested near Guguletu and charged that 'she being a Bantu wrongfully and unlawfully and without permission of the Municipal Labour Officer remained for more than seventy-two hours in the prescribed area of the Cape Peninsula and failed to produce on demand to an authorised officer her permission to be in that area'.

Elizabeth Pikashe pleaded not guilty to both charges, was found guilty by the Bantu Affairs Commissioner for the area and sentenced to R20 or forty days' imprisonment. On advice, however, she appealed and in 1975 the Supreme Court upheld her appeal. Mr Acting Justice Broeksma set aside her conviction for being in the prescribed area for more than seventy-two hours without authority. Elizabeth Pikashe had only been out of the area for the four years during which she was at boarding school in the Transkei. The Appeal Court judge ruled that when someone was temporarily absent from an area for the purposes of education that person always manifested an intention to return to the area. Lawyers pronounced this unprecedented judgement 'highly significant'. Thereafter the implication was that it was not the length of time a person was absent from the area but the absence of any intention to return that lost him or her the right to stay. As Noël Robb later explained, 'If you packed up, sold your things, gave up your home, went to the Transkei, hated it and came back after a week, you would have lost your rights. If, on the other hand, you still had your home but you went to stay in the Transkei for a month to look after your sick father, and in the end you stayed two years because he took two years to die, then you would not lose your rights because your intention was to return.' The Cape Town advice office had to deal with many instances of people who had been sent to school in the Transkei, and this precedent was used on numerous occasions.

Much later, in 1983, the case of black engineering worker Mehlolo Tom Rikhoto would severely dent the pass laws when he contested the refusal of his local municipal office to grant him his right under section 10(1)b to remain in a white area for more than seventy-two hours because he had worked there continuously for one employer for not less than ten years, on the grounds that although he had worked for one employer for ten years, he had renewed his contract every year and therefore his employment and residence had not been 'continuous'. The Supreme Court ruled in favour of Rikhoto in what was to prove an historic decision. According to a subsequent government statement this meant that 143,000 migrant workers would immediately qualify to live permanently in the urban areas and would be entitled to bring their wives and children to live with them under Section 10(1)c of the Act. In the first weeks after the judgement, labour offices were inundated with people asking for their 10(1)b endorsements, but despite Dr Koornhof's announcement that the Appeal Court's ruling would be accepted, only a negligible number of applications were granted and each day dozens of people crowded into Black Sash advice offices to complain that their rights had been denied them. On 26 August 1983 the government promulgated an amendment to Section 10, removing the right of husbands and fathers to have their wives and children live with them in the urban areas whether or not they had a house or even a lodger's permit. The Black Sash set about exposing this promulgation as a breach of promise and assisting migrant workers to obtain their endorsements through the Legal Resources Centre, an independent body providing free legal assistance established in 1979 in Johannesburg and in 1983 in Cape Town.

Between 1960 and 1980 it was estimated that 2 million people were convicted under the pass laws. Finally, in 1986, in response to the President's Council's report on 'An Urbanisation Strategy for the Republic of South Africa', the outlines for a new vision of 'orderly urbanisation' were drawn up. On 23 April 1986 the Abolition of Influx Control Bill formally repealed 'the laws relating to influx control in respect of black persons', which in practice had broken down some years earlier. The new vision, the Black Sash would then announce, far from being the piece of legislation for which it and a host of other opposition voices had been struggling for years, would still define, limit and control the access of black people to the urban areas and the opportunities of life there. People still could not live anywhere they wished. The Group Areas Act remained intact and controls relating to squatting, slums, health and trespass had been reinforced.

In 1986 The Prevention of Illegal Squatting Act of 1951 was amended. The Squatting Act already had exceedingly harsh provisions allowing, among other things, the removal of people from where they were to another place decided by a magistrate. The 1986 amendment would in fact, the Black Sash pointed out, give additional powers to the Minister and increase penalties all round. The Bill gave certain government officials the power to decide whether to 'prohibit' people from settling or congregating where they were. Section 3 allowed the Minister of Constitutional Development and Planning to prohibit anyone who owned, let or controlled land which was not zoned for black occupation, from permitting people to 'congregate or settle' on that land. His power to prohibit them was based on his 'opinion'.

As of 1986, under the Identification Bill, all South Africans regardless of race would be entitled to the same identity document, but even this innovation was not without certain undesirable features, most specifically the fact that race classification, the very foundation of apartheid, was to remain and that the taking and storing of black people's fingerprints, which had been implemented since 1952, was not to be abolished, but would instead be extended to all races.

By 1986 the Black Sash was able to speak out with exceptional authority on the basis of its unique experience accumulated in the advice offices. According to Sheena

Duncan, who for many years directed the Black Sash advice office in Johannesburg, already by the late 'sixties the press had taken to telephoning the Black Sash whenever an incident occurred. Through its advice office work the Black Sash could keep a unique finger on the pulse of what was happening in the black communities even when restrictions on the media denied such information to other parties. The advice offices dealt with the problems of individuals, and if it was found that a particular problem was common to a great many people then the people themselves were encouraged, should they wish to do so, to take up that problem as a community issue. The advice offices could thus mobilise and 'conscientise' both those who worked in them and the people who came for assistance.

Furthermore, the information the organisation gained by this means became the starting point for various strategies employed to force the government to act, strategies in which the essential ingredient was public knowledge. The initial step was invariably to inform the public of carefully substantiated facts of which, in segregated South African society, it might otherwise be totally unaware, and so to raise public concern about a particular grievance. Deputations and appeals were made to Cabinet ministers. The Black Sash supplied information to opposition members of parliament who raised questions in the House on the strength of it. The Progressive Federal Party MP Helen Suzman, who for thirteen years was the only liberal opposition voice in parliament and who in May 1990 would be made an honorary life member of the Black Sash, provided an effective voice for the issues which Black Sash activity brought to light. Other options included taking legal advice and testing the real parameters of the law in the courts, negotiation with the authorities, public meetings and the provision of practical support to people in whatever course of action they themselves had chosen.

It was on the basis of years of this process of listening, advising, mobilising and conscientising that in 1986 the Black Sash expressed serious doubts about whether President P.W. Botha's replacement of the pass-law system with what was to be called 'orderly urbanisation' would in fact do anything to diminish problems with which they had long been concerned, the problems of state control, squatting, forced removals and homelessness.

Chapter Four

New home – old story

The problem of homelessness had always been inextricably interwoven with the policy of influx control. In 1957 Dr Verwoerd, then Minister of Bantu Affairs, announced that the government's new housing policy was that houses for families were not to be built in the urban areas, that housing moneys in urban areas were to be used for the building of hostels and that money for family accommodation must be expended within the homeland borders. This housing policy was very much part of the control mechanism which denied freedom to black South Africans. Together with the pass laws, it was intended to ensure that blacks other than those required as workers would remain in their tribal homelands regardless of how ill-equipped the infrastructure of those homelands was to support millions of unemployed Africans.

Relocation was also a necessary part of the apartheid programme. It began in earnest in the 1960s. Blacks were moved from rural areas, towns and cities which were set aside for whites. Coloureds and Indians were moved into group areas on the edges of white towns and cities, and Africans were moved to bantustans. A report by the Surplus Peoples Project produced in 1983 with the help of members of the Black Sash stated that in the years since 1960 the South African government had moved more than 3.5 million people, and even that figure did not include those endorsed out of urban areas on conviction for pass-law offences, for the simple reason that it was impossible to establish with any degree of accuracy how many people actually left in those circumstances. The single biggest category of those moved from white rural areas was that of ex-farm-workers who were generally poverty stricken and found themselves evicted to unfamiliar bantustans. The largest category of people moved from urban areas during that same period was that of Group Area removals. More than 860,000 coloured and Indian people were involved, and many Africans had to be moved as a result of the deproclamation or official non-recognition of townships, mainly in the Transvaal and Orange Free State. The people who lived in and around the small towns had to move to bantustans, from where the workers commuted or migrated back to their jobs. Another large group moved out of white urban areas were the squatters. It was impossible to assess how many people in the informal settlements through-out South Africa were subject to enforced removal. The Surplus Peoples' project also stated that facilities and com-pensation provided for those undergoing these removals varied according to the status the government accorded to those they moved: 'Whites get the best deal (compensation for their farms and inconvenience), coloureds and Indians get more than Africans, and Africans who qualify to be in white urban areas get more than those who do not.' Lowest on this scale of treatment were inevitably the 'illegal' squatters.

Of the people who found their way to the big cities to work, those 'legals' who lived in hostel accommodation provided for migratory workers were regarded as fortunate, but through their contacts in the advice offices the Black Sash became increasingly conversant with what life in such accommodation was really like. They knew that for its occupants there was no privacy, that clothing frequently had to be hung up on string, benches in the communal kitchens were nailed to the floor, the electricity often failed and the limited number of communal toilets were grossly inadequate. They knew that, for example, in Langa, one of the black townships outside Cape Town, there were approximately 19,000 'bachelors' of whom 68 per cent were married men living away from their wives. They also knew that as a consequence of this fact alone somewhere in the country there were nearly 13,000 families having to survive without a father.

Frequently, however, work-seekers had no alternative but

to squat in the hundreds of informal settlements on the edges of South African cities. Even those who qualified under Section 10(1) to work in the cities could not necessarily find accommodation deliberately kept in short supply in South Africa. Even those blacks who could have afforded it were not allowed to own property in the coloured labour preference area of the Cape. Those reduced to squatting lived in shacks made out of corrugated iron, sacking, plastic sheeting and anything else they could come by, and were liable to enforced removal. Enforced removal could mean the arrival of bulldozers which levelled such pathetic homes to the ground and destroyed the acquisitions of a lifetime in minutes. The government began a process of busing illegals to the homelands, even those who had lived all their lives on the outskirts of South Africa's cities and knew nothing of their supposed 'home'. Only rarely could that homeland offer them the opportunity to earn the humblest of livings or the most rudimentary roof over their heads.

Like the right to move freely, the Black Sash regarded shelter as one of the basic human rights. People were entitled to a roof over their heads, and ways had to be found of forcing the authorities either to provide that shelter or to provide land on which people could build their own. The Black Sash conducted campaigns designed to induce the government to provide houses for the homeless and against forced removals. Information received in the advice offices and through relationships established on an individual basis was collected and collated, and the process of 'conscientising' the public began, particularly among the white electorate but also among black communities who sought to know what rights they possessed. Information was fed to the press. Talks were given by members of the Black Sash to business groups, church groups and any others prepared to listen. There were, as Sheena Duncan later pointed out, strategies that could be used to influence government action:

One can seek action in court that will lead to an order being made that will instruct government to do something. One can force government to do things by raising sufficient pressure in the electorate and amongst members of parliament for policy to be changed or if, as in South Africa, the majority of people do not form part of the electorate, then one has to find the strategies where government will eventually have to say: 'We will have to accept this position and change our policy towards homeless people'.

On 12 November 1968 the Black Sash in conjunction with the citizens' action committee presented a petition and a memorandum to the State President's secretary:

We, the undersigned, ask you to show concern for the fact that in the name of the law and for the sake of ideology, hundreds of thousands of South Africans are being arbitrarily uprooted and removed from their homes with disregard for their material and spiritual needs and their means of livelihood; denied the right to live together with their families; expelled from urban areas where they have been living and working and turned into displaced persons without concern for their aspirations and security and the suffering caused. We believe that justice and the need for stability in South Africa can best be served by having secure communities and stable family life and that the matters complained of strike at the roots of our society. We urge you to exercise your powers and influence to stop these grave wrongs which are being perpetrated on our non-white fellow countrymen.

On this occasion only 22,000 signatures were achieved. Petitions, it was decided, were not a very successful strategy, and the petition against removals proved to be one of the last the Black Sash would organise.

The Black Sash made it a rule that an invitation to take up the issue of a community's removal must come from the community concerned. Once the organisation had been approached by people from a community that had been informed it was destined for removal, it would then obtain all the necessary information about that community. Did the people in question own the land? For how long, for how many generations had they been in that particular place? Did they hold title deeds? It would then put the community, especially in the case of rural communities with no access to resources, in touch with legal advice. Every attempt would be made to raise public interest in the threat hanging over the people concerned. Interested parties would be taken out to meet them and hear the story at first hand and see the location to which the community was to be moved. Black Sash members would write articles for the press, publish pamphlets, books or booklets about a particular place or removal programme. Black Sash pickets were held to protest against civic removals, and in general members did their best to raise a public outcry.

In the case of squatters or homeless communities the Black Sash would assist the people concerned towards some form of initial community organisation. Squatter communities were not close communities in the way that rural, land-owning communities were. Often they were very disorganised. They would come to the Black Sash in desperation when their shacks were suddenly demolished. Sometimes members would receive telephone calls in the middle of the night from women announcing that all their men had been arrested and that they had been told their makeshift homes would be demolished in the morning. A meeting would be swiftly called and the people affected informed that the first thing they must do, if they wished to address their problem successfully, was to elect a committee of their own, a body through which they could negotiate with the authorities, make decisions about seeking legal advice and about what their actual demands were. Sometimes what they wanted was to be left where they were with security of tenure; at others they were content to negotiate that they move, provided that they were offered a site or accommodation in the vicinity.

One criticism put forward by a police spokesman was that the Black Sash ladies only listened to one viewpoint in relation to removals, that the authorities wanted to 'uplift' the places concerned and that such a process could not be achieved in dribs and drabs, that for every person who did not wish to move, he could find another who did, who wanted to be 'uplifted'. The presence of Black Sash members at the scene of removals was a source of irritation to police undertaking a difficult operation. The Black Sash response was that their involvement was strictly at the request of the people concerned, that their role was only to support that community in the choices the people themselves made, and that their presence was justified if, when all else failed, the bulldozers and the trucks and the barbed wire were brought in, because experience had shown that the presence of articulate white witnesses had an effect on the manner in which the removal process was conducted.

Among the first group of squatters with whom the Black Sash became closely involved were the occupants of the illegal shack settlement of Crossroads. It was in 1975 that the name Crossroads was first heard mentioned in the Cape Town advice office. By that time the advice office had been moved from Athlone to the premises of the Christian Institute in Mowbray, two doors away from its present location. Noël Robb recalls being taken aback by the answer to her routine question as to where various applicants for advice lived. 'Crossroads? That was a new one on me. Where's Crossroads?' In fact Crossroads had its roots in late 1974 as a place where 'illegal' Africans were herded together outside Cape Town as a first step to repatriation to the Ciskei and the Transkei. The boom of the early 1970s had meant that the flood of illegal labour had remained staunchly undeterred by apartheid laws. By 1974 there were an estimated 90,000 illegals in the Cape Town area and squatting was mushrooming. The boom ended but the illegals stayed, and because not a single house had been built for blacks between 1970 and 1980 the squatter problem was becoming an ever-greater thorn in the flesh of the South African government. Africans living in the Philippi bush, an exposed expanse of sea sand on the Cape Flats, where only an idigenous bush would grow, had been told to erect shacks on 'black land' near the Lansdowne Road/Klipfontein Road crossroads, hence the name given to the settlement, which although only one community among many to undergo similar treatment, would become a symbol of the black struggle to resist removals.

The majority of Crossroads residents arrived during 1975 not, as one Crossroads resident explained, from the homelands, but from other parts of the Cape Town area: 'When Crossroads was started in 1975, the people who came here were not from the Transkei, but from Cape Town. That was the time when the Afrikaners were trying to clean up the town. The people who came here in 1975 were those who did not qualify to be here. I was born here [Cape Town], married here and my husband was qualified to be here. We moved to Crossroads because I was not qualified. We fought being sent elsewhere.'

Squatting was regarded by the government as a health hazard. As potent evidence of the enormous contrast between the miserable circumstances of the homeless and the affluence of many established residents, it was also, and probably more significantly, looked upon as a potential awakener of revolutionary conditions and activity. Clearly visible from the main road between Cape Town and the city's airport, it was furthermore an embarrassment and a political threat since its very existence implied the breakdown of influx control in the Western Cape, the failure of the Coloured Labour Preference Policy. The more the residents of Crossroads became resolved not to be moved, the more the authorities raided the camp and made arrest upon arrest. The Black Sash duly opened special files for the people of Crossroads: 'The men were being had up for harbouring their wives and the women were had up for running little shops without a licence. There were charges of trespass, in fact anything the authorities could find.' For a while the advice office was taken once a week to Noxolo School in Crossroads, and the Black Sash made themselves responsible for finding legal representation for the people arrested. At one time they had seventy-two Crossroads cases pending simultaneously. R3,000 were collected from members to cover legal fees and when that ran out an attempt was made to raise a further

R2,000. Finally, one of the lawyers concerned suggested that a panel of friendly lawyers should be formed to conduct such cases free of charge. This was done on condition that the advice office took on a special clerk to deal with the clerical work involved.

By February 1978 the government had stated explicitly that Crossroads must go. Despite the sustained resistance encountered, Dr Vosloo, Deputy Minister of Plural Relations and Development, quashed any idea of a reprieve for the squatter camp. Demolition raids were stepped up. Bulldozers moved in to destroy the improvised homes. The community responded by consolidating its own internal organisation. Having formed their panel of lawyers and worked directly with the squatters, the Black Sash arranged for the defence of around 1,000 people. It estimated that 40,000 Rand was milked out of the Crossroads people in fines during that period. 'Mamma Robb', as the occupants of Crossroads came to call her, derived a certain satisfaction from the reaction of the small commissioners' courts which dealt with Africans accused of such offences, to the arrival of unexpected QCs in their trailing gowns: 'Our lawyers came to courts all over the place and they brought advocates who were their friends. When the magistrates, who weren't actually magistrates but commissioners who were not properly trained at all, saw these Supreme Court advocates appearing in their little courts, they nearly died of fright.'

Other concerned outsiders rallied to support the squatters in their struggle to stay in Crossroads. A 'Save Crossroads Campaign' was instigated with public meetings, pamphlets, bumper stickers and petitions to mobilise public support. Crews arrived from all over the world to make films about the residents' plight. Because of her relationship with the people of Crossroads, Mamma Robb found herself featuring in a number of them: 'I personally took part in dozens of films for all sorts of countries. They all had them at the ready, and if Crossroads had been demolished they would have been shown.'

As it transpired, they did not need to be. The process of

raising public awareness appeared to have worked. In November 1978 Dr Piet Koornhof, then Minister of Cooperation and Development, met the Crossroads residents to ask them to submit a proposal to him for discussion. Dr Koornhof swiftly became the community's hero. In what looked like a government reprieve, he announced that people who had been living in Crossroads since 31 December 1978 could stay. Gradually, however, the people began to doubt that they could trust the apparently sympathetic minister who became known as 'Piet promises'. What he was actually offering them, it emerged, was a new model township to be built nearby. New Crossroads would accommodate certain categories of resident but not:

(a) Those who had been convicted of a crime involving a fine of over R500 or six months imprisonment. Africans who qualified under Section 10 (1)b of the Urban Areas Act (through long residence) lost this qualification following such conviction.
(b) Those falling within a vague category of Africans who would be offered jobs and homes in the 'homelands'. This concerned 'a substantial number of particular Crossroads families'.
(c) Vagrants and persons or families with no visible means of support which render them a burden to the community itself.

In order to categorise residents and establish either their right to remain or their liability to be removed, the Administration Board drew up a questionnaire, but problems immediately arose in persuading people to answer it without fear of the consequences. If, for example, they were working illegally the natural reaction was to deny it. Yet it was in their own interests for those illegally employed to say so, as it showed that they had some means of support. In the black townships it was illegal to be self-employed, especially as a hawker or trader, without a permit. It was therefore natural for people to deny that they were self-supporting, but equally essential that they should admit it. Above all, there was considerable

fear not only of the questions but also of the officials. To
allay this a team of Black Sash members and others drew up
a simpler form of questionnaire. In two weeks some 3,000
families were interviewed and valuable records obtained.
Perhaps most significantly, the Crossroads residents were
advised by women they had come to trust to cooperate with
the Administration Board's questionnaire which followed on
the heels of the Black Sash survey.

Temporary permits to live in Crossroads were then issued,
but the next hurdle of which the Black Sash became aware
was that permits were not being provided for work. Employers tried hard to register their illegal employees but were
refused permission. After long negotiations, Dr Koornhof and
the local officials of the Department of Cooperation and
Development and of the Administration Board made statements to the press to the effect that they would not arrest
Crossroad residents working illegally. Nor would they prosecute their employers. Hundreds of photocopies were made of
a montage of these statements which aspirant employees
could show to prospective employers. By this means many
Crossroads people found jobs and the Black Sash received
numerous requests from large firms for any available workers
from Crossroads. The opportunity to engage good workers
informally, on the spot, was too good to miss. Hundreds of
other enquiries came to the advice office from people who
had missed the questionnaire and so had no permits, from
nervous employers and from would-be employees who
needed help to find work.

Gradually, however, towards the end of 1979 differences
arose between two sections of Crossroads. They were based
on friction between two leaders, Oliver Memani and Johnson
Ngxobongwana, representing the squatters occupying two
different parts of the camp and holding two different lists of
people to be considered for 'legality'. In the end this friction
ended in violence and the death of at least one man. Every
effort had been made by the Churches, the Urban Foundation
(a private-sector agency channelling aid to black communities), Friends of Crossroads and the Black Sash to iron out the
difficulties, but in the end the Black Sash deemed it wisest to

withdraw and allow the factions to settle their own disputes. For this reason they stopped taking the advice office to Crossroads, although they continued to advise residents who came to the office in Mowbray with their problems.

In April 1980 the advice office did reopen in Crossroads, but very rapidly the number of people seeking advice became unmanageable. It was found to be more practical for Cross-roads residents to come to the Mowbray advice office every day instead of a group of Black Sash people going to Cross-roads once a week. Still they were inundated with people claiming long residence who had managed to miss the survey. Advice office workers saw as many as eighty-eight people in one day and a total of more than a thousand in just over a month. A list was produced in alphabetical order, providing the salient facts in each case and recommending that many of the people should be given permits. Many others were obviously not eligible because they had been away for long absences or had entered Crossroads after 1978. 'As soon as Dr Koornhof said he was going to reprieve Crossroads and build New Crossroads the cousins and the aunts moved in,' said Noël Robb. Crossroads, she would reflect, was something of a watershed for the Black Sash, because it was perhaps the first time that, although in many instances people were advised that the law could offer them no solution, the people concerned decided to make a stand anyway. 'Then after our survey we found that many of the people involved had been in the Cape Town area in various other little squatter camps for years. It was only that they had moved together and come out into the open in 1975.'

In November 1980 the first families, those less intent upon making a political point, moved into the initial 750 houses built in New Crossroads. Dr Koornhof failed none the less in the people's eyes to live up to his promises. There were no buses, no crèches, too few schools, no promised market place and, most significantly of all, the rent for the houses was too high for people to pay. Finally, in June 1983, the Chief Commissioner confirmed what most people already knew: the second phase of building for New Crossroads would not be implemented. All this occurred against a background of raids and internal fighting. Attempts had been made to form a unified Crossroads committee, with Ngxobongwana as chairman and Memani as vice, but committee members were divided and disunity set in, fed by uncertainty over legal status, the desperate need for proper housing and a succession of broken promises which added to people's insecurity. It was also exacerbated, in the Black Sash's experience, by the fact that the authorities persisted in holding separate meetings with the chairman and the vice-chairman and causing trouble by telling the one what the other had allegedly said.

Violence and turmoil once more came to a head in April 1983 when fighting left seven people dead and twenty-six others wounded. Once more, each side blamed the other. No one was actually able to pinpoint the source of the flare-up and the faction fighting would continue. In September of 1984 the Black Sash would be involved in drawing up a constitution for a unified Crossroads committee and invited to monitor elections. As director of the advice office, Noël Robb informed the two parties that the Black Sash could only do this with the willing cooperation of both sides and on condition that the election was fairly and honestly run. When only Oliver Memani's group turned up to discuss the elections, the Black Sash declined to proceed on the grounds that it would defeat the object of having an election if only one party was involved.

The division and disruption which persistently plagued the community meant that there were those in Crossroads who were prepared to cooperate when, instead of fulfilling its promises for New Crossroads, the government came up with a much more grandiose scheme. It was called Khayelitsha (meaning 'new home'), and it was the government's ultimate solution to the problem of weeding out those blacks whose labour was not required and consigning those who were needed to an area far removed from the city, where it would be simpler to control and administer them and where 'unrest' could be more effectively quelled without disruption to the life and economy of Cape Town. On 4 March 1983, P.W. Botha, *en route* to survey the expanding eyesore of Crossroads' 100,000 shacks, flew over the sandy wastelands of

Cape Flats on the coast at False Bay some twenty-five miles from the city centre. The fortuitous siting of an expanse of windswept sand dunes previously used for military exercises seemed to offer a solution to what had by now become a source of embarrassment at an international level. A preliminary survey revealed that 1,070 hectares of this government-owned land could be developed. Accommodation in the form of 'high rise/density and selfbuild housing under control' was envisaged for 250,000 people over a twenty-year period. The established black townships of Langa, Nyanga and Guguletu, closer to the city centre, would be destroyed. Their residents would be compelled to move to Khayelitsha, as would the 'legal' occupants of Crossroads, who would then be dispersed throughout the vast new black city to squash their spirit of defiance. Such was the original intention. Township unrest with the eyes of the world upon it, however, combined with an international outcry over apartheid and the relocation policy in particular, meant that the government found it expedient not to be seen to be too obviously breaking up existing communities and forcing them to move elsewhere.

Shortly after the Crossroads eruption of 1983 it was announced that the established communities of Langa, Nyanga and Guguletu would not be required to move to Khayelitsha after all. Five days after that came a reprieve for Crossroads itself. Redevelopment of the site was to be allowed, but in order for upgrading work to be implemented many of the squatters would still have to go to Khayelitsha. An additional incentive was offered in the form of the provision of 'legal' status for 'illegals' who were prepared to live there, provided that they looked for work during the ensuing eighteen months, after which their situation would be reviewed. The tacit implication was that even unemployed Khayelitsha dwellers would not automatically be sent to the homelands. It was enough of an assurance for thousands of squatters to overcome their reservations relating to involuntary removals and the creation of a new home far from the city with only, initally at least, the most rudimentary services, and voluntarily to leave the squalid, broken life of Crossroads for what was sold to them as a location which, according to a statement recorded in Hansard, the government was going to make 'such an attractive and complete community that it will act like a magnet and can become the consolidated black township *par excellence* here in the Peninsula'.

A new era, it seemed, had begun. In a way the story of Crossroads was a success story. The Crossroads squatters had undoubtedly won, and the winning of the battle would prove to be a hole in the dyke of influx control. The Black Sash would number its role in 'taking up' the cause of Crossroads and bringing it to the attention of the media, at a time when other organisations were doing nothing about its predicament, among its more tangible achievements. The days of the removals brought about by bulldozers, dogs and armed police appeared to be numbered. Hennie van der Walt, Deputy Minister of Development and of Land Affairs openly acknowledged the folly of previous forced removals:

> I readily admit that we made mistakes in the past. So much so that black communities had to be moved by force and often resettled in critical circumstances. Our biggest mistake was that we did not undertake these resettlement actions in cooperation with the black authorities. A lack of consultation between the government and the black people concerned led to numerous unfortunate incidents.

Thenceforth people were to be moved 'nicely'.

Circular 2 of 1982, for the Department of Cooperation and Development had already stipulated, however, that: 'Motivational efforts must be made constantly by district officials in collaboration with administration board officials in order to persuade those qualifying in terms of Section 10(1) (a) or (b) of the Urban Areas Act to settle voluntarily in a national or independent state or in a South African Development Trust area.' Despite the government's attempts to appear reasonable, evidence brought to Black Sash attention suggested that it was no less determined that people should be moved and that 'motivational efforts' and other forms of intervention meant that even voluntary removals were not always what they might appear. The organisation set about exposing what it saw as a myth.

In the case of Crossroads, the Black Sash had good reason to deduce that the government was not entirely without a vested interest in the friction between the conservative element, the supporters of Johnson Ngxobongwana who had become self-appointed mayor, and the other occupants of the squatter camp, particularly in the satellite camp known as KTC because that was the name of a grocer's store round which it had sprung up. Tension, which began in January 1986 when Ngxobongwana's committee failed to return bail money collected the previous year or to explain what had happened to it, mounted gradually until two New Crossroads residents were killed on 19 March and houses in that area were attacked and burnt. Next day hundreds of Ngxobongwana supporters – so-called *witdoeke* or vigilantes – assembled in Old Crossroads to go to New Crossroads to retrieve belongings from the attacked houses. They were met by massed forces of 'comrades' and a pitched battle ensued leaving seven *witdoeke* dead. In the days that followed the Black Sash was actively involved in taking statements from people on both sides of the conflict and speaking to whoever they felt could influence the situation. 'There were allegations that the police had been in support of the *witdoeke* as they marched from Old Crossroads,' the 1986 advice office report stated. 'What is clear is that they did not prevent the fighting that erupted.'

The Black Sash attempts at conciliation failed. In May the *witdoek* vigilante grouping launched a massive attack on the newer satellite camps around Old Crossroads, setting fire to the primitive shacks. 3,000 homes were razed to the ground and thirty-three people died. Some 30,000 others were left homeless. 'This devastation,' stated the same report, 'was wrought under the eyes of the police, who claimed they were powerless to stop it.'

Advice office workers and other Black Sash members joined the South African Red Cross and other relief and welfare agencies in the mounting of a major relief operation. Accommodation was arranged in township schools and church halls throughout the peninsula. Emergency kitchens remained in operation for six months, funded by local agencies, foreign governments and other concerned South African people. Meanwhile, the South African government remained adamant that all the refugees must move to Khayelitsha. Only there would official help be available. Workers from the advice office and a Black Sash's township liaison project helped the Legal Resources Centre, the University of Cape Town's Department of Criminology and a number of lawyers in the taking of approximately 3,300 affidavits from people left destitute by the 'war'. More than forty affidavits alleging Security Force participation were filed in the Cape Town Supreme Court.

Senior Counsel representing the squatter leaders stated in court that there were strong indications that the army and the police 'flagrantly flouted' a provisional order issued in May to restrain police and vigilantes from attacks on KTC. From the affidavits and the subsequent legal action taken against the Minister of Law and Order and the *witdoek* leaders, it seemed clear to the Black Sash that 'the whole exercise tied in very conveniently with the government's long-term aim to reduce the size of the squatter camp at Crossroads and force the removal of the bulk of the people to Khayelitsha'. In the event some 3,000 did move to the tent town provided at Khayelitsha. Most who had lost their homes and their few possessions, however, remained reluctant to go there, convinced that it was firmly in the control of the *witdoek* vigilantes with the tacit support of the officials and the police.

The reduction of 3,000 homes to ashes, and the violence that had occurred with the balance of power, particularly of firearms, with the attackers, had taken place under the July 1985 to March 1986 State of Emergency. Since the instigation of that State of Emergency the entire area of Crossroads and its satellite camps had been sealed off. According to official reports, it had been subjected to intensive security operations, including house-to-house searches for firearms and suspects. Calls for the area to be declared a disaster area, for judicial investigation of the pogrom and for state assistance, especially in restoring the sites to refugees, fell on deaf ears. 'Go to Khayelitsha,' was the official refrain.

'Who benefits?' enquired Margaret Nash of the Black Sash in a subsequent report. 'An obscene question yet one that must be asked. Certain parties do stand to gain.' Quite apart from the advantages to be gained by Johnson Ngxobon-gwana's core group who laid claim to the whole area, she pointed out other relevant interests: 'The authorities do not face the same organised opposition as previously. In place of cohesive resistant squatter groups who refused the eighteen-month permits with sites at Khayelitsha and were holding out for full urban and political rights, there are tens of thousands of dispersed, disorganised and impoverished refu-gees desperately struggling to survive.' The security forces no longer faced the hazard presented by masses of tightly packed shacks into which stone-throwers and gunmen could easily disappear and where arms and explosives could be con-cealed. The official developers of Khayelitsha were looking for an increased population, who as commuter workers would provide the volume and passenger revenue for the R62,000,000 railway spur due to be provided over the sub-sequent eighteen months. They too were among those who stood to benefit.

Following the events of 1986 the Black Sash withdrew from its more direct involvement with Old Crossroads. Noël Robb, with the sense of what was and was not fair play character-istic of her generation of Black Sashers, no longer officially went there: 'I loved Crossroads but after that bit of behaviour I just thought it was impossible to be friendly with them. I've said I won't go back to Old Crossroads until they give back the land and possessions to the people they burnt out.'

There were times when, because of internal township tensions, David Viti, a Xhosa interpreter who worked along-side her in the advice office, advised her not to go to other black townships. A report by Margaret Nash to the Black

Sash national conference held in Johannesburg in March 1988 pointed to the fact that tensions within the black communities ('fathers' versus 'comrades', one squatter group against another, Old Crossroads against New Crossroads) were increasingly being expressed in violent clashes using a range of weapons. Struggles for power, for access to and control of resources and for the right to organise were endemic. Furthermore, Cape politics were notorious for factionalism. The UDF/ANC trend in the area was very strong, but there were other tendencies, including the Azanian People's Organisation, the Cape Action League and the South African Communist Party, which shared an aggressively Marxist-socialist orientation not always compatible with the multi-class composition of the UDF. Word would usually reach the advice office that particular areas were temporarily unsafe, but Noël Robb related in a very matter-of-fact fashion the story of how on one occasion she and another Black Sash lady had turned up in a newly fledged squatter camp on a day when the bulldozers were due to arrive. 'The squatters were very angry. Their blood was up. If someone in the crowd had not recognised us, it could have been quite nasty.'

In both 1988 and 1989 I had the privilege of going with her to Khayelitsha. By then an advice office was being opened in the township itself three times a week, run by the local community with the support and guidance of the Black Sash. The population of Khayelitsha was estimated at over 200,000. Development of the third of four proposed towns with a railway line running through the middle of them had begun. Mrs Robb had closely monitored that growth. She was all too well aware of its deficiencies and was still energetically determined to bring pressure to bear to have them rectified. Her grey hair and her long years of resolute action on behalf of the residents gave her, it seemed, an almost unlimited licence. Together we strode into hospitals, crèches and even people's private living-rooms:

> They've colour-coded departments and routes in the
> hospital to help people who can't read find their way
> round, but they've even got that wrong . . . Those flats

and the shops they built with accommodation above them are standing empty because people just don't like living on more than one storey. They will not learn to ask the people what they really want . . . Look at this. It doesn't matter how clean people try to keep their homes. The sand gets into everything.

Khayelitsha, with its ubiquitous wind-swept sand, was in no way comparable to the white suburbs. 'Green Point', the emergency camp which grew up after the burnings in Crossroads and KTC in 1986, had some 20,000 residents and seemed to grow steadily every day. The majority of people in the informal settlement would never manage to find formal employment and thus earn the money necessary to purchase even a core house, a two- or three-room structure supplying the most basic shelter; but the improvised stalls selling goods of all kinds, the boards erected outside the most unlikely cardboard and plastic-sheeting creations advertising all kinds of services from hair perms to tyre repairs bore witness to the ingenuity of the dispossessed and the fact that at least here, unofficially, some sort of living could be made.

There were large areas of semi-permanent shacks supplied only with bucket lavatories and communal taps, but the very presence of even such basic amenities implied that their occupants were not due for forcible removal. On the vast flat tracts of land, with their infrastructure of roads and rudimentary services, stood row upon row upon row of monotonous core houses. Elsewhere, lines of concrete lavatories flanked the neat tarred roads, supplying water-borne sewage systems in readiness for people to erect adjacent to them whatever form of shelter they could afford. Still, schools were plentiful, there were sports facilities and in Town One alone forty-six sites had been allocated for churches. There was also an area where houses more spacious than the core houses were being built out of klinker bricks by people given a three-week training course as part of the Department of Manpower's programme for the unemployed. The quality of building might be dubious, but they were at least being constructed with bathrooms and kitchens.

Most significantly of all, the Abolition of Influx Control
Bill might well not have been entirely devoid of the kind of
doublespeak of which the Abolition of Passes and Coordination of Documents Act had been guilty but it had at least
allowed for certain changes. The reinforcing pressure of
demographic forces had rendered them virtually inevitable.
The population growth figures for Cape Town between 1904
and 1985 were revealing. Statistics showed that in 1904 there
had been 104,421 whites, 62,534 coloureds and Asians and
7,492 Africans. By 1985 there were 606,090 whites, 1,057,500
coloureds and Asians and 568,170 Africans. A growth rate of
3.2 per cent per annum overall and 6.1 per cent for Africans
was anticipated up to the year 2000. During the years 1980
to 1985 the *de facto* black population in greater Cape Town
had virtually doubled. Nationwide the black birth rate was
higher than any other. This – combined with the fact that, as
Black Sash research revealed in 1988, more than 5 million
people in South Africa were homeless, and one out of every
six Africans was without proper shelter or was living
'illegally' somewhere he was not supposed to be – had
brought irresistible pressure to bear on a policy which in its
original conception had not allowed for the pressures which
any country must experience during a period of change,
growth, industrialisation, economic boom or decline and the
attendant movements of population.

In August 1988 the government brought before parliament
three new Bills dealing with the enforcement of Group Areas,
control over squatting and the control of slums. The Prevention of Illegal Squatting Amendment Bill transferred the onus
of proof from the prosecution to the accused to show that he
or she had a lawful reason or the necessary permission to
enter a land or building, and introduced heavier penalties for
infringements. It also denied people the right to bring an
action for a court interdict against unlawful demolition if
they could prove some right or title to the land. The Slums
Bill denied people who were ordered by a local authority to
vacate premises any legal protection. The penalty for any
resistance to such an order could be a fine of R4,000 or
imprisonment for up to one year. Again, in the case of the

Group Areas Amendment Bill, a person accused of owning or leasing or occupying any property in a wrong 'Group Area' (an area set aside for occupation by a race group of which he was not a member) would be presumed guilty unless he could prove otherwise. Although at the same time the Free Settlement Areas Bill provided the machinery for opening some areas to all, the 1988 amendment also tried to give the Group Areas Act more teeth by removing the previous element of discretion allowed to magistrates and making eviction the compulsory penalty for persons found guilty of living in a wrong group area. It introduced harsher penalties for landlords who rented to people of the wrong colour.

There was vigorous condemnation from both right and left. The Conservative Party condemned the provision for opening some areas to all races; the Progressive Federal Party predicted that if applied the Group Areas Bills were so harsh that they would provoke rioting. The Bills were passed without the harsher measures for offending landlords and with provision for the introduction of 'grey areas'. Black Sash members had compiled and distributed 15,000 pamphlets on the subject in the Transvaal region alone. They had briefed the press, diplomatic staff, church and professional groups, appeared on Radio 702, and held a shack sit-in to raise awareness of the plight of homeless people. They had stood with posters in the suburbs from which fellow South Africans had been expelled under the Group Areas Act, displaying the words: 'Group Areas hurt.' They had pointed out that in effect the Bills reintroduced the state's power to remove any group, tribe or black person from any area to another area. To little avail.

Nevertheless, despite what the Black Sash saw as an attempt to reintroduce influx control, 'abolished' two years previously, the continued and apparently undisrupted presence of the squatters in Khayelitsha, and the fact that since 1986 blacks had been able to purchase homes in the townships of the Cape, bore witness to certain changes. Since the 1986 changes in legislation controlling the development of land and the provision of houses in the black areas, private enterprise had become involved. Property developers were now building in Khayelitsha. At the top end of the scale were 'proper houses' with three bedrooms and 1½ bathrooms for over R70,000. The price meant that virtually only those people eligible for large government subsidies, such as teachers and government servants, could afford to buy them, and there were many reluctant to involve themselves in such dependence on the government, but at least the option of home ownership was now there. Noël Robb sees this as a far from negligible achievement: 'I get annoyed when people say nothing has changed. A lot more needs to be done, but it's an enormous change from saying nobody can get a job or has a home to go to, everybody's a temporary sojourner and nobody can actually own property or land, to being allowed to own your home.

Chapter Five

'Voluntary removals'

Such changes as had been achieved had been a long time coming. For the Black Sash a not insignificant part of the interim years was devoted to exposing the gulf between avowed intentions and actual practice, between reported, and indeed unreported, events and the reality as its members experienced it. The problems of forced removals were by no means confined to the Western Cape, any more than they were confined to urban areas. Despite the government's expressed regrets in 1983, despite its professed intention to bring about removals through cooperation with black communities rather than by force, it was the Black Sash's experience that, by means ranging from direct force to the application of more subtle persuasive tactics, a systematic assault continued to be made even upon the most settled and prosperous of the black rural communities wherever their presence was found to be in conflict with government plans. Their evidence suggested that this was true even as forced removals began ostensibly to be transformed into a more sympathetic and respectful settlement process.

Exposing the 'myth' of 'voluntary removals' meant drawing public attention to the fact that, for example, in 1982 in Kimberley in the Northern Cape rents for some township houses were increased to over R50 per month, an increase which forced pensioners, the unemployed and those on low incomes, to move 150 miles north to the independent homeland of Bophutatswana, where rents were less than half that amount. It meant ensuring that the fact that in Mgwali in the Eastern Cape in 1983 drought relief was only given to those who agreed to move and/or were members of the only Ciskei party, did not pass entirely unnoticed. In the same year, the Black Sash reported, in Driefontein in the Eastern Transvaal the leader of a resisting committee, Saul Mkize, was shot dead. A murder charge against a member of the SAP followed. In Natal, also in 1983, it was pointed out, only one of the nine bus services in the Ladysmith area was subsidised by the government. That service, it so happened, ran to the relocation areas of Ezakheni and Ekuvukeni. Black Sash records reveal innumerable examples of similar 'motivational efforts' in rural areas, where in the absence of advice centres and legal resources people were in some way even more vulnerable than in an urban environment.

In time, Black Sash advice offices throughout the country would recognise the need for field-workers to take up the problems of rural areas on a paid and full-time basis. Johannesburg was the first in 1983 to provide this kind of response to the fact that the removal issue was becoming critical. It was then that the Transvaal Rural Action Committee, which is part of the Black Sash but also part of the 'National Committee against Removals', was formed, precisely because rural communities had been coming to the Black Sash with problems amongst which forced removals featured very prominently. It had become impossible to deal adequately with serious, explosive issues arising in distant locations with voluntary workers alone.

In the Transvaal Rural Action Committee office on the floor above the advice office in Johannesburg, Aninka Claassens was one of a team incorporating three field-workers and an administrator employed on a full-time basis to deal with such issues. She was one of the more recent generation of Black Sash members. After leaving university she had sought solutions to the 'crushing poverty and powerlessness of people' by working in the trade unions in the belief that 'in the unions the balance of power was being addressed and the issues were being confronted in a less piecemeal way than in rural development'. The subsequent opportunity to work in TRAC had brought with it the promise of 'combining organisation with making a real impact in rural areas'.

TRAC's role was not to initiate resistance but to respond

to requests for assistance, always providing they were consistent with Black Sash principles. It helped people to set up channels of consultation, conduct surveys, organise meetings. Frequently it was a rather intangible role, so much less visible, particularly to the white community, than the protest stands, that it gave substance to the remark made by one white commentator: 'I know what the Black Sash stands for but I don't know what they actually do.' Yet, like the immeasurable process of 'conscientisation', it was no less real. Often the most important part of TRAC fieldworkers' activity was sitting down with people and really trying to understand what they wanted to do and why they wanted to do it, discussing the feasibility of what they proposed and then helping them to implement what they had decided upon. In Johannesburg there were plenty of people who shared their commitment to helping those in rural areas. TRAC was there to set up the link between people wanting to build a school and the builders to do it, between communities wanting publicity and interested journalists, between sick people needing a clinic and doctors prepared to give medical care. Often the resources needed were available. It was a question of liaison and establishing continuity.

Requests for help came mainly, in the first instance, from land-owing communities who had purchased their land before the Native Land Act of 1913. The Land Acts as the legislative basis for forced removals were a focus of ongoing attention for the Black Sash throughout the country. In June 1983, the seventieth anniversary of the Land Act of 1913, the Black Sash held a special week of protest against forced removals. The campaign was spearheaded in the Transvaal region, where a five-day vigil was organized from 8 a.m. to 8 p.m. with a photographic display. Throughout the vigil, Gill de Vlieg, a Black Sash member and professional photographer, fasted on a daily cup of tea and a slice of dry bread, which she had discovered was more or less all that some of the people of the rural community of Dreifontein had been able to eat while purchasing the title to their land many years previously. In a circular letter the Transvaal region appealed to thousands of people in religious groups, community bodies, political organisations, the press, trade unions, schools, business organisations and embassies, asking them to join the vigil. The response from press, public and schools, who sent pupils to listen to lectures on the subject was encouraging. Discussions and prayer sessions sparked off dialogue between all kinds of disparate people.

Among Port Elizabeth's contributions to the week of protest was a stand held at seven strategic points in the city during the early-morning rush hour with posters reading 'Removals destroy family life.' Cape Town had lunch-hour presentations in St George's Cathedral with an opening talk about the struggles of rural people faced with removal. In one of the wettest weeks for many years, protestors stood throughout the suburbs with posters showing an outline map of South Africa, the Black Sash logo and the words 'One people, one land'. In Durban a day-long vigil was held which drew not only studied indifference but also waterbombs, poster-tearing and verbal hostility. Thousands of pamphlets were handed out, roughly two hundred of which were confiscated by security police. In Pietermaritzburg, dry bread and tea were served after a member of the Association for Rural Advancement had presented slides which documented recent removals in Natal. In Grahamstown, Black Sash members concentrated on sending people into schools to outline the harsh facts relating to removals under the Land Acts.

The Land Act of 1913 actually defined the scheduled native areas down to the last farm or lot and stipulated that only blacks could acquire land in those areas. It also stipulated that in the remainder of the country no black could acquire land save from another black, and only a black could acquire land from a black. In 1913 blacks were allocated 7.3 per cent of South Africa's land. In 1936, with the passing of further legislation, the Native Trust and Land Act, this portion was increased to 12.3 per cent. The 1936 Act also provided for control over the residence of blacks, for the registration of squatters and for summary procedures for the removal of 'illegals'. Most significantly of all, it provided the legal foundation for the whole policy of removals by empowering the Governor General to remake boundaries by excising land from the black area and replacing it with other equivalent land. What then of those black people who had purchased their land communally prior to the Land Acts, whose tribal chiefs held deeds signed by a government minister? One of the numerous communities with which TRAC and the Black Sash worked closely was that of Mogopa, some 130 miles south-west of Johannesburg.

The Bakwena tribe members had lived in the valley of Mogopa ever since they bought the land in 1911. They had developed it into a flourishing community. They had sunk boreholes for water and built houses and churches, but then the authorities, apparently oblivious to their title deeds, their achievements and the human consequences of uprooting people from their homes and carting them off to a strange place where they must start the building process all over again, decreed that they must move to Pachsdraai, a place due to be incorporated into the homeland of Bophutatswana, where only tin shacks and a limited water supply awaited the majority of them. The people resisted the move. They even boasted about the number of officials they had managed to send packing over the years. In September 1981, however, the tribe voted to depose their headman, Jacob More, for corruption and failing to respond to tribal discipline. The local commissioner refused to accept their decision and created a furore by using his legal authority as an agent of the State President who is, officially, Paramount Chief of all blacks, to announce that he decreed that More would rule until he died. A commission of enquiry was set up to investigate the headman's financial dealings, hundreds of men came to give evidence over several weeks and during this time the Pretoria officials returned and informed the people that they would have to move. There was the customary outcry and refusal. This time, however, the officials did not go away. They stayed to negotiate with Jacob More.

Secretively, behind closed doors, the Black Sash report revealed, the removal was negotiated between Cooperation and Development officials, Bophutatswana officials, and the deposed headman and some of his cohorts, named a 'planning committee'. The Mogopa people applied to lawyers to have the meetings made open to the villagers, but to no avail. Then, in June 1983, bulldozers smashed the schools and churches at Mogopa and some of the houses. Less than half the villagers moved to Pachsdraai, where Jacob More, the deposed headman, and his 'planning committee' were empowered to allocate all the facilities. They allocated themselves the white farmhouse there. The doors and window frames and roofing materials from the smashed schools at Mogopa were subsequently found in a large shed in the deposed chief's yard at Pachsdraai. Mogopa had been bought communally and divided equally between the buyers, but at Pachsdraai the fields and grazing land were to be controlled by Jacob More, a man rejected by his people for the corrupt use of the tribe's resources.

It was in August 1983 that representatives of the majority of Mogopa villagers who were still resisting removal – despite the fact that much of the village had been destroyed, the engines from their water pumps had been removed and their buses stopped – made their appeal to TRAC. The Black Sash managed to muster considerable publicity for the villagers' plight by staging a vigil. A number of residents chose to leave Mogopa, but not for Pachsdraai. Instead they went to Bethanie, where there were no facilities, no water and no grazing land, but where they would be nearer to towns where job opportunities might emerge, and far away from Jacob More. The Black Sash helped them with their move. After the June raid a bulldozer had been left near a demolished school at Mogopa. A removal squad remained parked on Mogopa land. Legal action was taken to have it removed on the grounds of trespass. With the help of TRAC coordination the case was won, but no sooner had the removal camp been dismantled than the villagers received an order signed by Dr Koornhof that they must leave Mogopa by 29 November 1983 and never return. The Commissioner who read the order told them that if they did not leave voluntarily they would be loaded up and removed by force.

With a concerted effort on the part of the Black Sash and others to raise public awareness, there was an international outcry. Journalists, students, political groups, the Reverend

Allan Boesak and other church leaders – including Bishop Tutu, who much later would comment on the 'quite remarkable way' in which the Black Sash used the right sort of publicity to achieve their ends – camped out on the hillside overlooking the Mogopa valley waiting for police to arrive and forcibly remove the remainder of the people. As a result plans were changed. The police did not come. Instead, only a handful of government officials appeared, attempting peaceful persuasion. State tactics in those days were simply to wait. There was, after all, a limit, TRAC would point out, to how long people could live without schools, without pensions, without migrant labour contracts and with daily uncertainty about their future. Nevertheless, in early December the remaining Mogopa villagers met to decide upon joint action to rebuild the village. They installed a new pump and raised funds to build a new school. In January they went to the Commissioner about their pension problems and managed to solve these. Men and women left their jobs to work full-time on the reconstruction of buildings and roads, and in a month the new school was finished. Surely now they would be left in peace. Had not Louis Nel, the Deputy Minister of Foreign Affairs, told them in front of the foreign press that they would not be thrown into the street. Had not Dr Koornhof said that the era of forced removals was over?

In the early hours of 14 February Mogopa was surrounded by armed police. At 4 a.m. the villagers were informed through a loud-hailer by Jacob More that they must load their possessions into trucks and go to Pachsdraai. A Black Sash report recorded that:

He took the police and the officials to the houses of all the leaders first. They were handcuffed and put into police vans. Their families refused to pack their possessions. Government labourers did so. Women were carried on to the lorries and buses. People tried to run away and children were loaded with the furniture and despatched to Pachsdraai. All of this happened in the presence of scores of armed policemen who had dogs at their disposal. People caught standing together outside

their houses were beaten with batons. Parents desperate
to find their children got on to the buses at Pachsdraai
to look for them.

Outsiders, including members of the Black Sash and the
press who tried to go to Mogopa, were turned away at the
entrance to the village. Those who managed to sneak in
through the back door were caught and charged. Photographer
Gill de Vlieg managed to speak to people on the buses. She
visited Pachsdraai on the morning of the 'peaceful and
orderly' move. She and others recorded the pathos of hands
reaching out to vehicles to women recognised as Black Sash
members with cries of, 'We are being taken away. What is
going to happen?' and people sitting amongst their belongings
in the knowledge that the next rainfall would ruin what it
had taken a lifetime to collect. Black Sash fieldworkers drew
up detailed lists of possessions lost and broken in the course
of the move. As a result no doubt of worldwide publicity, the
compensation for individual Mogopa houses was much more
substantial than in the case of any other removals known to
the organisation, but still it was not enough to replace
anything like the original homes, to say nothing of the
uncompensated loss of life-supporting fields of mealies, sun-
flowers and beans.

Aninka Claassens reported to the 1984 Black Sash national
conference that Mogopa was representative of numerous
other communities in terms of the various stages of persuasion the state had employed. In many cases the timing of the
first real move was geared to coincide with evidence that the
community which might have been told years previously
that it was under threat of removal was in a weak position or
was subject to some form of split. Pursuing a policy of 'divide
and rule', 'consultation' would then take place with a person
the state – and not necessarily the people – recognised as
'chief', a leader who would reap the benefits of all sorts of
perks in exchange for cooperation. Once this leader had
agreed to move and the new area had been bought and
developed by the state, the resisters, even if they were in the
vast majority, were reduced to a state of insecurity. This

insecurity would be exacerbated by restrictions in the threatened area. In many instances people resisting removal were not allowed to hold public meetings to discuss their situation and plan their response – even when these meetings were held indoors on their own land. At Mgwali in the Eastern Cape at one stage church services had become the only public means of communication. When Saul Mkhize was shot dead on the Easter weekend of 1983 while addressing a gathering inside the school grounds, the meeting was considered 'illegal' because he had not applied to the magistrate for permission. An earlier application for permission had been granted on condition that only 'landowners in Driefontein will attend the meeting', a provision which would ensure the exclusion of many interested parties. The severing of services and pensions was also a widespread tactic, and if that did not work then so too was the ominous presence of removal squads camped at the entrance to a location. Then came the waiting game, and finally the open display of the brute force which in the Black Sash's experience actually underlay every step of the 'process of persuasion'.

'There are laws remaining on our statute books which make talk of reform and voluntary removals utterly ridiculous,' Aninka Claassens concluded her report to the 1984 conference. There were too many to list in their entirety. One at least, the Black Administration Act, which empowered the State President to order any black tribe or black person or group of blacks to move from any area to any other area, was put to the test in the Mogopa case. Lawyers for the Mogopa villagers argued that the order must be discussed by parliament before it could be executed, but the argument was rejected by the Supreme Court and the lawyers were refused permission to appeal against this judgement.

Six years after the evictions TRAC were still working with the people of Mogopa, who, after many court cases, were still busy reoccupying their village. 'In a way the Mogopa issue was the most depressing,' Aninka Claassens later acknowledged. 'There was enormous resistance to the removal and a lot of publicity, and that focus precipitated a very vicious reaction by the state.' Yet, although the people concerned had suffered terribly, the publicity given to the removal and the organisation of the people had never allowed the issue to die down. That fact had changed the arena of other communities under threat. The people of Potsdam, the Moutse and Qwa-Qwa people, had been reprieved: 'In fact there has been a very high success rate in terms of change. Partly that change has been due to the political climate but partly also to the fact that once people saw that victory was in their grasp, it inspired other communities to fight as strongly.'

The work of TRAC, as of fieldworkers elsewhere in the country, had extended over the intervening years to deal with assaults and evictions by farmers, the problems not so much of rural land-owners but of rural dwellers. It had also altered in response to the changes in the strategies of the state. In Aninka Claassen's words: 'As communities began to fight more strongly, the state resorted to a less direct strategy and started using vigilantes to wipe out the community leaders. During the period from 1986 to 1987 it was much less tangible and much less easy to deal with, and it caused havoc in certain areas. Now another kind of angle is being used: the redrawing of homeland boundaries to incorporate communities into a bantustan.'

By 1986 TRAC and the Black Sash were already attempting to alert the public to the fact that another method of eradicating black people from the map of white South Africa had been devised. This new method was much less messy than forcing people on to trucks, sometimes at gunpoint, and then driving them miles to dump them in a 'foreign country'. 'The government simply draws a line around the particular black community it wants to extricate on the map,' asserted a TRAC report. 'It then colours in the space to show that the area is part of one of four territories to which it has already granted independence, viz Transkei, Ciskei, Venda or Bophutatswana.' A law entitled the Borders of Particular States Extension Act granted the government the extraordinary power to do this, and an amendment scheduling yet more areas for 'incorporation' was passed in 1986. TRAC was working with three communities, Bloedfontein in the central Transvaal, Braklaagte in the Marico district and Machakaneng near Brits, whose people were about to become alienated from the land of their birth in this way. The result of such annexations of small segments of South Africa and the people in them to 'foreign countries' would be that white South Africa would no longer be responsible for them. Roads, schools, hospitals, pensions, unemployment insurance, passports, voting rights, all became obligations that the 'foreign' country must shoulder, despite its economic inability to do so.

The Black Sash had been campaigning for many years on the homelands issue as part of the policy of 'separate development' which it rejected as inimical to justice in South Africa. Members had spoken out vehemently against the Bantu Homelands Citizenship Act of 1970, which stated that every black South African was a citizen of one of the homelands even if he had never been to any homelands or had anything to do with one, and which decided his citizenship by the language he spoke. Inevitably the question of removals, Group Areas and the homelands overlapped. Essentially the Black Sash took the view that people should not be removed from where they lived in the pursuit of an ideology based on race, that people should be left where they were regardless of whether their presence did not fit in with government plans, particularly in relation to the homelands. The evil done by the uprooting and removal of communities was so great that it could not be justified for any political purpose whatsoever.

The year 1976 brought a particular focus to the Black Sash's attitude to the homelands when the areas in question began to take independence. Shortly before the Status of Transkei Act gave independence to Transkei that year, the Black Sash compiled a memorandum which was sent to the Transkei leader, Chief Matanzima, explaining the organisation's anxiety with regard to the future of the homeland in the event of its becoming independent. Nevertheless the Transkei did opt to become independent, Bophutatswana followed in 1977, Venda in 1979 and, despite written evidence submitted by the Black Sash to the Quail commission looking

into agricultural and economic conditions in the Ciskei prior
to its independence, so too did the Ciskei in 1981.

By 1982 the President's Council, a body which, as part of
President P. W. Botha's reform programme, replaced the
upper (Senate) house and consisted of sixty white, coloured,
Indian and Chinese representatives appointed by the State
President, had been charged with the task of drawing up a
new constitution for the country. This reformed constitution
would take account of the requirement for coloureds and
Indians to have political representation, but not for the
representation of the substantial number of blacks. The
country's black population was gradually being deprived of
its South African citizenship. Its political representation was
destined to lie not in 'white South Africa' but in the tribal
homelands. The Black Sash's intent was sharpened by President P. W. Botha's proposals for a new constitution and three-
chamber legislature for whites, coloureds and Indians – which
still made no provision for the blacks who represented 73 per
cent of South Africa's population to have a vote in South
Africa – and by the proposed Orderly Movement and Settlement of Black Persons Bill. In 1982 it published one of a
series of booklets the organisation has produced over the years
designed to explain in simple language the meaning and implications of various pieces of legislation and legal procedures
for the benefit of those most likely to be affected by it.

'You and the New Pass Laws' compiled by Sheena Duncan,
explained in easily comprehensible terms the consequences
of homeland independence and of what the Black Sash saw
as a new and worse form of influx control for their citizens.
This booklet was disseminated free of charge to those who
could not afford to pay the requisite twenty cents via the
advice offices. On the day of independence, it pointed out,
every single person who was a citizen of that homeland in
terms of other legislation ceased to be a citizen of South
Africa. By this means, between October 1976 and December
1981, 8 million black people had become 'foreigners' in South
Africa, and if you were a foreigner in South Africa you could
not claim a share in political power. You would never have a
vote in the central government. You could not claim a share

in the land and wealth of South Africa. You could be deported if you did things which the South African government did not like. You had no right to have a South African passport if you wanted to travel. In short, you were an alien in the land of your birth.

People in the homelands were poor. By 1984 the Second Carnegie Inquiry into Poverty would establish that 80 per cent of people in the homelands were living below the urban breadline. Between 1960 and 1980 the number of people without any income in the homelands rose from 250,000 to 1.43 million. In the space of the same twenty-year period 2 million black people were resettled into the homelands. Rapid population growth aggravated already impoverished areas, and migrant employment was vital to the survival of many. The proposed new Orderly Movement and Settlement of Black Persons Bill would, 'You and the New Pass Laws' explained, make it impossible for black persons to stay in a town without a permit. Whereas in the past the thousands of people who had gone from the homelands to the towns without a permit to find a job had been able to remain there illegally because in practice influx control had not worked very well, now they would be required to have both a permit to look for work and a permit to stay in town between 10 p.m. and 5 a.m. the following morning. What was more, they must also have approved accommodation. Worst of all, the penalties for breaching the proposed new legislation were to be far more severe both for the black person found working or residing in a town without a permit and for those people who allowed him or her to stay in their house or gave an unregistered black person work.

'We are to be the policemen. We will turn people out because we do not wish to incur the penalties,' wrote Sheena Duncan in a 'Comment addressed to the Churches' on 31 August 1982. 'What is the Church going to say about this? A copy was sent out to the various Churches. She also wrote an analysis of the Bill in what she described as a 'lay person's legalistic terms':

'This Bill is terrifying in its implications for people who have to live within the homelands. It can only serve to increase the dire poverty already existing in those areas. It greatly increases the efficiency and rigidity of influx control. Far from leading to any kind of control over the urbanisation process, it slams the door shut in the face of landless rural people who have come to town to seek survival.'

This document was also widely disseminated. The 50,000 or so copies of 'You and the New Pass Laws' which were printed and distributed further informed readers what they could do:

Ask your Trade Union, Civic Association, Political
Party, Church Minister, Church Women's or Men's
Group, Housewives' League or any other organisation
you belong to, to study the laws and to call meetings of
members about it . . . Write to Dr Koornhof . . . Talk to
people who live in the homelands . . . Ask your Church
Minister or Bishop or Moderator or other representative
to talk to the Church Synods or assemblies . . . Talk to
your fellow workers about it, then go together to your
employer to tell him what you think about it . . . Teach
everyone you know about it.

The Urban Foundation also set up a committee to work on the Bill in which the Black Sash was actively involved. The Churches spoke out very strongly about it. Trade unions addressed their employers and the employers' organisations about it. Opposition to the Bill was widespread throughout South Africa, and in the end the government was persuaded to withdraw the legislation.

The struggle to expose the real implications of the home-lands policy went on. Through the pages of newspapers and magazines, through its own distinctive methods of protest and through widespread communication with the general public, the Black Sash continued to direct its energies towards informing both black and white communities of the consequences of the homeland policy in terms of poverty and exclusion, denationalisation and the new constitutional system in South Africa and, above all, towards exposing to the world at large the fact that, although the language might be different, the policy remained the same. During the years 1983 to 1985 its campaigning was particularly related to the removal of people into or to the edges of the homelands as part of the government's attempt to consolidate the territory of the homelands. The purpose of the campaigning in general was ultimately to persuade the government to abandon its homelands policy altogether. The Black Sash was compelled to recognise the independent states as legal because they had been established by law, but it did not recognise them in the 'moral' and 'legitimate' sense. In 1986 Sheena Duncan would give evidence for the defence in the so-called 'Delmas trial', the trial of twenty-two UDF members accused of treason. In the course of her evidence she was pressed to explain that non-recognition. In response she pointed out that the Black Sash had even changed its constitution because of the question of homeland independence: 'Our constitution says that we will work within the Republic of South Africa, and after the independence of Transkei we changed that to say that we will work in the Republic of South Africa as defined in 1910. That is what I mean by non-recognition.'

If the Black Sash's long-term goal was the repeal of the Status Acts which gave the independent states their independence, in the short term it was a question of trying to monitor what happened in those states, providing on-going support for local problems, sometimes running advice office sessions for people who were being denied pensions, having difficulties in relation to their unemployment insurance benefits, or other similar practical day-to-day problems. 'But how will this question of pensions and all that stuff that you mentioned now assist you in the question of the independence of that state?' came the pertinent question from the prosecution to Sheena Duncan at the Delmas trial. Sheena Duncan's reply was characteristically realistic. It also provided the key to the crucial relationship between the advice office work and the role of the Black Sash as a political pressure group:

> It probably won't, but if you are trying to mobilise
> public opinion about those independent states the fact
> that people in Bophutatswana only get an old-age

pension of R40 a month as compared to the current
R117 for black people in South Africa, is a bit of very
important information that enables one to explain how
the homelands policy excludes the people who live in
those areas from access to the wealth and resources of
South Africa, that they become cut off and that people
who live there and whom we regard as South Africans
are deprived because of the homelands policy.

In East London, a small coastal town sited on the brief
corridor of South Africa in between the Transkei and the
Ciskei, the advice office, opened in 1986, and its skeleton
staff of four paid workers and nine volunteers, was particularly involved with the consequences of homeland independence and its curious, shifting boundaries. At the time of my
1989 visit the increasing number of cases of extreme poverty
coming to the office was becoming a source of growing
concern. The queue of desperate people began to form each
day at 4 a.m. Anything up to eight people in a family could
be living on one person's pension. By that time a pension was
R150 a month. That was assuming that the individual concerned was eligible for a pension in South Africa, and even
then blacks were frequently disadvantaged by comparison
with whites. In Port Elizabeth white pensions had been
computerised. This meant that applications could be pro-
cessed within forty-eight hours. Blacks had to wait for nine
months and often even longer. In the homelands, pensions
were smaller and payouts were unreliable. Many advice office
hours were spent helping people to prove that they actually
lived in South Africa.

When somebody goes along to get a pension, they are
required to produce evidence that they live in East
London, otherwise it's: 'Oh no, you know these blacks.
They'll draw a pension in the Ciskei and then come and
get another one here.' Providing proof is all very well if
you have a house, but by far the majority of black people
do not have houses. They live in shacks or under
bushes, so how can they prove residence and become

registered residents? We have people in the office who
are sixty-five wanting to apply for a pension. They were
born in East London and have lived there all their lives,
but they've never had a regular house so how can they
prove it?

Much of the advice work had been devoted to inducing
officials to accept such credentials as people had.

Another task undertaken by the relatively small number of
Black Sash members in East London was that of taking
visitors into the neighbouring townships to make them aware
of conditions there. I was driven to King Williams Town by
Sue Power, daughter of Cape Town's Noël Robb, and an
equally dedicated Black Sasher whose professional life was
devoted to running a Workbench Centre providing sheltered
employment for the mentally handicapped. *En route*, as we
crossed in and out of scattered pieces of the Ciskei with
nothing substantial to mark where this independent state
began and ended, she recounted, not without some amusement, the story of how she and another Sash member who
had a strong Scottish accent had taken one male representative from the British embassy on a conducted tour, only to
meet with the question, 'What's a nice Scottish girl like you
doing in a radical organisation like this?' One of the problems
the Black Sash encountered in bringing pressure to bear on
the South African government in relation to what was happening in the homelands arose, ironically, out of the failure
of foreign governments to recognise the so-called independent states. Because of this non-recognition, embassy officials
were not really supposed to go into the homelands. Consequently, they did not put pressure on their own governments
to pressurise the South African government.

As far as the Black Sash was concerned, the world outside
South Africa needed to take more notice of what was happening in the homelands and not simply to accept the South
African government's line that the violence that was taking
place there was the inevitable consequence of black people
being left to their own devices: 'The point is that the real
leaders of the people are in jail.' The people who were

wreaking such destruction were men who, like Jacob More, had a vested interest in acting as a puppet of the South African government. Pretoria could hardly be unhappy that the independent homelands were slipping into chaos and anarchy, thus demonstrating to the world what happened when blacks were granted self-government and so, by inference, what would happen if the same system were applied to South Africa as a whole.

The Ciskei was the object of particular concern. Our destination was a church hall in white South Africa's King Williams Town which was providing emergency shelter for nearly eight hundred black people from Peelton, originally part of South Africa, subsequently consolidated into the Ciskei and now being persecuted by supporters of the homeland's leader Chief Lennox Sebe. There had been conflict in the Ciskei ever since Chief Sebe had opted for independence against the wishes of the majority of the Ciskeian people. Nepotism had prevailed within the Ciskeian government, a number of trade unions had been banned and government opponents detained. In October 1983 a researcher for the Centre for Applied Legal Studies at the University of Witwatersrand in Johannesburg, while compiling a report on human rights violations in the Ciskei, had spoken of Sebe resorting to 'desperate measures' to control his subjects. Helen Suzman, opposition MP, had publicly described him as a 'vicious tyrant'.

On the way to King Williams Town we paused in Bisho, with its renowned Amatola Sun Casino, currently being boycotted as a protest against what was happening to the people in the church hall in King Williams Town, and in the homeland's capital Mdantsane with its grandiose development of government houses and offices complete with animal heads adorning their façades. Just down the road from this incongruously glamorous capital, which took no account of the pitifully poverty-stricken lives of ordinary people, an enormous plush new hospital was being constructed despite the proximity of King Williams Town's newly revamped hospital, for which there were insufficient staff. One of the consequences of independence was the 'necessity' to construct and run all facilities independently with money which

could have been used for more urgently needed development
and the upgrading of the large numbers of poor. Also 'just
down the road' from what Sue Power described as 'this
ridiculously palatial lunatic place' lay East Peelton, the home
of the refugees I was about to meet. In Mdantsane no one
could rent a house without producing a membership card for
Sebe's party. Without a party card it was almost impossible
to live. So it was that Sebe could claim the support of the
majority of his people, but not all of them. The people of East
Peelton had refused to join the party and pay the Ciskei taxes
which financed the showpiece capital at the expense of
people who could ill afford it.

East Peelton had been incorporated into the Ciskei on 12
August 1988. The views of its people had never been canvassed by the South African authorities. A request for the
land by the Ciskei government had been considered sufficient
to warrant the incorporation, and a petition signed by almost
the entire community, rejecting the Ciskei, had been dismissed out of hand by South Africa's Minister of Cooperation
and Development, Gerrit Viljoen. One constructive fact did
emerge out of the resulting parliamentary debate, however,
namely Minister Viljoen's assurance that the incorporation
would never affect the residents' right to South African
citizenship. From the day that the Ciskei officials and police
moved into East Peelton there had been conflict in the area.
The residents had adamantly refused to accept Ciskei authority, insisting that they were South Africans. The Ciskei's
response had been heavy-handed. Members of the residents'
committee had been periodically detained, residents had been
harassed and assaulted and the community had been denied
basic facilities such as access to the cattle dip. An appeal was
made to the South African government to reverse the incorporation, but the government continuously argued that the
matter was internal to the Ciskei, an independent homeland.
Although the residents carried South African identity books,
the Department of Foreign Affairs issued statements saying
that they were Ciskeian.

On Monday, 16 October a State of Emergency had been
declared in the Ciskei, covering the three villages of East

Peelton. Next day demolitions began in one of the villages, Nkqonkqweni. Houses were bulldozed and trucks began dumping residents on the South African border. The demolition work had continued all that week. On Thursday, 19 October the State of Emergency had been extended retrospectively, to enable the Ciskei authorities to evict people in the affected areas, to demolish their houses and dump them anywhere in the Ciskei. Trucks started taking people and dropping them together with their possessions in remote rural areas. The people who had taken refuge in the Catholic church hall in King Williams Town had seen their houses flattened and Nkqonkqweni reduced to a ghost town.

In conjunction with the relief organisation Operation Hunger, the Border Council of Churches and a number of other local organisations, the Black Sash had helped to arrange aid in the form of food and clothing for the flow of Peelton villagers who managed to find their way across the invisible border back into South Africa. Press coverage was not always readily forthcoming in what was sometimes regarded as something of a backwater. The peace march which had taken place in East London that September, during which 40,000 people had taken to the streets, had barely warranted national coverage. Nevertheless provision was being made for journalists to see the people concerned and publicise their predicament.

In a room in a building adjacent to the church one reporter questioned a dozen of the people who had been granted temporary refuge in the nearby church hall. A boy of thirteen recounted in monotones how he had been taken from his home by police for allegedly burning down houses. He told of how he had subsequently been removed to Frankfurt where he had been slapped and beaten with a buckle. At Zwelitsha, he said, he had been beaten again, this time with an empty bottle and with chairs. Because of the beatings and because he was frightened, he had admitted to burning the houses. He had appeared before the court at Zwelitsha, been released on bail and then made his way to King Williams Town. The Black Sash ladies who stood bail for him had told him his people were at the church. There were no visible signs of the beatings he claimed. It was hard to tell what lay at the root of those monotones. Anger, frustration or stoical acceptance of the inevitability of injustice? Time and again in South Africa I would hear first-person accounts of extraordinary human suffering told without trace of emotion. If the belief that such misery was inevitable lay behind the lack of passion, then it was part of the role of the Black Sash, one advice office worker in Grahamstown would inform me, to teach people otherwise, to show them that there were ways in which they could help themselves.

The other four members of that boy's family were among the people waiting in the church hall itself and the yard outside to know their future. Grubby children with smiling faces played amongst the piles of blankets which had to be unfolded each night and stowed away each morning. Washing fluttered from pieces of string strung haphazardly across the church yard, while beneath it old men sat in a circle on wooden chairs. They waited quietly in the knowledge that in Peelton the livestock in which they had invested so much and which for rural people like them was a bastion against starvation, was dying. With their owners turned out, the animals themselves would be starving. The Black Sash had tried to obtain permission for an animal care organisation to have access to them, but permission had been denied. Rural people, as Sue Power pointed out, for all their lack of money, actually have a reasonable standard of living thanks to their animals and the vegetables they grow. 'But if you're going to kill off their animals or shunt them all into towns where they can't keep animals, they are not going to make it.'

All the Peelton people wanted was the right to remain South African. By comparison with life in the Ciskei, life as black people in white South Africa seemed to them desirable. Asked what it was they hoped for as they waited in the dusty heat of that overcrowded churchyard, they expressed only the desire to remain together and to go back to their home location, provided it was to be under the Republic of South Africa. The Black Sash had been invaluable in making their predicament known to the people of South Africa. It was, they announced, 'a progressive and good organisation'.

Next morning I was taken by Sue Power and one of the residents of East London's black township, Duncan Village, to see the living conditions of people in South Africa who had held out for years against removal. For years the whole of Duncan Village had been under threat. White East London had expanded to form a horseshoe round the township, and its presence had become offensive to many of those who did not have to live there and who regarded it, not without justification but possibly without undue thought for the reasons behind its condition, as unhealthy and overcrowded. The virtual creation of slum areas was, it seemed, another state tactic to persuade people to move. In some cases, where communities had been resisting removal for over ten years, the facilities in the area, such as schools and roads and clinics, had not been extended or maintained by the local authorities. Duncan Village was a case in point.

I, a total stranger, could have drawn a line unprompted across the road at the point where the adjacent coloured area under the jurisdiction of the white municipality ended and black Duncan Village began, so abrupt was the transition from, albeit imperfect, tarmac road to a dirt track in which attempts to repair the deep and all pervasive potholes with inadequate materials had all too evidently failed. It was impossible to put a figure on the population of the township, for every day a new shack appeared among the closely packed improvised shelters, and in those shacks as many as a dozen people made their home. Duncan Village, in all its poverty, highlighted the tragedy of destroying the homes of people like the Peelton villagers who had actually had decent brick houses in which to live. There were houses: one-roomed, windowless structures of perhaps ten feet by ten, with appended to them 'extensions' built of corrugated iron, wood or whatever other materials had been found available. Some of them had been built in the 1940s; some in the 1960s as emergency accommodation provided with the promise of better things to come. Many of the residents had been born in Duncan Village, but the government regarded them as illegal squatters. No more land was to be provided in that area for blacks, and so Duncan Village grew progressively more congested. A nursing sister earning a good salary lived in a 'house' without running water or a lavatory because there was no land on which to build alternative accommodation. To have the smallest of gardens would have been to deprive another potential resident of space in which to erect his home.

In the end the government had apparently relented. Officially Duncan Village could stay. Better housing was built, but it did not solve the housing problem because the cheapest cost in the region of R3,000. Few people could afford to live in them and they took up valuable space. So it was that Duncan Village consisted for the most part of acre upon acre of rows of shacks separated by mud pathways in which there was only room for one person to walk abreast. Their occupants shared a tap in a small open-air wash area with several stone tanks for all-purpose washing. They also shared the desperately inadequate number of communal toilets that were almost constantly blocked and overflowing because the water supply was not functioning or simply because of the amount of use.

Sue Power had little patience with the blanket condemnation of black people as dirty: 'Recently the water was cut off in Duncan Village for several days. After a day the toilets are overflowing and people go on the floor of the toilets but what else can they do? Where can they go? If they go into the bushes it's actually quite dangerous. If you talk to people, they'll tell you that at night you can be raped or attacked. So what do you do?' People used drains outside their homes or went to the filthy public toilets and added to the mess that was already there. 'So the place is a pigsty and people point a finger and say: "Look what these blacks do." ' It was true, she said, that the townships were often in a mess but the villages in the rural areas were not dirty – there school children emerged from the neatly thatched round huts in immaculately laundered uniforms – and if you took into account the density of the population in the townships and the fact that the rubbish was only collected once a month instead of once a week, whites in similar circumstances would probably create not dissimilar conditions. The independent homelands would probably create not dissimilar conditions. The independent homelands and the black local authorities who since 1971 had been expected to be responsible for raising their own money to cover the needs of their own communities did not have the necessary funds. A rubbish truck would cost Duncan Village approximately half a million Rand. 'The people here simply haven't got that sort of money.'

Nor did Sue Power have any sympathy for the line of thought which held that as fast as schools were built for township children, people burned them down, so they must now provide their own. Many communities did provide their own schools. Schools in many of the villages around East London had been built at the villagers' own expense, but if one considered the schools which the government had provided it was hard to blame people for burning them down. Sue Power's own children went to a government school which she had not had to build. That school had every facility, including squash courts, while just a mile away in one of the Duncan Village schools which was subsequently burnt down, pupils had sat for their lessons in the sand between the floor supports. The floor boards had simply rotted away and never been replaced. There was one table for the teacher. Now black children were receiving free books, but prior to many of the burnings they had not: 'My kids used to come home at the beginning of the year with a whole suitcase full of hard-cover books, scribblers – all for nothing. By the end of the year they would not have used half of them, while just down the road the black schools which had no money received no free books. Black pupils knew that their white counterparts had so much for nothing.'

Over the years the Black Sash had made a point of publicising the conditions of African schools: the overcrowding, the inadequate equipment, the scarcity of books, the limitations of the syllabuses and the high drop-out rate which condemned a large part of the African population to a state of semi-literacy. It had uncovered the need for textbooks, uniforms and funds for school lunches. It had protested against the injustices of a system which provided free compulsory education for the comparatively affluent white children but not for their African counterparts. Sue Power had taken the headmaster of her children's primary school to see the conditions in Duncan Village's school. He was appalled. Why did the black headmaster not keep up the maintenance of the school so that jobs did not become too large or too expensive? It was pointed out that in a white school there was a caretaker and/or a handyman and the funds to undertake the necessary work. In Duncan Village the teachers had to do the maintenance jobs themselves and pay for it out of their own pockets. 'They all get tired and disgruntled and you can hardly blame them. It's so depressing.'

I saw an unusually large number of people in Duncan Village with scarred faces and hands. The scar tissue was frequently the result of shack fires. Paraffin lamps were often the only source of light in the township homes. Accidents were far from rare, and because of the close proximity of the shacks and the absence of readily available water, when one caught fire so too did countless others. Through darkened doorways I heard the sound of voices not raised in anger or in pain but apparently talking of ordinary things. In such conditions people went about the activities of their daily round: sleeping, eating, doing homework. When it rained, Sue Power informed me, the mud of the narrow alleyways washed up to the level of what little furniture the houses contained, carrying the effluence from the overflowing drains with it. It was a miracle that there were not more incidences of typhoid. It was drizzling as we were about to leave Duncan Village. A young man with a smiling face and something missing from his mind waved frenetically. A middle-aged woman, recognising the van, came to ask for plastic sheeting. Operation Hunger might still have some, the woman was informed. Sue Power would make enquiries on her behalf. Plastic sheeting, it seemed, was like gold dust. For many it was the only protection against the potentially hostile elements.

On the edge of the township, clearly visible from the road leading back to East London, was a small area of grassland set aside as the black cemetery. Like a South African pension, the right to burial in that cemetery was dependent upon registration as a South African citizen and all the necessary and sometimes impossible proofs which that entailed. The Black Sash advice office had been the last resort of many a grieving widow not permitted to bury her husband, on the grounds that the deceased was not a South African citizen and must be taken to the Ciskei or the Transkei. The black burial ground was small. The shortage of land was becoming critical and the black local authority's attitude was that if everyone was allowed to be buried there, they would soon run out of space. The Black Sash was adamant that they must ask for more land and not just 'sit there and say we can't bury you'. With funds secured through Lawyers for Human Rights, the organisation had recently made an urgent application to the Supreme Court in Grahamstown on behalf of a man who had lived in Duncan Village for thirty years but had not been registered. After his body had been lying in the mortuary for two weeks – and hours before the case came to court – the Gompo Town Council settled with costs. Small triumphs such as this brought hope for the future, but that did not wipe out the pain of the past.

   That night the wind blew and the rain beat down without interruption. I thought of the woman in Duncan Village with her unpressing request for plastic sheeting and I knew I had glimpsed something of the causes of 'moral outrage', something of what it was that made the women of the Black Sash take up the day-by-day, minute-by-minute challenge as South Africans to work for a different kind of society.

Chapter Six

A watchdog not a lapdog

The magistrate entered the small dreary courtroom, the court rose and the business of the day began. One by one the prisoners, who had been waiting in an enclosure fenced in with high wire netting, were brought in: neatly clad urban workers, ragged rural immigrants or roughly dressed mineworkers. The charge was read out and interpreted to the accused; he replied, again through the court interpreter. The magistrate might ask a question or two, or the prisoner might elect to enter the witness box to give evidence on his own behalf, and then sentence was passed – £3 or three weeks in prison, £8 or eight weeks in prison, £5 or five weeks, wih monotonous regularity. Each case occupied, on average, approximately two minutes of the court's time.

Gradually a pattern appeared to emerge; failure to produce a reference book, £5 or five weeks; possession of a forged permit, £8 or eight weeks; mine employee, book left in compound, £1 or seven days. Sometimes, however, sentences varied inexplicably. Why was one man fined £8 or eight weeks for failure to produce his reference book, when he had lost it, according to his evidence, and been arrested on his way to report that loss? Sometimes the accused had been arrested for failure to produce his book and produced it in court, completely in order. Sometimes a man claimed that the policeman arresting him did not give him time to fetch his book. If he elected to have the policeman in question summoned to give evidence, his case was remanded for a day or two, and he was returned to the cells to spend a further period in jail. Too often, a prisoner was re-arrested soon after his discharge from jail, before he had had time to collect the reference book for non-production of which he had just served a sentence.

These things were witnessed by a Black Sash member of the Transvaal region who, in August 1960, sat on the wooden form along one wall provided for members of the public in one of Johannesburg's four Commissioners' Courts. Since first they had gone into the pass law courts in Cape Town to assist black women needing bail, Black Sash women had taken to monitoring the Native Commissioners' Courts in the Cape and in the Transvaal. What they had seen was a revelation to women accustomed to a world in which people in trouble simply engaged a skilful lawyer. They had become acquainted with the summary forms of justice meted out to undefended Africans, and with the vulnerability and ignorance of people so unaware of their rights that they became the victims of unfair and even illegal procedures.

The organisation began wherever possible to send representatives to sit in on a daily basis on the succession of cases which were hurried through the courts with indecent haste. There were occasions when the magistrate barely even appeared to look up from his bench to cope with his quota of the 1,500 offenders who were at one time tried daily in the Native Commissioners' Courts. At the court in Cape Town's black Langa township, an unpretentious structure made up of two austere little rooms with a tin roof, sometimes as many as sixty cases were heard in a morning. The accused were mostly women, charged with being in the area without a permit. This law only applied to blacks over the age of sixteen, so sometimes the Bantu Affairs Commissioner would cross-question the accused to make sure he or she was a 'Bantu'. As to determining a young person's age, sometimes when there was no birth certificate available, the Commissioner would order an examination of the accused's teeth.

A typical case was a woman who had come with her children to Cape Town because she had no work or income in the Transkei. Her husband, a migrant labourer, had stopped sending her money. She was arrested before she managed to find him and, in the absence of the requisite stamp in her pass book, was found guilty. She had no money to pay the fine so went to prison with her young children and was told to leave the area immediately on completion of her sentence. She was thus compelled to leave without knowing whether her husband was dead, in prison, or now living with another woman. Quite often people were given rail vouchers to leave Cape Town and go back to the Transkei.

Frequently an accused woman would plead not guilty on the grounds that she had come to Cape Town for medical treatment for herself or her child. Even if the woman had a letter from a doctor recommending treatment at a hospital in Cape Town, such mitigating circumstances were usually dismissed because the Commissioner considered that there were adequate facilities in the Transkei. On one occasion a woman collapsed and fell to the floor of the dock whilst trying to plead her case. The court officials did nothing until two Black Sash monitors went to her aid and demanded that they call an ambulance. The officials would not even produce anything for the woman to lie on, so the court monitors did their best to make her comfortable at the back of the courtroom. Finally she was taken to hospital, still unconscious. As far as the officials were concerned, however, the general attitude seemed to be 'assume everyone is lying unless proved otherwise'.

By the early 1980s conditions in the courtroom at Langa had scarcely improved. Cherry Fisher, who joined the Black Sash in 1981, recalls attending it as one of her first assignments:

> To me it was almost a send-up of a court. The court interpreter was there, but he was already a marked man because he was working for the state. A woman would come in with two children clinging to her and another on her back. She wouldn't really look much more than twenty-two. The Commissioner would then bark at her in Afrikaans, asking whether she spoke English or Afrikaans. Invariably she wouldn't understand because she'd come straight from the homelands. Then there would be wisecracks going on between the Commissioner and the interpreter: 'Hm, three down below and another in her belly, and you've come here to have another.' He would humiliate her terribly. Then he would ask her why she was here. In her own language

she would explain that she had come to look for her
husband and she'd claim an excuse, and you knew that
she was just playing for time and that all she and many
others really wanted was to be near their menfolk.
Always the response was that they had come to be a
burden to Cape Town, either by having more babies or
by looking for work when there wasn't any for them.

In personal terms for the court monitors, the experience
was also a heart-rending one. By then the facts of injustice
were not new to them. What hurt was the 'actual sight of
these sufferers, these patient pathetic people, dully and hopelessly accepting their bitter lot'. Black Sash members were
on the whole realistic enough to know that some of the
accused were rogues and that all might technically be law-
breakers, but mostly they were simple, inoffensive human
beings caught up in troubles not of their own making and
against which they had no defence. So depressing was the
prospect of the procession of prisoners through the courts
that there were times when volunteers who could muster the
heart to witness proceedings were in short supply, but the
Black Sash struggled to hold on to the belief that their
presence was important. They had discovered that the critical
observation by white women of what was happening in the
courtroom, like their witnessing of 'voluntary' removals,
exerted a certain influence over the manner in which proceedings were conducted. Furthermore, simply by being there,
they served as a reminder both to official white South Africa
and to the apartheid victims in the dock that one element at
least of white South Africa still protested against apartheid.

In March 1984 in the Native Commissioner's Court in
Langa township, together with a Canadian visitor, the day's
Black Sash duty observer watched a succession of accused
blacks appear before a white Commissioner* and a white
prosecutor. The Commissioner and the prosecutor talked
together in Afrikaans. The interpreter and the undefended

---

* Commissioners, although also referred to as magistrates, were bureaucrats,
employees of the Department of Cooperation and Development which administered blacks, and frequently had only minimal legal qualifications.

accused spoke in Xhosa. The interpreter then translated into English for the Commissioner, who answered in English. The Canadian visitor took out a stopwatch and placed it on the bench beside him and the Black Sash monitor timed the beginning and end of each case:

First Case: Fuzddi Mbunge, a young man in worn khaki overalls, wringing his hands, said he had travelled from Johannesburg to Cape Town to tell his father, who worked there, that the young man's mother was sick. The man's Reference Book did not say he had authorisation for the trip.

Commissioner Fourie told him that his father should have gone to visit his wife. He imposed a fine of R70 or seventy days' imprisonment but suspended the sentence for twelve months. Disposition time: eight minutes.

Second Case: Nancy Makidwa, said she came (illegally) to Cape Town from another community to visit her brother. When apprehended by police, she was unable to produce her pass book. She was fined R60 or sixty days. Disposition time: five minutes, and four seconds.

So the docket of a total of eight cases went on. In many respects, from a Black Sash point of view, these cases were just a demoralising repetition of thousands of others that had passed through the pass-law courts over the years. Having come to the end of the docket, however, Commissioner Fourie addressed the Canadian visitor. 'I see,' he said, 'that once again there are people in the court timing the proceedings. For their benefit, I will point out that there were eight cases. In total they took thirty-two minutes, which is an average of four minutes a case.' He also pointed out that it was ridiculous to measure the workings of the court on the basis of one day's timing. Some cases, he claimed, took hours, even days. He then left the court, but shortly afterwards he caught up with the Canadian visitor outside and invited the latter to see the figures for the whole of 1983 for his court. A cumbersome ledger revealed that it had disposed of 144 cases where evidence was heard, 59 cases where no evidence was heard but the Commissioner had asked questions of the accused, 7,282 cases where guilty pleas were accepted without evidence or questions, and 3,411 cases which were withdrawn. The total court time had been 630½ hours. Discounting the withdrawn cases, that worked out at five minutes and five seconds per case. On 30 March a report of what was happening in the Langa Commissioner's Court appeared in Canada's national paper *The Globe and Mail*. As for the Black Sash, its members were delighted. The episode with the ledger was an indication that the presence of visitors in the courtroom was a real source of worry.

This was only one example among many. The Black Sash monitors knew well the evident satisfaction of the court officials when the accused was found to be under sixteen, the case had therefore to be held *in camera* and the white women looking on could be required to leave the court. David Viti, who had first come to work as an interpreter in the Cape Town Black Sash advice office in 1962 and who subsequently served as interpreter for the small panel of lawyers prepared to act in the accuseds' defence, described how in the days before the Black Sash women's practice of attending the courts four, five or six defendants would sometimes be packed into the tiny docks at any one time and asked *en masse* whether they pleaded guilty or not guilty. The response was invariably 'guilty' because to plead 'not guilty' meant being remanded in custody for several days, followed almost inevitably by a sentence. As the courts became more and more congested, David Viti would go regularly to the Commissioners' Courts in the Cape Town area if there was the slightest chance of a lawyer being required. David was black. His leg was in a calliper. His presence in the courtroom did not have quite the same effect as that of the Black Sash women themselves and when he was there in their absence he was able to note the difference.

As more and more illegals poured into the Cape Town area and the pass-law offences in Johannesburg increased, the Black Sash monitors' purpose was still officially to act as a spur to the consciences of official white South Africa and to highlight the extreme distress caused by the imperfections of the legal system. Officially they were also there to draw attention to the fact that most people were still undefended and that in many cases those who attempted their own defence were unnecessarily remanded in custody while their stories were checked in the minutest detail by the authorities. Unofficially their purpose was to 'gum up the works', to slow down the proceedings of the courts as much as possible until the point came where the system simply could not cope with the endless conveyor-belt of pass-law prosecutions and influx control would be found to be unenforceable. Sure enough, that point, long hoped-for but never quite envisaged, was reached. Yet with the abolition of the pass laws in 1986 the role of the court monitors was by no means exhausted. Although the role of the Black Sash as witnesses to courtroom proceedings may have begun with the victims of influx control, it did not end there. Even before the 'abolition' of influx control the organisation had begun to try and extend its, albeit thin, monitoring resources to courts other than those devoted to the pass laws. The sight of Black Sash women in the public gallery with their notebooks at the ready became an increasingly common one at those trials which became labelled 'political' because in them the relationship between the government and the governed became a key issue.

1976, the year in which the issue of compulsory teaching in the Afrikaans language sparked off the Soweto riots, setting off a nationwide wave of violence, was a crucial year in South Africa. General Stadler, in placing the Black Sash in the context of the revolutionary plan of the ANC/SACP Alliance to overthrow the South African government, would cite it as a year in which 6,000 young black people left South Africa. They were not all necessarily pro-ANC, but as far as the South African Police were concerned they were anti-white and anti-government, for the most part subscribers to the full spectrum of black consciousness groupings whose shared attitude was that 'whites are part of the problem so they cannot be part of the solution'. The SAP had records of just over 2,000 who had joined ranks with the ANC and received training in Angola, the Soviet Union and the

German Democratic Republic. In 1975 Mozambique had received its independence. The ANC thus found itself equipped with both a substantial number of very militant people and a forward-base which could be used as a spring-board into South Africa. Hitherto its attempts to infiltrate large numbers of people into the country had failed: 'They had tried their utmost but all their people had been arrested by police.' Prior to the advent of the Black Consciousness movement General Stadler felt that the ANC had virtually lost control of the 'internal dimension'. From 1976 onwards, however, the position was very different.

> One of the lessons they had learned from Soweto was that they could not hope to create a revolution in South Africa unless they could unite the masses behind them. During 1978 an ANC delegation led by Oliver Tambo conducted research in Vietnam into the methods employed by the Vietnamese in the revolutionary struggle against South Vietnam. They concluded that the armed struggle had to be combined with political action (important components of which were mobilisation, organisation and protest) in order to bring about a decline in South Africa's military, economic and social abilities. The ANC leadership therefore decided on a three-year programme of organising and mobilising the masses that would have culminated in 1982 with the anniversary of the ANC.

From then on the strategy was to make South Africa ungovernable by destroying the structure of government and law implementation, bringing about a people's war and set-ting up alternative structures. As far as the forces of law and order were concerned, that strategy meant an escalation both of 'unrest' and of acts of terrorism. '1976 was the first time Communist acts of terrorism were committed in South Africa.' Some called those acts 'guerilla warfare', some called them 'freedom fighting', some 'armed propaganda', but as far as the government and the police were concerned the bomb-ing of cars and other similar incidents of violence were 'acts

of terrorism', and between 1976 and 1984 they slowly esca-
lated. After 1985 they increased more dramatically. In 1984
there were 44 such incidents, in 1985 136, and by 1986 236.

Widespread unrest provided the ANC with the opportunity
to infiltrate more of its people into the country. It had also
been able to form cell systems and recruit and train more and
more people inside South Africa. The Security Forces felt
they had lost their grip. According to General Stadler: 'Our
intelligence network broke down. I was officer in charge of
the Intelligence Unit of the South African Police so I know
what I'm talking about.' In the period leading up to the 1986
State of Emergency, the General claimed, there had also been
396 necklace murders: 'Almost 400 murders by burning, not
to mention other murders that took place, of which there
were more than 1,000.' Law-abiding members of the public
needed to be assured of their safety. This was the justification
for ever-more stringent attempts to enforce law and order.

The imposition of a partial State of Emergency from 20
July 1985 to 7 March 1986, and then of a full State of
Emergency on 12 June 1986, would ultimately be regarded by
the SAP as the reluctant but necessary response to the
breakdown of law and order in the form of school boycotts,
rent and consumer boycotts, mass stayaways and the revolutionary and radical rise of people's power. In 1989 General
Stadler spoke of how people of all races appealed to police for
protection with tears in their eyes. What was more, he was
emphatic that without the state of emergency 'we would
have been very much worse off than we are now'. Between
1984 and August 1989 the SAP had been able to recover 2,329
hand grenades, 4,330 other bombs. As a result of their
Emergency powers police had been able to eliminate 400
alternative structures and 'people's courts'. Statistics showed
that the almost 15,000 incidents of unrest in 1986 declined
to 5,000 in 1987. At its Arusha conference in 1987 the ANC
itself acknowledged that the 'people's war' strategy had
failed. To bring that failure about the South African authorities had needed to implement more rigorous control.

In 1982 the government added the Internal Security Act to

an all-embracing network of security legislation. In the conviction that the violence in the black townships was the
result either of plain criminality or of a carefully planned
campaign by the ANC and the South African Communist
Party, the government rounded up the supposed ringleaders
of the conspiracy and put them on trial for high treason. The
strategy of bringing court cases against activists was one
which it had used in the past, perhaps most notably in the
1956 treason trial. Legislation encompassing the Suppression
of Communism Act of 1950, the Criminal Law Amendment
Act of 1953 and the Unlawful Organisations Act of 1960, had
led to the banning of the African National Congress, the Pan-
African Congress and the South African Communist Party
and also, much to the outrage of some Black Sash members
who had found even activities which they regarded as merely
in the interests of human rights being tarred with the broad-
sweeping brush of communism, made provision for extreme
penalties for anyone found guilty of any action which could
be remotely interpreted as communist.

From 1982 onwards the Internal Security Act was used for
the arrest of suspected political agitators and to prohibit anti-
government activities which the Black Sash considered
should be regarded as part of the normal democratic process.
As far as it was concerned the Internal Security Act cast the
net so wide as to include as criminal and subversive conduct
regarded as perfectly legitimate and lawful in normal societies. It provided the authorities with a useful device to
prosecute selectively with no effective safeguards. The Black
Sash took the view that this led to the criminalising of
legitimate opposition, the use of the law courts effectively to
neutralise opponents who were awaiting trial. (In many
instances bail was refused, thus disguising the ever-increasing number of detainees.) It also resulted in the courts
themselves being used to subvert the rule of law while
apparently observing the due process of law.

When on 20 August 1983 the United Democratic Front, a
broad alliance of anti-apartheid bodies inspired by Allan
Boesak, was launched to lead extra-parliamentary opposition
to the government's new constitution, it was a move which

the Black Sash wholeheartedly applauded. It shared the UDF's opposition to the government's reforms on the grounds that neither the tri-cameral parliament, nor a referendum by which President Botha had hoped to obtain a clear mandate for the new three-chamber body, had taken into account a substantial proportion of the potential electorate. The government's response to the formation of the UDF, however, was to attempt to link its leaders with the outlawed ANC and SACP. As far as the Law and Order Minister Louis Le Grange was concerned, the UDF had the same revolutionary aims as the South African Communist Party, declared unlawful by the 1950 Suppression of Communism Act, and the ANC, banned in 1960: it was actively preparing a revolutionary climate. He claimed that 90 per cent of the UDF's office-bearers had previously been involved with these banned organisations. The next move was to arrest sixteen of the UDF leaders and charge them with high treason. The 600-page indictment contended that the sixteen had supported a 'revolutionary alliance' comprising the SACP, the ANC and the South African Congress of Trade Unions, but no hard evidence was produced and by June 1986 the state had dropped charges against all the accused.

In January 1986, however, in the 'Delmas' trial, the state once again brought charges of high treason against members of the UDF, including Patrick 'Terror' Lekota, the organisation's publicity secretary; Popo Simon Molefe, national secretary; and the former UDF secretary of the Transvaal region, Moses 'Moss' Chikane. On this occasion the state alleged that the UDF was actively involved in the murder of five township residents in the Vaal Triangle and the destruction of homes and shops, school boycotts and unrest, intimidating black community councillors to resign and indoctrinating the youth and women. It was in what proved to be the longest political trial South Africa had ever seen, that Sheena Duncan actually gave evidence for the defence of the twenty-two accused. The intention was to show that the UDF's attitudes and actions were not dissimilar to those of the Black Sash, a legal organisation of which the state was manifestly not over-enamoured but which it evidently did not consider to be guilty of treason.

Mr Justice K. van Dijkhorst, presiding over the Supreme Courtroom where, in 1963, Nelson Mandela had been found guilty of high treason, eventually found that the state could not prove that any of the accused were directly responsible for the death of any councillors. He also found, however, that they had encouraged the masses to revolt and that, by calling for a stayaway and protest marches, they had incited people to violent confrontation. He further found that the dominant part of the UDF had acted as the ANC's internal wing and concluded that the UDF had accepted violence as the only justifiable option open to the ANC, who had attempted peaceful protest for nearly fifty years. Eleven of the accused were acquitted, six were convicted on alternative charges of terrorism and five, including the key UDF men, were found guilty of high treason. An Appeal Court subsequently quashed the convictions of the five and set their sentences aside, following a campaign on behalf of diplomats, Churches and political and human rights organisations, including the Black Sash.

What was apparent from this and other 'political' trials was that the dock provided a platform from which political activists could make their views public in a way that they could not elsewhere. Like the contact made with the black community through the advice offices, the reports of court monitors thus had a profound impact on the Black Sash's understanding of the situation of thousands of people. Whether in the pass-law cases or in the 'political' trials, the conflict between the people and the state was made visible and audible through the legal proceedings. In the course of those proceedings defendants also frequently spoke of precisely the inadequate living conditions, forced removals, discriminatory education and denial of human rights which the Black Sash was committed to exposing. This fact, combined with the organisation's commitment to educating itself and others, meant that the Black Sash saw the gathering and publicising of information relating to the trials as of considerable importance, although the number of women available to sit in on proceedings on a regular basis, particularly in the

Eastern Cape where members were few and the consequences of membership frequently tough, was invariably limited.

By February 1986 a project involving some thirty volunteers had been initiated in the Western Cape. It was particularly concerned with the charges covered by the blanket designation 'public violence', many of them involving children, which had been filling the courts since the massive arrests had begun in 1985 of those involved in the politics of overt oppostion to the apartheid state. Information which emerged from the records they maintained kept the Black Sash aware of situations which were ever less in the public eye because under the State of Emergency they had been made subject to media restrictions. The information, the statistics derived from it and the conclusions reached were of particular value because they were the result of direct experience.

A report from Muriel Crewe, a retired school mistress, in charge of court-monitoring in the Western Cape, to the Black Sash conference of 1987 recorded the fact that it was appalling to

> note the number of individuals who allege brutal violence on arrest, in *casspirs*, and in police cells – including incidents of torture. The assaults ranged from kicking and beating – with quirts, fists or rifles – to teargassing and close-range shooting. (In a few cases doctors' certificates, photographs and slides were offered as evidence.) There were reports of inadequate food in police cells, rudeness and obstructiveness towards parents seeking their children, opposition to bail applications and protracted detention. Many claimed that the statements they had made, which were used by the state as evidence, had been signed under duress. We have seen detainees brought into court manacled or in leg-irons – even before the charges against them had been framed.

As with the pass-law cases, the length of time proceedings took was again a cause for concern. Here, however, the monitors were highlighting the fact that some cases were dragging on for more than a year because of repeated remands. The worst instance they had on record was of twelve remands. Many of these were requested by the state because their witnesses, usually policemen, failed to appear. Frequently the reason given was that the charge sheet was not ready. Sometimes the defence lawyers saw the charge sheet for the first time on their arrival in court. They then requested a remand in order to be able to study the charges. Delays arose for a multitude of reasons. 'The whole process,' Muriel Crewe concluded, 'smacks of purposeful delay, or suggests that there is a very real problem in framing charges against people arrested in random fashion.'

The consequences for both the accused and their families of such delays were often excessive trauma and hardship. There was loss of schooling; possible loss of several days' salary, when leave had to be taken to attend court; actual loss of employment when employers were unsympathetic; heavy expenses incurred in travelling, which could be especially serious in rural cases often very deliberately heard in towns far removed from the accuseds' homes, in order to diminish the likelihood of demonstrations of local support. The very real difficulties facing the authorities of preserving public order were not accorded priority by Black Sash members in contact with individual suffering. Psychological and physical strain was marked among the accused. The Black Sash had heard complaints of insomnia, headaches, shingles rashes and of an epileptic who had a fit at each appearance. It had further established that over 80 per cent of the 483 individuals who appeared in the 141 cases monitored had been found not guilty or the charges had been withdrawn. Additional analysis showed that the number withdrawn was far greater than the number found not guilty. It seemed reasonable to infer that innocent people were being arrested in a random fashion and charged on evidence that could not stand up to examination in court. They were thus being made to endure a protracted period of punishment by process with little hope of redress. Claims had been brought against the Minister of Law and Order, but these seemed generally to be settled out of court without open admission of wrongful arrest or unwarranted assault.

By 1987 it was still the Black Sash's experience that many of the accused lacked legal defence, especially in rural towns. Current legislation overrode the principle that the accused was entitled to legal defence and should be made aware of this right. It was even legally possible for children as young as seven to be arrested, detained, tried, convicted and sentenced without their parents' knowledge. The bail system was found to be confused, arbitrary and often excessive. It was true that young children were generally given free bail in the custody of their parents, but the Black Sash monitored one case of five schoolchildren aged between fifteen and seventeen who were refused bail for almost three months in 1985, released without being charged, detained again early in 1986 and refused bail for a further four months because it was alleged that if they were released they would start a boycott. A seventeen-year-old was given bail of R200 on a charge of throwing a stone at a *casspir*. Three young men, accused of being in the forefront of an unrest crowd had bail set at the impossibly high sum of R1,000. A student, accused of arson, could not pay the bail set at R2,500 and spent some time in Pollsmoor prison just south of Cape Town, only to be subsequently acquitted of the charge. Clearly, the Black Sash deduced, bail was being seen as part of the punishment process. In many instances it was only with assistance from the Western Province Council of Churches that bail money could be paid, although often the necessary funds were raised through community effort.

As to sentencing, when the accused were found guilty, the sentence frequently stated that there should be no remission or parole for people convicted of unrest-related crimes. In general it seemed clear that such crimes were being viewed as more serious than even the most brutal actions against the public, such as rape or murder. 'Public violence' offenders, even when there had been no damage to property or injury to persons, were treated in the same way as common criminals. Minors accused of stone-throwing, who were first-time offenders, could find themselves given prison sentences without even the option of a fine. In Muriel Crewe's words:

> According to established legal procedure, punishment should fit the criminal as well as the crime, be fair to the society, and be blended with a measure of mercy according to the circumstances. The crime in most public violence cases involving children is stone-throwing. The criminal is a youth between fifteen and seventeen years of age who has not committed any earlier misdemeanour. What society is being considered and which circumstances? Mercy? One magistrate in Cape Town on 3 September 1986 was reported to have said that he could not be influenced by 'maudlin sympathy', although he sympathised with the children.

One thing was becoming particularly apparent to Black Sash monitors from their regular contact with those at the sharp end of the state's attempt to curb public violence, namely that for most of those people there was no distinction between the different departments involved in the legal process. The courts were perceived simply as an extension of the police and the prison system. Because of this the Black Sash made several approaches to the Minister of Justice, requesting an interview in order to bring its findings to his notice. Despite persistent efforts the interview was made subject to indefinite postponement. Black Sash reports would continue to comment on this perception of the courts as a branch of the state, police and prison system – a state in which the majority of the governed were black and unrepresented in the legislature, while those governing were white. This divide was clearly reflected in the courts, where all the judges and most of the magistrates and prosecutors were white, while 80 per cent of those appearing before the courts were black. 'The question thus arises,' the Black Sash pointed out, 'by whose measure are the actions of the accused judged? And, when the state persecutes on behalf of the society, which society is being considered? Without providing freedom with justice to all citizens and without meeting the

1a Members of the Black Sash (then the Women's Defence of the Constitution League) camp outside the Union Buildings, Pretoria to protest against the Senate Bill, 28–9 June 1955.

1b A vigil in Bloemfontein marking the announcement of the dissolution of the Senate, November 1955.

2a An early haunting:
Minister of Justice C. R. Swart arriving in East London.

2b The East London convoy joining the great protest trek
to Cape Town, February 1956.

3a Cape women stand in mourning over a book draped with a black sash, symbolising the Constitution, February 1956.

3b Members of the Black Sash stand outside parliament in protest against the General Law Amendment Bill, 1964.

4a and 4b Over the years the Black Sash advice offices have helped people
of the black communities through the maze of apartheid legislation.

5a Sheena Duncan helping a black family with a pass-book problem.

5b A Black Sash member talking to women in the Driefontein community about their problems connected with receiving pensions and disability grants.

6a Noël Robb, a founder member of the Black Sash and for many years a leading advice office worker in Cape Town.

6b Damage caused to the Port Elizabeth advice office on 21 October 1989, in what was believed to have been an arson attack.

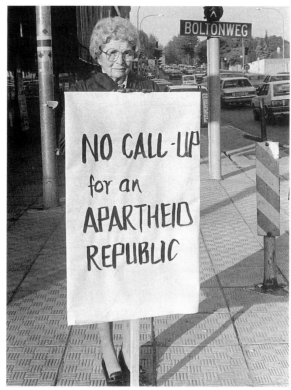

7a Jean Sinclair, a founder member of the Black Sash,
stands in individual protest against enforced conscription, May 1985.

7b Black Sash women stand in illegal protest
against the death sentence imposed on the Sharpeville Six, March 1988.

8a A march by Crossroads residents, supported by the Black Sash, demanding the readmission of their children to a local high school.

8b Black Sash members sit in a 'shack' to publicise the plight of the homeless.

8c The vigil held at Mogopa on the eve of the anticipated removal, November 1983. It was attended by political and Church leaders, including Bishop Tutu.

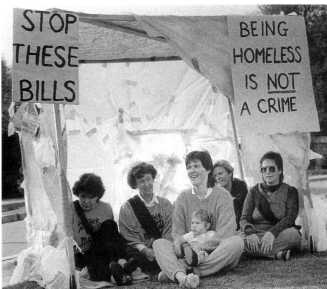

9a A former Mogopa resident outside the home he built in Bethanie, March 1984.

9b A Black Sash member listening to a woman from Mathopiestad, which was designated for removal but later reprieved.

10a Molly Blackburn attending a funeral
of unrest victims in the Eastern Cape, July 1985.

10b The funeral of Molly Blackburn, killed in a head-on car collision,
at St John's Methodist Church, Port Elizabeth, January 1986.

11a Black Sash delegates with Oliver Tambo at the Five Freedoms Forum conference in Lusaka, June 1989. (*From third left*): Joyce Harris, Beverley Runciman, Judy Chalmers, Judith Hawarden, Jenny De Tolly.

11b Mary Burton and Di Bishop at the Black Sash conference, Durban, March 1989.

12a Illegal multiple stand in support of the
Mass Democratic Movement's defiance campaign, Cape Town,
August 1989.

12b On the steps of St George's Cathedral, Cape Town,
Black Sash members take advantage of the right to stand together again
to urge for the repeal of remaining apartheid laws, February 1990.

basic needs of that 'other society', how can the state demand its loyalty?'

The experience of court-monitoring was not all negative. Even in the Commissioners' Courts regular court visitors had established contact with the court officials and made a point of reporting also the least change for the better in the depressing surroundings of the overcrowded courtrooms. Court-monitoring reports did not fail to take account of the fact that they had found prosecutors who had been cooperative, magistrates whose summing-up had been fair and impartial, occasions when magistrates had reprimanded police for not framing charges more expeditiously. Monitoring provided an opportunity to establish cordial relationships with attorneys and advocates involved in cases. Monitors could facilitate communication between overworked lawyers and their clients, a process which was in the interests of all concerned parties. Sometimes they could negotiate with the prosecutor to reschedule a case when a lawyer was delayed. They could assist in obtaining legal defence for people appearing in court who were ignorant of how to set about such an undertaking. They could help to make it clear to people overawed by members of the legal profession that their lawyers were there to act for them. Court-monitoring thus proved to be a significant avenue still available for contact across the colour-divide.

Attendance at court had opened up other areas of commitment for many members of the Black Sash. From the days when David Viti first used to interview defendants brought from Pollsmoor prison or the jail in Langa to the two small rooms that formed the 'cells' for the Commissioner's Court, the Black Sash women and those who worked with them had been concerned about the conditions under which prisoners were kept. David Viti later referred to the fact that these defendants could not be called 'clients'because they were not paying for the services the lawyers and the Black Sash were providing. Instead they were known as 'our people'. 'Our people' were often manifestly hungry. The township women who sat with their third-rate fruit outside the courtroom did a good trade. One of the resolutions taken at the Black Sash national conference as early as November 1959 was that the 'diet of prisoners should be investigated and raised at least to government standards'. Another was that 'the Black Sash enquire into the jail and prison system and see whether conditions in jails are regularly inspected, as it appears they should be by law.' By 1960 it had been agreed that every region should endeavour to draw up a report of prison conditions in their area. The reports were then presented in one complete document to MPs, health officers, Penal Reform, the National Council of Women and the Race Relations Institute, so that these conditions could be exposed and improved.

The Black Sash had called for better standards of interpreting. It had made a point of finding out what rights prisoners awaiting trial actually had, and had then undertaken to ensure wherever possible that prisoners were conversant with their rights. Individual Black Sash members were also members of Dependants' Conference, an organisation which gave support to the families of prisoners. In Cape Town, Tish Haynes worked in Cowley House, a rest house for visitors to political prisoners in the Western Cape run under the auspices of the Church of the Province of Southern Africa. Her first-hand experience of transporting the families of prisoners in Pollsmoor prison, Brandvlei prison or on Robben Island, of the sadness and joys of these difficult visits, supported her in what she was doing as a member of the Black Sash. At the same time she found that her membership of the Black Sash gave her a starting point for a relationship of trust with the prisoners and their families.

Both in the courtroom and beyond it, people in helpless situations were encouraged by the presence and assistance of white women who could sometimes offer practical help and who were at the very least concerned. 'Now I truly believe in God,' was the response from one mother to a court monitor who had succeeded in persuading a lawyer to appear for her son, 'Thank you so much. My prayer is answered.' 'The reason why we are still strong,' wrote another woman on trial for furthering the aims of the ANC, 'is that we hear your footsteps behind us all the time, mornings and night.' Again and again it was made clear to the Black Sash that it mattered to the accused and their families to know that there were white people who cared about their situation. Black Sash women for their part were made keenly aware of the black community solidarity that could be forged in the face of trouble, and of the courage which emerged among those put through the trauma of arrest, detention, court appearances and possibly imprisonment. Through these opportunities for contact, they were kept continually aware of what it was like to live in communities that were constantly patrolled, constantly under surveillance, constantly in fear of the midnight hammering on the door.

In November 1988 I had the opportunity to witness some of this 'bridge-building' for myself. By that time cases involving substantial numbers of children were causing Black Sash monitors special concern. They knew from contacts in the townships that all was far from well for township children, that several township schools were in turmoil and under siege. Yet little of what was happening was being reported in the press. All that appeared to be important was that there were fewer disturbing accounts of scholar–police confrontation. Instead, accounts had been emerging of escalating gang warfare. Gangs were not a new phenomenon on the Cape Flats. What was new was that the gangs appeared to have multiplied. Reinforced by the school-drop-out situation of the previous few years, combined with the coercion exercised on youngsters to join, they were also becoming more powerful and more dangerous. What the Black Sash regarded as a strange development was the kind of publicity which was being afforded to them by the media: articles with colourful groups of smiling faces and maps of their 'territory', together with interviews with the leaders, were according a form of glamour status to the gangs.

Yet in the Cape Town advice office, workers were all too familiar with the anxiety of distressed parents who described what life was like in the face of the reign of terror organised by young thugs. In Guguletu, where gang warfare was a relatively recent phenomenon, Mrs Malindi offered a glimpse of the causes of what was happening in her township: 'Frustration, no work, no school, nothing to do. I think it started with those who dropped out of school fighting those who chose to stay.' The two groups had resorted to being gangsters and fighting each other. It was worrying for mothers, not only because of the risk of injury to their sons and the possibility of arrest, but because when their children took refuge at home, pursuing gangsters threw stones at the windows or even set fire to the house. Mrs Malindi had known instances of people asking others to look after their furniture because they knew their children were involved: 'But we can't keep their furniture. If we do they're going to know who's keeping it and we too are going to be victims.'

The Black Sash knew what kind of world produced young thugs on a large scale. It recognised also that the police and society had a very real problem in the form of a whole generation brutalised by contact with violence, and that this problem must somehow be tackled. Women like Noël Robb freely acknowledged that children who found themselves arrested for stone-throwing and other public-violence offences were 'very naughty': 'I've taken affidavits from kids who have been badly treated by police, and I can tell you that their whole attitude was so anarchist that I was really alarmed. Obviously what had happened was quite wrong, but so was their whole attitude to life.' Nevertheless, the Black Sash took the view that the thugs in question were still somebody's children, and the treatment they received at the hands of the police was often out of all proportion to the offence. Advice office records in Cape Town include a number of affidavits taken from juveniles by four advice workers. One of them was Mrs Robb.

> I took one of the affadavits in which a youngster
> claimed that among other things the police did to him
> was urinate in his mouth. I took it in a building in a part
> of Cape Town some distance from Mowbray.
> Meanwhile, three others had come to Mowbray to the
> advice office and three other women in the office took
> affadavits from them. I didn't believe the youngster. I
> couldn't believe that it could be true, but when I came
> back and read the other affadavits I discovered that

these kids had all been together and claimed the same thing had happened to them. They didn't know each other either before or after, but the story was so consistent that we realised it had to be true.

In the courts monitors were seeing something of the other side of the situation as it was presented in the media. There, large groups of distressed parents were trying to understand what was happening to their children. In November 1988 the case I attended at the court in Athlone in the company of Ros Bush, one of Cape Town's court monitors, involved the arrest of sixty-five people after a funeral in Guguletu, when a member of a rival gang was killed as an apparent reprisal. Of the sixty-five arrested, fifty-five were children aged between thirteen and seventeen. There was no institution available in the Western Cape for juvenile offenders, and so these children had been kept in custody in Pollsmoor prison since July, this despite the fact that headmasters and teachers in Guguletu were prepared to vouch for some of them. In the case of two sixteen-year-olds their parents claimed to have letters from their employers vouching for their presence at work on the day in question and many of the children were allegedly arrested because they were 'fingered' by others in the hands of police. This explained the Black Sash's involvement with a case which was strictly criminal and not political. Prison, the organisation maintained, was simply not a place for children. Rather, it was a place where 'the deviant are likely to become worse and the good risk injury and corruption'.

Initially, the children involved in the Guguletu Funeral Gang case had been without any legal representation at all. Because this was a criminal case as opposed to a political one, defence finance could only be obtained through state legal aid. In such cases the amount granted could well be inadequate to cope with the expense involved in the defence of so many accused. Government funding could be as little as R375 for ten clients. For busy lawyers such cases, compared with the far more lucrative political cases, were simply not worth while. Those progressive lawyers prepared to sacrifice financial interests for principle were often overburdened. If, therefore, the Black Sash could undertake some of the spade-work, it helped. Particulars in respect of the accused were collected for the use of the attorney when a large number was involved and the time and effort made the task difficult for the lawyer to handle. In general the Black Sash could facilitate communication and thus expedite proceedings.

On the morning in question I followed Ros Bush past the policeman on guard duty, who waved us by without searching us as he searched others seeking to enter, through the maze of corridors of the Athlone Court, up a narrow staircase lined with anxiously waiting relatives of the young accused. There had already been several remands and on each occasion, I was informed, the mothers or grandmothers had all been there at the court waiting to know what was to happen. 'Are you a lawyer?' I was asked in Xhosa. 'A lawyer,' Ros explained, 'is some kind of genie who can make sons appear.' A whisper of 'Black Sash' was passed along the expectant line. Ros had been doing her spade-work on their behalf, gathering information needed by the lawyers and relaying progress reports to the parents of the accused. Her information was that the Attorney General had been telephoned and he had said that the children could not simply all be released on bail. The lawyers would have to make individual applications, although legal defence had not as yet been arranged for all of them. She broke the bad news gently to the crowd that pressed around her. According to one of the mothers, her imprisoned child was mentally handicapped but she had no social worker's report to prove it and her word was not enough. A grandmother explained that she was there in lieu of her daughter because her daughter's shack had just been burned down.

We waited outside the courtroom and when, eventually, a defence lawyer emerged, it was with better news. All except two were to be released from Pollsmoor into the custody of their parents. Ros Bush would relay the lawyer's message to the parents. 'I can't bear it,' came her aside. 'Now I have to break the news to the families of the two who are going to be kept in Pollsmoor.' Slowly and carefully she explained first the implications of release on bail to people who evidently had no idea what was entailed and who, with the highest possible intentions, were considering sending their children 'up country' to keep them out of trouble. That they must keep their children out of trouble at home, available for questioning or court appearance, seemed to come as a revelation. Otherwise, it was elaborated, a warrant would be issued and the children would be taken back into custody. Some of the children could not get home from school without crossing another gang's territory. Keeping them out of trouble would be far from easy, but they must understand that they could not send their boys 'up country' even for their own good until the court had cleared them.

The mood of euphoria which accompanied the long-awaited rush of fifty-three youngsters into their relatives' arms and then into several waiting 'combis' was not untinged with sadness and a sense of hopelessness. Doubt hung even over the chances of the children returning from the court to their homes without some incident occurring. The sister of one of the accused, a thirteen-year-old boy who had been denied release on bail because there were other charges against him, stood quietly weeping, excluded from the scenes of happy reunion. Her mother too was devastated. Next week, Ros tried to reassure her, another application would be made for bail. In the meantime she must do everything she could to find any documentation she had – her son's birth certificate, anything to show that he had attended school regularly, evidence that he came from a stable home and could be guaranteed to appear when he was needed at court. One year later, when I returned to Cape Town, the Guguletu Funeral Gang case was still in progress.

In the interim the Black Sash had continued to report with increasing gloom on the diminishing legal rights they were witnessing. In several major political trials the courts had in effect been adjudicating between the regime and the resistance, and although in the shrunken space left to them there were still those whom the Black Sash could applaud for endeavouring to protect individuals against a string of laws

which the Black Sash saw as having demolished the 'rule of
law', the State of Emergency had on the whole created the
framework for some 'alarming judgements and protracted
proceedings'. Since monitoring of non-pass-law cases had
begun in earnest in the Western Cape in 1986 after the
imposition of the second State of Emergency, it had identified
among progressive lawyers in Cape Town a sense of being up
against the odds. Persistent efforts had been made to obtain
interdicts against police/vigilante harassment of individuals
and communities. They had seen considerable success in
getting courts to rule in their favour; but the Black Sash had
also seen with how little regard for the law such ruling was
flouted and ignored. The case of the burning of the Crossroads
satellite camps, despite a restraining interdict, was only one
in point.

The sentencing in several cases against policemen, involving serious assault, culpable homicide, attempted murder,
theft and defeating the ends of justice, also provoked comment from the Black Sash. In one case a policeman was
found guilty of culpable homicide for assaulting a farm
labourer and then dragging him behind a tractor. The sentence included the option of a fine: R2000 or 500 days.
Despite the increasing tendency to disillusionment the Black
Sash struggled to hold on to its vision of the law courts as
'virtually the only arena where State injustice and violence
can be openly and safely challenged.' Muriel Crewe wrote in
February 1988:

> Mr Justice Berman pronounced clearly on the role of the
> courts in a summing-up delivered in the Supreme Court
> in April last year. He quoted first from Lord De Villiers'
> view, 107 years ago, that the troubled state of the
> country ought not to influence the court, 'for its first
> and most sacred duty is to administer justice to those
> who seek it'. He went on to say: 'Where it is sought to
> control, in troubled times, the exercise of the
> fundamental rights of free men, the function of the
> court is to act as a watchdog and not as a lapdog.' We

have seen the lapdog syndrome in operation, but there
are fortunately also the watchdogs who remain vigilant.

By 1989 Black Sash court monitors in the Western Cape
were able to speak of their encouragement at the ever-more
courageous stand being taken by the legal profession at all
levels. They had also seen a fall-off in the courts in the
number of those charged with public violence offences. When
charges were brought now, it seemed, they were better
substantiated, and their own feeling was that the Black Sash's
publication at the end of 1986 of the fact that 80 per cent of
those charged were found not guilty or had had the charges
against them withdrawn had in some way contributed to this
improvement. Certainly, it would have been surprising if
the police had not been anxious to avoid the repetition of
such embarrassing statistics. The obverse of this, however,
was the large number of detainees held and eventually
released after protracted periods of time without ever having
been charged because no case against them could be
substantiated.

Furthermore, when court-monitoring reports from the
Transvaal, the Eastern Cape and Grahamstown were taken
into consideration (Durban had been unable to produce a
court report because it had been wholly involved in trying to
alleviate the plight of victims in the strife-ridden townships
round Pietermaritzburg and Durban) it became apparent that
the old umbrella charge of public violence had actually given
way to far more menacing and well-defined charges – treason,
terrorism, murder, subversion and arson, together with illegal
gathering, intimidation, incitement and the possession of
banned literature. To this could be added additional charges
of furthering the aims of a banned organisation and conspir-
ing to prevent the end of the State of Emergency. Conditions
in the Eastern Cape were generally worse. There were more
prolonged detentions, more unrest-related trials involving
large numbers of people, more severe prison sentences and a
large number sentenced to death (forty-four in Grahamstown
in the year 1988–9). Even when the accused were found not
guilty they had in all probability spent months, even years,

in jail – a substantial proportion of which may have been passed in solitary confinement under the provisions of the notorious Section 29.

Section 29 of the Internal Security Act provided for detention without trial for interrogation purposes. Under it a detainee could be kept in a police station or security-branch office until such time as the security police were satisfied with the answers given to their questions. There was nothing new about this breach of the right of habeas corpus. In 1964 the General Law Amendment Act had introduced the infamous 'ninety-day clause' which granted police the power of arrest without warrant of anyone suspected of sabotage, and enabled them to detain him or her for interrogation purposes for ninety days without bringing the subject before a court. In 1965 that period of detention had been extended to 180 days by the Criminal Procedure Amendment Act.

Then the Terrorism Act of 1967 had stipulated that a suspected terrorist could be detained indefinitely without trial, and that no information about the detainee need be made public. The regulations governing the State of Emergency delared on 12 June 1986 provided one more set of rigorous controls over individual freedoms, justified, in the eyes of the authorities, by the need to root out armed terrorists and obtain information relating to the location of arms caches, contacts, the reason for a suspect's entry into the country and the nature of intended targets. Under the Emergency Regulations a person could be arrested without warrant if such arrest was deemed necessary by the arresting officer for either the maintenance of public order, the safety of the public or the person himself or the termination of the State of Emergency. He or she could then be detained on a written order in custody in a prison for fourteen days, which period could then be extended without reason for as long as the State of Emergency lasted.

The Black Sash had long been concerned with the plight of people not even afforded the opportunity to put their case before a court. It had protested vociferously against the introduction of the General Law Amendment Act and subsequent security measures. It remained staunchly unimpressed by protestations that the police did not want to keep people in detention for indefinite periods, that the detention of children was necessary because some of the necklace murders were known to be committed by 'children'. It did not accept the argument that extreme circumstances demanded extreme measures. Rather it had used the fact that in 1984 there were an estimated 1,149 detentions, the highest number since 1976–7, to point out the 'hollowness of the government's pretensions of consensus rule and reform'.

The Black Sash was particularly concerned about the conditions under which detainees were held. 'Since 1963 more than 5,000 people have been detained without trial' announced the organisation's magazine, by then known simply as *Sash*, in February 1983. 'What percentage of these can be said to have emerged without permanent damage, whether physical or mental or both? . . . Can you tell us, Mr Le Grange?' it enquired of the then Minister of Law and Order. During April 1982, a memorandum, prepared by the Detainees' Parents Support Committee claimed that systematic and widespread methods of torture were employed by the security police during the interrogation of detainees. The Minister of Law and Order, to whom the memorandum was presented, rejected the allegations, although a CID officer was subsequently appointed to investigate them. The fact did not escape mention in *Sash*, nor did the names and any other available details of detainees who had actually died in detention: Solwandle Ngudie died 5/9/63, cause of death 'suicide by hanging'; Bellington Mampe died ?/9/63, cause of death 'undisclosed'; James Tyita died 24/1/64, cause of death 'suicide by hanging'; Suliman Saloojee died 9/9/64, cause of death 'fell seven floors during interrogation'; Ngeni Gage died 9/5/65, cause of death 'natural causes'; Solomon Modipane died 28/2/69, cause of death 'slipped on soap'; James Lenkoe died 10/3/69, cause of death 'signs of electric shock, but verdict of suicide by hanging'. The sinister list went on through the years: Steve Biko died 12/9/77, cause of death 'Brain injury after a scuffle in interrogation room'; Lungile Tabalaza died 10/7/78, cause of death 'jumped from fifth floor, Security Police Headquarters, Port Elizabeth'.

Black Sash policy was not to allow these people simply to

disappear without trace. In the case of Steve Biko, the Black Consciousness leader who was held in jail in Port Elizabeth and visited by two white doctors who failed to have him undergo proper medical examination despite evident head injuries, and who was found dead on arrival in Pretoria after being taken naked in the back of a police vehicle on a journey of several hundred miles, the Black Sash provided a faithful presence at the inquest. Black Sash members made 250 wreaths and laid them at key public places. Sheena Duncan and Joyce Harris (national president from 1978–82 and an office-bearer in the organisation for many years), together with another member, took it in turns to stand outside the University of the Witwatersrand with a placard saying 'Steve Biko dead. Why?' The Black Sash requested an interview with Jimmy Kruger, Minister of Police and Prisons, who declined to see its representatives, whereupon members wrote letters and statements to the press, most of which were published. Sheena Duncan was invited to sit on the platform during the PFP's protest meeting at the City Hall in Johannesburg, and another Black Sash member provided the lawyers for Steve Biko's family with all the relevant press clippings. The inquest concluded that no officer was criminally responsible for Biko's death. Eight years later, the two doctors who had supposedly examined him were found guilty by a medical board of disgraceful or improper conduct, and one of them was struck off the medical register.

It became regular Black Sash practice for the names of those who had died in detention to be read aloud at the beginning of monthly general meetings and at the annual national conference, followed by a minute's silence as a poignant reminder of the continuing need for the organisation's existence. It also became Black Sash practice to make a point of trying to monitor detentions by telephoning the security police regularly to enquire about the well-being of persons held in detention, although there were times when such enquiries received no response. The regulations governing the 1986 State of Emergency determined that no person was actually entitled to any information relating to a detainee. In fact it was an offence to disclose the name of a detainee without the written consent of the Minister, unless the name had officially been released. Emergency detainees had no actual right to see a lawyer, although police could give permission for them to do so, and in practice usually did after the lawyer had made a written application.

Section 29 detainees also had no automatic right to see a lawyer, and although again police had the power to give permission for a lawyer to be seen, that permission was rarely granted. Emergency detainees had no automatic right to see members of their family, but in practice police usually granted permission. In the case of Section 29 detainees even that concession was usually withheld. A chart entitled 'Your rights behind bars', produced by the Legal Education and Action Project at the University of Cape Town and widely distributed by, among other organisations, the Black Sash, painted a pathetic picture of the rights that Section 29 detainees did not have: no right to outside physical contact (often they were held in solitary confinement); no right to see a minister, priest, imam or rabbi; no right to write or receive letters; no right to reading matter other than the Bible or the Koran; no right to outside food or drink. Under the final heading, 'Discipline' came the despondent directive: 'The law says nothing about punishment for misbehaving. You can try to make a complaint if you are assaulted.' Conditions for detainees under the Emergency Regulations were only marginally better.

Time and time again the Black Sash would hear former Section 29 detainees tell of the horror of their experience of complete sensory deprivation, to which was added the constant fear of what, it was repeatedly alleged, might happen in the process of interrogation.

Gille Skweyiya, a black activist from the Eastern Cape and a long-standing friend of the Goniwe family, was detained in August 1986 in St Alban's in Port Elizabeth: 'When I arrived there were over 2,000 of us. I've never seen so many people detained without trial. The majority naturally came from Port Elizabeth. Old people of almost seventy were detained because they happened to be on street committees.* There's

* Street or people's committees were secret alternative local government

an old man who's still there. He has entered now his twenty-eighth month. He passed greetings only recently to me – heart-breaking.' For Gille the worst part of the experience had been not knowing when he was going to be released: 'I remember being sentenced to eighteen months' imprisonment and I wondered if I could take it, and then they left us there. We were still there when others were being released, some on parole. At least they knew when they would be leaving. We didn't know, and every time they read out the list of detainees to be released it was nerve-racking.'

We met in November 1988. He had been released in March of that year. In a way, he felt, his detention, though terrible, had been an enriching experience because there had been so many people involved. They had been able to be philosophical about the dreadful food: 'We used to remind ourselves of the many hungry stomachs who could not even afford this and then we'd go at it.' And through it all the Black Sash who, in the absence of any formal Detainees Parents Support Committee or other support structures in Port Elizabeth, had stepped into the breach, had been 'wonderful'. 'I still have the tracksuit there in the township which I got from the Black Sash. They brought them to us in detention, and Christmas cards came from all over in the Black Sash'.

The Black Sash had come to appreciate how important it was for detainees to feel that they were not forgotten. As an organisation it continued to do its utmost to ensure that grievances were not stifled and injustice hidden. In July 1985 Mary Burton, a former journalist and the Cape Western regional chairperson who in 1986 would succeed Sheena Duncan as national president, had written to the editor of the *Cape Times* in protest at the onset of the First State of Emergency:

---

structures to the black local authorities placed in power by the Nationalist government and looked upon by the black communities as 'sell-outs'. The establishment of people's committees was regarded by the authorities as part of the ANC's attempt to organise inhabitants of black residential areas at ground level in order to implement the 'people's war'.

The historical evidence of detention without trial is not calculated to reassure us about the safety of people being held. Many were in detention before the announcement of the State of Emergency, now there are and will be many more . . . In the face of the naked power of the authorities the average citizen feels helpless to do anything to improve the situation. We look to you and to the fellow-members of your profession, to continue to do the utmost to provide the public with the facts.

In the meantime the Black Sash pledged itself to continue to struggle for a resolution of the conflict through genuine negotiation towards justice and the rule of law. 'We shall,' it announced, 'endeavour to make our contribution by seeking out and proclaiming the truth of our situation. We shall not rest until South Africa is a country of freedom, democracy and peace.'

Seeking out and proclaiming the truth, the determination to maintain its role as 'watchdog', meant the direction of considerable energy into the general monitoring of the erosion of human rights. 'We, the Black Sash, repeat our condemnation of the practice of detention in the overall state strategy of silencing opposition,' announced a statement from the 1988 national conference, subsequently issued to the press. 'We note that an estimated 1,500 people are still incarcerated in political internment in South Africa, many of whom have been held for twenty months. We also condemn the silencing of all organisations which have had the courage to explore the scale and depth of inhumane treatment of the detention strategy. We reaffirm our commitment to monitoring and opposing ever-increasing repression in South Africa.'

As individuals and organisations were increasingly restricted, the monitoring of detentions, restrictions, instances of public violence, capital punishment, arson and state-instigated violence assumed even greater importance. In Natal a group of volunteer workers was assigned to collect information falling within these categories from people coming into the advice office, through community contacts

and from press clippings taken from a wide range of newspapers. The resulting statistics, together with some analysis
and assessment of trends, was then published in a bi-monthly
bulletin and circulated to a restricted mailing list. It was sent
to people who supplied it with information, to certain academics, to lawyers, to foreign embassies, to bodies such as
Amnesty International, the Human Rights Commission, to
Africa Watch.

The copy for even this restricted circulation did not mention names unless the people concerned were dead, because
the Black Sash could not take the responsibility for jeopardising their safety, but one version complete with names was
kept on file. By 1989 this monitoring process had become so
demanding that it was felt that it could no longer be undertaken on a voluntary basis. One of the volunteer monitors
had had a baby, another was writing a thesis and the remainder could no longer cope with the volume of work. The plan
was therefore to take on a part-time employee, to include
affidavits in support of allegations and so to widen the
readership.

Chapter Seven

Mothers of the struggle

Perhaps nowhere was state repression felt more markedly than in the Eastern Cape. The Eastern Cape was traditionally an area of black political organisation. The main black political movements had a firm base in the area. It was the political home of Robert Sobukwe (leader of the Pan-African Congress), Steve Biko, Oliver Tambo, Nelson Mandela and Raymond Mhlaba. Its black university of Fort Hare had provided an education for many of South Africa's black leaders. Govan Mbeki, at one time appointed to the High Command of Umkhonto we Sizwe – the military wing of the ANC, established in the early 1960s by Nelson Mandela and other ANC leaders – and one of the political prisoners released in October 1989, studied there. Matthew Goniwe, the UDF activist, obtained his teacher's diploma there. In the township of New Brighton were several influential high schools producing well-educated and politically highly aware young people, destined for the most part, because of high unemployment, to join the long queues of jobless, there to have their political frustration fuelled.

For those who did find work there was also a strong history of trade unionism dating back to the 1920s, when giant motor companies like Ford and General Motors began to arrive in the area to take advantage of the shipping potential at Port Elizabeth, a port which in time would become the third largest in southern Africa. Unionisation and the concentration of a massive black workforce into a relatively small number of major companies produced strong worker solidarity and significant bargaining power for the numerous black organisers who held key jobs on the vehicle-assembly lines. Their cohesion was further endorsed by the fact that, by

contrast with the workforces in most major urban centres of
South Africa, in the Eastern Cape by far the majority of the
urban black population came from a single tribe. The vast
majority were Xhosa speakers from the Ciskei and the Transkei. The satellite townships of Port Elizabeth, townships
such as Kwanobuhle and Langa had some of the worst
conditions anywhere in South Africa. Thus, socially, economically and politically the blacks of the Eastern Cape had
long felt themselves part of a united struggle.

As a result it was also an area which the state watched
closely as a hotbed of ANC- and PAC-inspired black revolution, where policing was notoriously stringent and where
right-wing white feeling made itself potently felt. To join the
Black Sash in the Eastern Cape had always taken particular
courage. Membership figures had never been large. In 1989
Port Elizabeth had only about fifty paid-up members, by
comparison with between eight and nine hundred in Johannesburg. In 1980, when Molly Blackburn's sister, Judy Chalmers, joined, there were only about eight really active
members in Port Elizabeth. Small numbers made it easy for
the security police to keep close tabs on those women who
did become involved, and in the small-town communities of
places like East London and Grahamstown the consequences
of identification with an organisation perceived by many
members of the white community to be radically activist,
part of the 'total onslaught', allied to the South African
Communist Party and actively encouraging subversive activity, could be distressing and even dangerous.

A young Afrikaner wife of a minister of the Dutch
Reformed Church who opted to join the Black Sash in East
London was only one among many who discovered the consequences of such action in a very painful way. She found
that her every move had been monitored by a member of the
security police, who also happened to belong to her husband's
congregation. Marietjie Myburgh was editor of the women's
section of the *Daily Dispatch*, the East London paper for
which Donald Woods worked, whose wife Wendy was also a
member of the Black Sash prior to their enforced exile. When

Marietjie Myburgh joined the Black Sash, her husband's congregation simply, without any explanation, stopped coming to church. The minister's enquiries after the reason for this ostracism met with wild allegations about subversive activity and all the misunderstanding born of ignorance: 'The Black Sash was vaguely associated with the idea of women standing with placards or marching. Very few people knew what was being done in the advice offices, about the conducting of pension surveys and other similar "social service" activities, and if they did know they still suspected the offices of being a vehicle for instigating clandestine activities.'

Johann Myburgh was offered the opportunity to leave his ministry and work with the Institute for a Democratic Alternative for South Africa, a possible move which certain members of his congregation also viewed as alignment with 'evil forces'. He chose not to go but rather to make his stand for tolerance from within the Afrikaner community and church. This was in 1988, some years after Dr Beyers Naude had made his not dissimilar stand. By the autumn of 1989, despite his wife's attempts to confine her involvement to 'low profile' activities, a substantial proportion of his congregation had still not returned. For Marietjie Myburgh it meant a constant weighing-up of her loyalty and affection for her husband, and her belief that he too must be able to function properly in his calling, against her commitment, not to the violent overthrowing of the state, for she was not someone who could subscribe to violence, but to the cause of human rights. Forgiveness from her own community was dependent on her recognition that her commitment to the plight of domestic workers, or of people not receiving the pensions to which they were entitled, was the result of external political manipulation, a recognition which her own intelligence would render impossible.

Black Sash members could offer numerous other similar examples of the consequences of reaching out a hand to alleviate the miseries of the black communities in the Eastern Cape. The Black Sash advice office opened in Port Elizabeth in the 'sixties was compelled to close because of harassment. It opened again in 1982 on a once-weekly basis, but burning tyres put through the door forced it to change its premises. In 1989 the office was actually burned down, and once again the venue had to be changed. Yet it was in this kind of context, at this kind of cost, that the Black Sash undertook some of the work which served most effectively to reach across the racial divide in an area where that divide was potentially at its most expansive. The Black Sash today endeavours to be an organisation as committed to the democratic process in its own internal structure as it is in its political objectives. Decisions are taken to committee, and mandates obtained through regular meetings at branch and regional level with meticulous scrupulousness. Hours are spent discussing the wording of any statement made, any poster to be displayed. Individuals and their actions are not on the whole singled out for special attention, except where particular courage or harsh treatment demands special recognition or encouragement. In the area around Port Elizabth, however, the names of certain Black Sash individuals spring readily to the lips of township people, among them those of Molly Blackburn, her sister Judy Chalmers and her friend and close co-worker, Di Bishop.

Molly Blackburn did not join the Black Sash until 1982, the year in which an advice office was reopened in the town in which both she and her sister had been born. She had waited until then precisely because she wanted her involvement to be rooted in advice office work. 'She wanted,' Judy Chalmers would recall, 'to be really doing something, and it does make a difference if you are involved at grass-roots level as well. The protest work comes so much more easily if you are actually seeing and experiencing the problem.' Judy Chalmers herself had been working for the PFP for some years until, in 1980, as she sat filling in cards in a political office, she too had experienced the desire to be more actively and directly involved. Her conscience had been pricked by a Sash member who invited her to join a stand in protest against the Group Areas Act. Next day she found herself standing alone and being questioned by the police.

In 1981 both Molly Blackburn and Di Bishop found themselves elected to the Cape Provincial Council. At that time every parliamentary candidate had a form of junior partner who was a member of the Provincial Council, a second tier of government which administered provincial matters. Molly Blackburn was the PFP MPC for Walmer at a time when Andrew Savage was member of parliament. Much to her own surprise, at the same time Di Bishop, a trained social worker and former branch director of the National Institute for Crime Prevention and Rehabilitation of Offenders (NICRO), won the PFP provincial seat in Gardens. The simultaneous election of the two women to the Provincial Council was the first time they had met, but it brought the immediate recognition that they were kindred spirits and marked the beginning of a very effective partnership. From then onwards, at the age of fifty, Molly Blackburn was catapulted into what was for her a very exciting and vibrant, if at times distressing period of her life.

Di Bishop had joined the Black Sash in 1978 with the encouragement of her husband Brian, who was a leading member of both the Civil Rights League and the Institute for Race Relations, a tireless campaigner for human rights, and a great admirer of the Black Sash. The clinching factor in Di Bishop's decision, however, was almost accidental. She had interviewed what had seemed to her an eminently suitable candidate to provide her with secretarial help in NICRO, but objections had subsequently been raised on the grounds that the applicant was known to be a member of the Black Sash. 'It's strange you should have a problem with that', she had found herself protesting, 'because I'm a member of the Black Sash myself.' Next day she joined the organisation to ensure the truth of her own claim. Work in the advice office totally revolutionised her life. Nothing in her training as a social worker at university had been in any way relevant to the black Africa that existed in South Africa, and in the actual practice of her social work in the Cape the vast majority of the people with whom she dealt were coloureds. The office gave her the closest contact she had ever had with extreme suffering:

> It brought me face to face with women, not only
> women, but perhaps one was more touched and moved

by the suffering of women – by the encounter with
other women who were just at the raw edge of the
wedge and didn't know what to do about it. Physically,
emotionally and spiritually you began examining
yourself as a co-traveller, as a fellow South African,
although that citizenship was denied to so many of the
people with whom you came in contact. So what then
do you do about it? As a white person you think, 'But
whites don't know about this.' Your first concern is to
share what you have discovered.

In 1981, even before the July session of the Cape Provincial
Council had opened with all its pomp and circumstance, Di
Bishop had taken Molly Blackburn with her to the black
township of Langa outside Cape Town. A police raid had
taken place there during the previous week. The Black Sash
advice office had asked Di Bishop to help an eighty-year-old
man who had mislaid his daughter and grandchildren in the
course of the raid. Molly Blackburn promptly recorded the
results of their findings: the arrest of the man's daughter for
living illegally in the Western Cape, the experiences of the
courtroom and the conditions in Langa in an article entitled
'Life among the evicted in "the fairest Cape"', published in
the *Cape Times*. The fact that she was an MPC opened up
additional avenues for 'conscientising' the public. Neither
Molly Blackburn nor Di Bishop felt particularly at ease in the
sphere of party politics. Their first term as Provincial Councillors was frustrating. 'The Nats don't listen to a word Di or
I say,' Molly Blackburn complained. 'They sit there with
their feet up and snore. It's unbelievable.' Nevertheless, they
would both learn to use effectively the public platform which
their position as MPCs afforded them to highlight many
issues that were not related to the Provincial Council. Molly
Blackburn's dossier was related specifically to 'hospitals,
museums and libraries', but her interest and activity
extended well beyond her actual brief.
    Although many years younger than Molly Blackburn, Di
Bishop's work with the Black Sash had already shown her
something of the living conditions and deprivations of the

black communities. During the ensuing years she and others brought Molly Blackburn into increasingly close contact with the townships, black leaders and a new world, the world which 'as a white person one can spend a whole lifetime in South Africa and not get in touch with at all'. Gradually the people of the townships began to learn that here were women prepared to listen to their problems and to act upon them with the minimum of fuss. The calls began to come in from far and wide: 'How do we structure a committee?' 'How do we form a self-help group? We have so few taps, the roads are so terrible and the rents so high.' 'My child has been taken by police and he is only thirteen.'

It was in 1983 that Molly Blackburn first met Matthew Goniwe. Matthew had been born and raised in Lingelihle, the neglected black township near Cradock where in 1989 I joined the thousands of township dwellers on their dusty march along the rutted road to the town hall. After his teacher's training at Fort Hare, Matthew had taught at schools in the Transkei. In 1972 he and another Cradock stalwart had started a school in a dilapidated church hall in Mqanduli, some twenty-five miles outside the Transkei capital of Umtata, but as a teacher he had tried to provide his students with a wider understanding of the context in which they found themselves. He had introduced political analysis and discussion into his lessons and for doing so, in 1977, he had been arrested under the Suppression of Communism Act and spent four years in jail in Umtata. On his release he had taken up a post in Graaff-Reinet, where he swiftly became acting principal and in 1983 he returned to Lingelihle to take up the post of acting principal at Sam Xhalli Junior Secondary School. During that year, however, a new section of Lingelihle was opened. Rents plus service charges on the new houses, which were virtually identical to the old four-roomed houses, involved a payment of some R54 more per month. In a township with a chronic housing shortage, and where R40 was considered a good salary, people were forced to take the houses but were simply unable to pay the rents. In September a group of residents headed by Matthew Goniwe therefore asked Molly Blackburn to enquire officially into the structuring of the rents and to advise them on procedures for forming a civic association.

Molly Blackburn gave him the necessary information. She also wrote to the Chief Director of the Administration Board, asking for a copy of the sliding scale used to determine rentals and service charges in various Eastern Cape townships. She became an intermediary between him and Matthew Goniwe, while the latter played a central role in setting up CRADORA, the Cradock Residents Association which would subsequently affiliate to the UDF and CRADOYA, the Cradock Youth Association. On 7 December 1983 Matthew Goniwe telephoned Molly Blackburn to tell her that a tranfer to Graaff-Reinet had been served on him. She duly engaged the assistance of John Malcomess, PFP MP. The people of Cradock believed the transfer to be a political move to curb Matthew Goniwe's activities in relation to the rent increases. Matthew refused the transfer and was promptly dismissed. He reapplied for any post as a teacher in Cradock, 'even the lowliest', but his reapplication was turned down. It was this refusal, so Molly Blackburn wrote in *Sash* in August 1984, that was the catalyst in the decision the youth of Cradock made to boycott the schools. Townships all over South Africa were in turmoil. Discontent was prevalent over issues such as community councils, Bantu education, the new constitution, economic and social hardship, internal struggles within the black communities themselves and police and army conduct. The spark required to ignite so volatile an atmosphere need only be small. When Matthew Goniwe's application to be reinstated in a Cradock school was turned down, the township children boycotted classes and, although the teachers continued to report daily to schools, none of the pupils attended.

On 25 March students from seven schools held a meeting to discuss an ultimatum from the Department of Education and Training. Police converged on the gathering and ordered it to disperse. Before this could be done, Molly Blackburn reported, police shot teargas canisters into the hall, and chaos ensued. On 30 March Minister Louis Le Grange issued a banning order on all meetings for three months, and on the following day, Matthew Goniwe, his cousin Mbulelo Goniwe, Fort Calata (chairman of the CRADOYA youth group) and Madoda Jacobs (headboy of the high school) were arrested under Section 28 of the Internal Security Act. They were subsequently variously transferred to prisons in Cape Town and Johannesburg and held in solitary confinement. Madoda Jacobs was charged with public violence and acquitted. The Goniwe cousins and Fort Calata spent three months in detention, during which time Helen Suzman, Di Bishop and Molly Blackburn were granted visitors' permits to see Matthew. Molly Blackburn also took Ken Andrew, MP, the official opposition spokesman on black education, to Lingelihle township where he met CRADORA members at Matthew Goniwe's home. He would afterwards meet with V. Barend Du Plessis, Minister for Education and Training.

During the May/June Provincial Council session Mrs Blackburn was contacted two or three times each week by residents with reports of police brutality or requests for guidance on how to obtain assistance with rent relief. In response, as soon as the council session ended, she and Di Bishop and Judy Chalmers went to Lingelihle, where they taped personal accounts of violence at the hands of the police and recorded other cases in which there appeared to be a complete disregard for the normal processes of law. There was, *Sash* claimed, 'much evidence to show that official provocation has sparked off a pattern of violence and counter-violence in Cradock'. The sequence of events in Cradock's township was carefully recorded in the magazine as defence against the allegation frequently levelled against Sash members in such situations, namely that they were instigators.

Clearly angered by the intervention of Molly Blackburn, Di Bishop and Judy Chalmers, Minister Le Grange told PFP MP Andrew Savage that he should warn them and the rest of the Black Sash to keep out of Cradock township. Notwithstanding this indirect warning, Molly Blackburn and Di Bishop attended some of the trials arising out of the Cradock disturbances and became increasingly aware of the police harassment of the community. Molly Blackburn had for some time been warning that the status of the police as law-enforcement officers was being destroyed in the townships. In a memorable article in the *Cape Times* in May 1984 she warned that whites visiting black townships were no longer greeted with friendly waves but rather by skinny little arms raised in a clenched-fist salute. Yet she herself did much to change that. Gille Skweyiya later recalled the appreciation with which Black Sash intervention on behalf of township people was greeted.

> To those who read newspapers Molly's was a household name in the Eastern Cape, so when she came to Cradock she was already known to readers. Cradock is an Afrikaans-speaking community. The whites don't visit the township so they know nothing about what is happening there, but here was someone who was white who could actually sit in whatever chair you might find for her in the township, and could converse with children. People took to her at once. That was Molly. When so many of our youth were shot or detained she would take their part, the side of the underdog. That made her instantly popular and whoever came with her was welcomed.

On 19 November 1984 Molly Blackburn and Di Bishop attended a political trial of a Cradock resident which, like so many other such trials, was held far away from the township. On that occasion it was in Somerset East sixty-five miles from Cradock. Afterwards they drove Matthew Goniwe and two friends home to Lingelihle. In Somerset East, and when they stopped for petrol in Cookhouse, they realised that they were being followed by three security policemen. As they approached Cradock they followed the signposted road to Lingelihle with no signs prohibiting entrance. After dropping Matthew Goniwe at his house they found themselves arrested by the security policemen they had seen in Somerset East for being illegally in the township. Their case came to trial in Cradock on 19 December. It was a day which would remain indelibly engraved on Gille Skweyiya's memory because so many members of CRADORA and CRADOYA turned out to lend their support to the two white women on trial. The SAP tried to keep them out, but gave way when Brian Bishop responded that if they were denied entry he would recommend that the accused apply for a mis-trial. The public gallery was filled to bursting point with a massed display of CRADORA and UDF T-shirts. The accused were eventually found guilty, cautioned and discharged. They left Cradock court much moved by the fact that so many had been prepared to risk further harassment by showing their support.

In the spring of the following year the Black Sash held its thirtieth national conference in Port Elizabeth. It was to prove a conference very different from the usual annual event in that it actually drew those attending it into the unrest of the community around it. There were the usual presentations of papers of a very high standard and the usual impressive level of debate which newcomers frequently found so awe-inspiring, but it was also an experience which was, as one person who attended put it, 'much more realistic than sitting around listening to academic discussion'. The evening of the opening day, Thursday 14 March, found a number of people attending the conference, including twenty-one nuns and the Progressive Federal Party MPC for Walmer, left stranded in the pouring rain after the tyres of their vehicles had been slashed. Next day, they heard several black leaders, including Matthew Goniwe, provide an insight into what was happening in the township. At the time Matthew Goniwe was a listed person. He could not be quoted, but he spoke about the background to black discontent, of how the 24,000 inhabitants of Lingelihle had only two sources of income: poorly paid domestic labour in the small town of Cradock, and the railways which had been facing cutbacks. He spoke with quiet eloquence of how the huge army of unemployed in the township made the rent increases all that much harder to bear. He also asked to become a member of the Black Sash.

That same evening Molly Blackburn received information from a highly respected member of Uitenhage's Kwanobuhle black township, who had just been released from Port Eliza-beth's Rooihell prison, where he had been charged with public violence. He was deeply concerned because he had seen as many as a hundred children held in the prison. They had told him that they were being sodomised by older prisoners and were frightened. Next morning at the national Black Sash conference it was decided that an interview should be arranged with the magistrate. Contact would be made with bodies such as the National Medical and Dental Association, attempts would be made to arrange an interdict to get the children released, and a national memorandum about police conduct in the Eastern Cape was to be initiated. That afternoon three Sash members met Port Elizabeth's chief magistrate, the chief magistrate of Uitenhage, his assist-ant, the captain of the prison and four advocates. No attempt was made to deny the allegation that there were children in the cells, nor that they were very young. The magistrate said, however, that the abuse was impossible. He had visited the prison only the day before and no one had complained. Moreover, the captain claimed that children were kept com-pletely separately in cells away from adults. The Black Sash suggestion that the children might have been too frightened to complain to these white oficials was not accepted.

It was in the course of investigating another call for help arising during the conference from a group of parents who were fearful for the safety of their children that Molly Blackburn and other Black Sash members actually witnessed an assault on a sixteen-year-old black youth, Norman Kona. On Sunday 17 March a delegation from the Black Sash conference, including a medical doctor, Dr Liz Thompson, went to Uitenhage police station to enquire about the where-abouts of six chilren and were referred by a sergeant in the CID office to another section of the building to request permission to see the children in question. The group led by Molly Blackburn accordingly made its way to what she took to be the prison office. Her subsequent sworn affidavit records her reaction to what she encountered after knocking on the door and opening it:

I was deeply shocked to see a young man lying on the floor next to a table with his hands handcuffed behind his back and the handcuffs were behind the table leg . . . Bending over him was a black man in civilian clothes with a long orange plastic whip. I saw him assault this young man as I walked in. I called out, 'Dear God, what do you think you are doing?' I moved over to the young man, who was bleeding from lacerations on the left side of his face and had traces of blood on his mouth. He had also lost a shoe. The person who was assaulting him disappeared as my colleagues and some of the black parents entered the office. One of my colleagues asked the people in the office, who I presume were CID staff, whether this young man had been charged with any offence. They said no. There were three young men sitting on a bench against the wall. They were not handcuffed but appeared to have been assaulted.

After a heated exchange Molly Blackburn refused to leave the premises as requested until the station commander came. They waited about half an hour for the District Commandant to arrive in order to report the matter to him and ensure that Norman Kona received the medical attention he needed. In the interim, however, a policeman later identified to her as Lieutenant J.W. Fouché, the station commander from Kirkwood and the officer who on occasion was in charge of riot units in the Uitenhage area, entered the charge office and picked up an R1 rifle that was lying on the desk. In doing so he dropped a magazine of bullets on the floor. On the strength of this and what she considered loud and aggressive behaviour, Molly Blackburn told the Port Elizabeth magistrate who had come to the police station at the request of the Black Sash, that she wanted his condition placed on record: 'Lt Fouché, in a very aggressive manner, shouted at me and said he did not want to see me down at this end of the building. I told him not to shout at me as I was standing no more than one metre away from him. He continued to shout and I noticed that there was a strong smell on his breath. When he walked away I turned to the magistrate and said that I wished to record that it was my impression that the man had been drinking.'

As a sequel to this, in September of that year two court cases were brought before the Port Elizabeth Regional Court. One was a case of assault in which the state charged two black policemen, who in the interim had been suspended from duty, with kicking, hitting and beating Norman Kona with a sjambok. Key witnesses were Liz Thompson, Molly Blackburn and Audrey Coleman, another Black Sash member present at Uitenhage police station on that Sunday afternoon. This case was eventually discharged. The other case was one of *crimen injuria*, or, alternatively, defamation arising out of Molly Blackburn's allegation brought by Lieutenant William Fouché against Dr Liz Thompson and the MPC for Walmer. Both Black Sash members were finally acquitted and discharged.

In the meantime the Kannemeyer Commission of Inquiry into the causes of the death of twenty-one people in Langa township near Uitenhage on 21 March, four days after the Black Sash encounter in Uitcnhage police station, had revealed that Lieutenant Fouché was the officer who gave the order to shoot into a crowd of black residents marching towards the white suburb. The statement made to parliament on the afternoon of 21 March by Law and Order Minister Louis Le Grange had said that police had had 'no alternative but to order fire in self-defence' on a crowd of between 3,000 and 4,000 people armed with stones, sticks and other missiles including petrol bombs. This account had been swiftly challenged. In response to pressure to which the Black Sash with the parliamentary support of the PFP had substantially contributed, Justice Donald Kannemeyer had been appointed by the State President to be a one-man commission of enquiry. He made an *in loco* inspection, during which Molly Blackburn eased the tension by kneeling down among the crowd that had swiftly gathered. Despite the heat of the moment, a large proportion of the assembly quietly followed suit.

After carefully considering conflicting evidence, Justice Donald Kannemeyer ultimately laid the blame for the shootings firmly at the door of the police, although by no means

exclusively at the door of Lieutenant Fouché. Police claims
with regard to the weapons carried by marchers were, the
report found, grossly exaggerated. The report criticised commanding officers who allowed police to go out on patrol
without conventional riot-control weapons – tear gas, rubber
bullets or birdshot – but only with live ammunition. It also
criticised the conduct of several individual officers, including
a security-branch officer who had applied for a funeral due to
be held on 21 March to be banned. Black witnesses had been
able to show that the crowd marching towards Uitenhage
was not, as the police had apparently believed, intent on
attacking whites but rather on attending a funeral which
they had good reason to believe was taking place in the
nearby township of Kwanobuhle. Their only route to Kwanobuhle from Langa, where they lived, was through part of
Uitenhage.

The first the Black Sash knew of the incident at Langa was
via a telephone call to Molly Blackburn's home from a young
man in Uitenhage. Molly was at the advice office at the time
but her sister was asked to relay a message: 'Tell her to come.
They're killing our people.' By the time they reached Uitenhage the road blocks were up and it was impossible to gain
access. Mrs Blackburn spent three days searching hospitals,
police stations and mortuaries for the seventy-two people
who went missing after the shootings, at a time when the
authorities showed no inclination to help anxious relatives
locate them. By this time the Black Sash in the area had
acquired considerable skills in attracting the appropriate kind
of attention. Molly Blackburn in particular had a very meticulous way of taking statements, feeding information to
Andrew Savage, her member of parliament, or supplying
Helen Suzman, who at that time was Shadow Minister for
Police and Prisons, with well-documented accounts. She had
a natural gift for providing newsworthy statements and had
established useful contacts with the international press and
with numerous embassies. According to Judy Chalmers,
Langa was really a kind of culmination of her sister's skills
in 'the ways to proceed, the ways to document, the ways to

pressurise and push for publicity'. She was very much a factor in the international attention the episode received.

Because of the publicity given to the incident, the 'Langa massacre' and the Kannemeyer report – which was all the more potent an indictment of the police force because of its manifest fairness in considering the 'awesome dilemma' of police on the spot – did much to cast a serious shadow over President Botha's reform efforts both at home and abroad. Yet there were no resignations from the force and Minister Louis Le Grange, whom the *Cape Times* described as 'remarkably uncontrite', remained firmly in office. The Black Sash continued to make it one of its priorities to expose the abuse of police powers wherever it could.

Molly Blackburn was thrust into the limelight. She spoke out in the press, at public meetings, at women's groups and at funerals, and her fluency and stature grew with every appearance. Her efforts won her the constantly increasing appreciation of some. 'We salute you, comrade Molly Blackburn. The struggle continues. Amandla' was boldly inscribed in red spray paint on the walls along the highway leading from Port Elizabeth's city centre to Humewood, a white suburb. When she and other Black Sash women attended the funeral of the victims of the Langa shootings, 70,000 people stood up to greet them. Her work also earned her the animosity of the pro-government media, certain members of the white community and the government militia, but the knowledge that she was prepared to defy such opposition only drew her closer to others who were also the constant object of police surveillance. Among these were inevitably the Goniwe family. Alex Goniwe, Matthew's brother, would speak of how merely to be the bearer of the Goniwe name was to be the recipient of persistent unwelcome attention. Cars would drive past his house at night and direct a strong flashlight into his room. He received anonymous threatening phone calls. On one occasion five litres of oil were poured into his backyard. On another he claimed to have been arrested simply for washing his car in the street.

Matthew Goniwe's mother tells of an incident which

occurred in 1984 when Matthew was taking her into town a
little before 8 a.m.

> Before we left we saw security cars coming up the street
> and move slowly past us. We drove to the national road
> – the town is two kilometres away along that road. We
> were ordered to stop, this gentleman came out of a car,
> grabbed Matthew out of our car by the scruff of his neck
> and pointed a gun at his head, saying, 'I'll kill you, I'll
> kill you.' Matthew was taken to the security police car
> and we were told to follow to the police station, where
> the car was searched from top to bottom.

Matthew laid a complaint, but no more was ever heard of the
incident.

It was in June 1985 that Matthew Goniwe and the three
other UDF activists, Fort Calata, Sparrow Mkhonto and
Sicelo Mlauli, disappeared while driving home from a political meeting in Port Elizabeth. On Friday 28 June, the morning
after the meeting, Matthew's wife Nyami telephoned the
Black Sash in Port Elizabeth. That afternoon Matthew's burnt
car was found near the Port Elizabeth–Grahamstown road on
the outskirts of Port Elizabeth. In the evening Sparrow
Mkhonto's mutilated body was discovered some kilometres
from the burnt car. Judy Chalmers recalls the death of a 'dear
friend'.

> He and I went on a pensions workshop together in
> Grahamstown. He was quite a shy man, not very
> articulate, very powerfully built and just a very nice
> person. He died first. I think he must have put up a big
> fight because they found his body in one area and the
> others were in quite a different one. It looked as though
> he tried to fight his way out because there was a lot of
> blood and I'm sure Sparrow wouldn't have given up
> easily.

On Saturday 29 June the body of Sicelo Mlauli was found in

sand dunes at Blue Water Bay. He too had been stabbed, burnt and mutilated. Next day Audrey Coleman arranged for a forensic specialist to fly down to Port Elizabeth. Similar arrangements were also made with a pathologist. A Legal Resources attorney was engaged to help the families of the four men. Finally, on 2 July, when officers from the East Cape Murder and Robbery Squad together with local reporters and photographers searched the Blue Water Bay sand dunes, the bodies of Matthew Goniwe and Fort Calata were found outstretched on the sand. The bodies were so charred, Judy Chalmers reported, that it was difficult to see whether they had been mutilated.

'Such clues as there are,' she wrote in a *Sash* magazine tribute to the four men who had died, 'are obviously intended to make the crime appear the result of the UDF/AZAPO feud currently going on in the Port Elizabeth townships.' She added: 'We must bear in mind that in Cradock there has been no UDF/AZAPO feud.' Despite government protestations against what it claimed was a callous insinuation that it had been behind the tragic deaths, activists still blame right-wing assassins, agents of the state. Alex Goniwe, Gille Skweyiya and various other members of CRADORA and CRADOYA all referred to a man who at the time of our meeting was being held on Death Row and had stated that an officer in Pretoria had told him to eliminate those people who were creating trouble for the government. It is their conviction that those responsible for the four men's deaths would have liked them to disappear without trace, but the pressure to find them was too great. 'Molly was searching all over. The Black Sash members were phoning everywhere: police stations, hospitals – everywhere.

Matthew Goniwe, Judy Chalmers recalled, was 'physically quite slight with a wonderful smile and a very rational, reasonable way of thinking'. He had been a very respected and well loved teacher, whose personal life had been non-political. He had entered politics because of the popular pressure that had recognised his abilities and spurred him into forming CRADORA. He had hated violence so much that he had given up boxing for yoga, and his non-violent spirit had not failed to have an impact on Lingelihle. Early in

1985 the entire township council of Cradock resigned on the grounds that they had been rejected by the people and could no longer function. In what was seen as a symbolic gesture, young members of the community went at once to the councillor's homes and removed wire mesh nailed over the windows to protect them from rocks and petrol bombs as a sign that they were once more at one with their community. Matthew Goniwe could easily have been Minister of Education in the new dispensation but basically he was just 'terribly, terribly nice'.

It is customary for black people in South Africa to hold a vigil on the eve of a funeral. On the night before the funeral of Fort Calata, Sparrow Mkhonto, Sicelo Mlauli and Matthew Goniwe, some three weeks after they had first disappeared, a dozen Black Sash members stayed the night in a convent in Cradock's coloured township. That evening the unlit streets of Lingelihle were packed with people as buses poured in from black townships all over South Africa unloading their cargoes of singing, toyitoying mourners. For the Black Sash contingent arriving in their 'combi' to pay their respects to people in the 'incredibly traumatised homes with the widows just sitting there in a state of shock, among all the sadness and yet the excitement', the experience was a revelation. For the people of the township their presence was a source of astonishment. To see white people roaming the streets that evening as if they had lived there all their lives was, according to Gille Skweyiya, 'like giving us a picture of a free South Africa'. People in the township spoke about it for months afterwards.

Next morning, representatives from all the organisation's branches attended the funeral. The Black Sash women walked with their banner, bearing the words 'Women against apartheid for justice, peace and democracy', to Lingelihle's stadium. When they reached it, accompanied by a crowd of coloured people who had joined them along the way, two comrades took hold of their banner and led them in a lap of honour round the stadium to the accompaniment of cries of 'Viva Black Sash'. It was one of those occasions which gave deeply valued encouragement to people accustomed to working frequently without many tangible results.

The declaration of the State of Emergency in July 1985 and the presence of troops in the townships intensified the pressure not only on the black communities – on countless other families less well known than the Goniwe's but whose suffering was no less considerable – but also on those working with them. The Black Sash became involved in the establishment of crisis centres in most areas of the country, generally in conjunction with other organisations. In Port Elizabeth, however, the advice office itself took on extra personnel specifically to meet the extremity of the need. The office became a nightmare world. Parents sought detained children. Bereaved mothers told of children killed. An old woman was riddled with birdshot. A girl had to have scalp wounds stapled together. One man expressed the dilemma which every township resident shared: 'If you see the soldiers or the police and you stand still, they beat you. If you run, they shoot.' People slept with buckets of water beside their beds to alleviate the effects of teargas that seeped under their door. Between June and September of that year the Port Elizabeth advice office held 172 interviews with people affected by police action, detentions, alleged assaults and deaths. Molly Blackburn worked there every Thursday morning, and on those days the queue was half as long again. Calls for assistance came from ever further afield. Brian and Di Bishop, often aided by Molly Blackburn, travelled tirelessly from township to township tracking down victims of alleged police brutality, collecting affidavits and advising on legal and medical aid.

In the township of Fort Beaufort, following a very effective boycott of white-owned shops there, the Emergency Regulations gave power to police to close black-owned businesses supported by the black community and deemed to be a threat to any other business. Not only did they close one shop down but they also detained the shop-owner and his wife and other members of his family who stepped in to try and keep the business running. When Molly Blackburn and Di Bishop entered the township in response to an appeal for help, they found that they had done so in contravention of a regulation implemented only the previous day which required non-residents first to seek permission of the police. They were arrested for failing to do so, and the prospect of actually being locked up seemed more likely than usual. On this particular occasion, however, they had been asked to take with them an American appeal court judge, Nathaniel Jones, to provide him with an insight into conditions in the Eastern Cape. It so happened that Judge Jones was black. There was no such being as a black judge in South Africa. Nathaniel Jones was accordingly addressed in Xhosa and his response to questions concerning his name and occupation were treated initially with scathing incredulity. 'We were all charged,' Di Bishop would recall, 'but something changed their minds about locking us up. I think they must have decided it would be quite difficult to find a suitable place in which to lock up an American judge.'

Even their increasingly high public profile could not exempt them from the rigours of the Emergency. In July 1985 Molly Blackburn was arrested for attending a commemorative service for black leaders in Zwide. Ten days after the event the authorities alleged that this was an illegal gathering and arrested her at home. Inevitably the non-pro-government media took up her cause.

> The way Mrs Blackburn was treated (wrote the *Cape Times*) does no credit to this country or its administration. She was not summoned to appear on some future date. She was arrested at her home and whisked into court as if police feared she would otherwise evade their clutches. If the authorities had wanted to give the impression that they were singling out for harassment an opposition public representative who has done much to gather information about Eastern Cape unrest, they could not have done a better job.

They had also done it on a day on which Mrs Blackburn was due to keep an appointment with three former United States

cabinet ministers on a fact-finding tour for the Ford Foundation. 'Next time the government complains about a bad
foreign press,' the *Cape Times* concluded, 'it should look at
its own Ministry of Perfect Timing.' The PFP leader of the
Provincial Council challenged the police liaison officer for
the Eastern Cape to respond to claims that the arrest was an
attempt to intimidate Mrs Blackburn. The response, again
according to the *Cape Times*, was that investigations took
time to complete: 'It is not as easy as that to arrest a person,
formally charge him and take him to court.' When Molly
Blackburn attended New Brighton Magistrate's Court the
BBC was waiting to film her arrival. She was granted bail of
R100, the case was postponed and when it did come to court
she was acquitted. The following September a proposed
meeting in Cape Town at which Di Bishop was to address
white schoolchildren on the State of Emergency was banned.
Such treatment was not allowed to deter them, although by
this time anonymous phone calls in the night and vitriolic
letters, even death threats, had become a not infrequent
occurrence. On one occasion Di Bishop's car was set alight.
In October two teargas canisters were thrown into the
grounds of the Bishops' Oranjezicht home, making the house
temporarily unoccupiable.

On 28 December 1985 Molly Blackburn, Judy Chalmers
and Brian and Di Bishop were driving back from a day spent
in the black township of Bongolethu in Oudtshoorn. They
had gone there at the invitation of residents to discuss local
problems and they had spent the day taking affidavits and
hearing about the community's concern about the number of
young children detained in mid-November and held for long
periods in police cells. More than 250 people had been
rounded up in a door-to-door search by police following
allegations of murder and arson concerning a resident of the
township. Suddenly, on a straight section of the road near
Humansdorp, the car driven by Brian Bishop was involved in
a collision with another vehicle in which Molly Blackburn,
Brian Bishop and the driver of the other car, Michael Blesi,
all lost their lives. Di Bishop sustained serious leg injuries.

As news of the smash spread, Dr Gavin Blackburn, Molly's

husband, received anonymous, abusive phone calls at his home. The untimely death of two people who had maintained links across the colour line in the face of death threats, intimidation and harassment, however, stunned and saddened many South Africans of all race groups who shared their commitment to interracial justice. In a telegram from Lusaka the African National Congress said that it had learnt 'with shock' of the death of Mrs Blackburn and Mr Bishop: 'We dip our banner in honour of those two outstanding champions of democracy and justice.' The night before Molly Blackburn's funeral Gille Skweyiya professes to have been nearly killed in Cradock.

> We were busy organising transport for some of us to attend the funeral. It was not really a community project but people knew that Molly had passed away so the UDF, which was still operational then, sent a bus to Alex Goniwe's house. When the youth, who are very militant, heard this bus was for Molly's funeral we had to use our wits or we would have been assaulted. One bus would not accommodate them all. Why hadn't we organised more transport? All we could do was say: 'Don't touch us but visit everyone who has got a vehicle.' They went to everyone in Cradock who had a car and told them that transport was needed. Next morning every available Cradock car was in Port Elizabeth for the funeral.

It was a very hot day in the first week of January when a crowd of some 20,000 people clustered into the square near St John's Methodist Church in central Port Elizabeth. After the service, which was relayed over loud speakers, chanting black mourners hoisted aloft Dr Allan Boesak – who together with Sheena Duncan and the Methodist minister and PFP MP, Alex Boraine, had been among the funeral speakers – and toyitoyed round the square. An elderly bishop was caught up in the toyitoy, went round with the procession and came back with his eyes sparkling. There was a brief moment of near confrontation with police who had surrounded the square, but that was swiftly defused. Judy Chalmers remembers it as a day of extraordinary harmony. 'At first the whites were petrified out of their wits. They were locked up in their flats but after an hour or so, when nothing dreadful had happened and no stones had been thrown and nobody's windows had been broken, they actually started coming down and giving people water to drink, talking to people on the fringes.' There would be no other such occasion, no other opportunity for the white population of Port Elizabeth to be exposed to the discipline and mass of the black struggle until October 1989, when 70,000 people marched through the white area in the intense heat without a single incident of disharmony.

Brian Bishop's funeral service was held in Cape Town. A thousand mourners of all races packed St Mary's Cathedral. Many more could not find space in the building. They had come from Cradock, Uitenhage, Port Elizabeth, Johannesburg, Durban and elsewhere. 'White South Africans think that the gap between black and white is too wide to be bridged,' Molly Blackburn had once told her sister. 'I don't think this is so. If you stretch out a loving hand, somewhere on the other side a loving hand will take it, and that will be the beginning of a bridge.'

A small cross on a fence marks the spot where the car crash occurred. Judy Chalmers returns to it at intervals just to see that it is still there. For her a questionmark lingers over the nature of the accident, on the grounds that the driver of the other vehicle was widely known to be a non-drinker, yet his blood was found to contain alcohol: 'It amazes me that this fellow who had so much alcohol in his blood, which he clearly did, although it was said that he did not drink, circumvented a very windy bit of road and then when it straightened out – there he was suddenly in front of us. It's impossible to tell whether or not it was contrived, but certainly it was something that didn't break the hearts of the police.' Inevitably, in view of what had gone before, suspicion was widespread. 'When any person dies,' another Port Elizabeth resident explained, 'who is progressively minded, who aligns himself with the non-racial struggle and the underprivileged, it is understandable that people should ask the question: "How is it possible?"' The memory of what happened to Steve Biko is not easily buried.

At the age of thirty-six, Di Bishop picked up the pieces of her broken life and resolved to continue. There was still so much work to be done. When the second State of Emergency was declared in June 1986, it was, for the small number of workers in the advice offices, like being caught in a rushing stream, but the response by the black community to Molly Blackburn's life and death had been an inspiration and a confirmation for them. For many there was the omnipresent question, 'Are we ameliorating, are we really helping?' In a way, that question was the point of division between the two major streams of black political thought, between the Black Consciousness groupings who felt that there was no place for whites in the struggle and the Charterists who wanted whites to be part of the liberation process. Di Bishop did not know what the answer was. She knew only that as a South African she could not sit back and do nothing, and that what kept her actively involved was the richness of the contacts and the relationships that had become possible through the work, the demonstrations of solidarity with her when she had been suffering, when she had lost her husband and her friend. 'Once you are in it, you are held by a new community and I don't feel white in that community. I just feel part of that community.'

'So far I'm happy with the Black Sash as an organisation,' a young man of seventeen or eighteen in the crowd at Cradock confided. 'They are coming with us, they don't just give us their ideas, they come along with us in our struggles. Molly Blackburn, Helen Suzman, Judy Chalmers, all those old ladies – we call them our mothers.'

Chapter Eight

The violence debate

Over the years the Black Sash had attracted a substantial number of academics to its membership. The level of intelligence, knowledge and eloquence displayed at conferences and meetings had been impressive and, although it had never been necessary to be an academic in order to do worthwhile work in the organisation, the need for theory to inform its practice as well as practice to inform its activities as a political pressure group had grown ever greater. The necessity to think through what the organisation was really striving for and what would actually be feasible in a future South Africa had further tended to create an increasingly substantial role for the intellectually and academically inclined. Other socio-economic changes in South African society as a whole had contributed to a general alteration in the composition of Black Sash membership to include fewer of the leisured ladies with unlimited time to give to worthy causes, and a much greater number of working women whose additional salaries were necessary for the maintenance of home and family. Amongst these working women it was often those holding university posts who were in a position to juggle their timetables and make the necessary space in which to attend ever more frequent meetings, and who therefore found themselves occupying key positions within the organisation.

The result tended to be a reverence for the intellectual which some Black Sash members, some of them themselves academics, felt was at times unwarranted. There was too among many, it seemed, a reluctance to lay themselves open to accusations of being unduly emotional in a way which raised a questionmark over their rational credibility in a still strongly male-dominated society. In such a climate it was undoubtedly preferable to talk in measured tones of moral outrage, injustice, the onslaught on human rights. Beyond the figures so meticulously monitored, however, beyond the documentation despatched to the press, members of parliament, embassies and other bodies in a position to bring pressure to bear, lay a dreadful reality of suffering and of violence constantly there on the periphery of white lives, and most of those involved 'at grass-roots level' would acknowledge that it was their contact with suffering which fuelled the fire in their bellies.

In Port Elizabeth Judy Chalmers talked of the anger she often felt, of how in the never-ending contact with the horror of some people's lives it was possible to become 'burnt out', of how there were still times when she was reduced to tears. The week before we met she had been to a pension payout. Pension payouts were always terrible because they meant old people turning out to queue in the wind and the rain, often arriving in the middle of the night for fear that they would not otherwise receive the money they needed to survive. Usually the very frail sent a proxy, often a child, to collect the money on their behalf, but on this occasion it had been stipulated that all old people must come themselves to show that they were still alive and that there was no corruption afoot. So people were carrying their old people in on their backs, laying them over donkeys and putting them in the backs of wagons, and amongst all these elderly travellers there was one blind man just sitting there holding his wife's hand: 'He wasn't sobbing but his face was wet and the tears were running down his face. I said to his wife, who was equally aged and frail, "Why is he crying?" She told me he hadn't been out of the house for years and he was so frightened. That was too much for me. I just had a good cry.'

Inevitably perhaps, this encounter with suffering, the daily contact in the advice offices and through the courts with people who literally did not know where the next meal was to come from, combined with the fact that violence was increasingly being perpetrated not only by the repressive machinery of the apartheid state but by those combating repression, gave rise to the question of how far such suffering could be regarded as a justification for reactive violence. In the early 'eighties it provoked a debate within the Black Sash as to whether there was or was not such a thing as just war and just revolution, a debate about the justification of the use of violence in fighting repression or standing in judgement upon that violence. One of the principal protagonists in that debate was Jill Wentzel, who had joined the Johannesburg Black Sash as a young girl and become its organising secretary during its earliest years. In those years, as a socialist, she had found it quite amusingly conservative. From 1959 to the mid-'seventies she had not been very active in the Black Sash because of work undertaken first for the Liberal Party and then, following its disbanding, for Helen Suzman and the PFP. She had subsequently returned to the Black Sash and become at various junctures Transvaal chairperson, national secretary, national vice-president and magazine editor.

As far as she was concerned, the Black Sash's most important work had been done when, together with the Liberal Party, the PFP and a relatively small number of others, its members had really been the only people solidly campaigning and organising protests against the pass laws and forced removals, at a time when the 'wickedness' of apartheid was at its height. Then the Black Sash ladies had been 'tremendously solid, hardworking, down-to-earth, diligent and properly interested in the fate of all people'. For many years the Liberal Party and the Black Sash had held on, vesting much of their hope of bringing down the cruel inflexible monolith of apartheid in overseas pressure because nothing had seemed to be building up on the ground within South Africa itself, and in the course of a struggle in which all the odds had seemed solidly and malevolently stacked against them, the idea had evolved that 'somehow we were on the side of good versus evil'. From the early 'seventies, however, demographic forces had come to the aid of those endeavouring to combat apartheid. The explosion of the black population in contrast to a much more static white population had left the whites too thin on the ground to maintain the system. Despite the

most repressive rules, blacks had managed to organise themselves into trade unions. Employers who were already con-
travening the law by employing blacks in skilled jobs found
themselves helpless when black trade unions organised effective if illegal strikes. Dismissal of those involved would
mean the undesirable expense of training replacements. It
became in the interests of employers to negotiate, albeit
illegally, with illegal black unions.

These factors, combined with the fact that – because black
people were finding it preferable to come to the towns in
defiance of the possible penalties, actually go to prison and
still remain in town – the pass laws could no longer prevent
the influx of black people into urban areas, had contributed
to the crumbling of the apartheid system. At the same time
blacks had started moving into white areas in defiance of the
Group Areas Act, and white authorities had found it impossible to keep track of their movement. Various white schools
and universities had started taking blacks into their institutions, and again the government had found it in its own
interests to turn a blind eye because it could not cope with
the pressures of providing education for blacks. Doubtless, as
it became more and more interested in South Africa, overseas
opinion had also played its part in dislodging the confidence
of the apartheid ideology. All these forces had, as far as Jill
Wentzel was concerned, contributed to the loosening of
apartheid in such a way that the government's subsequent
so-called reform issues could be viewed as simply a reaction
to pressure. It was arguable that it did not really matter what
the government intended, whether it could be trusted,
whether or not it had really experienced a change of heart. It
really had no option.

What was significant was that the loosening of the apartheid hold began to happen in the 'seventies at a time when
the conventional wisdom among the increasing number of
anti-apartheid organisations was that there was no method of
combating it other than by violence. It was Jill Wentzel's
view that, at the very moment when all sorts of non-violent
possibilities were opening up because the ideology was less
confident, it almost became criminal to say so:

It was as though you were reneging, backing out. There was such an emotional hatred of the government that it became impossible to say to people objectively that now there were alternative options. There had been an influx into the Black Sash at that time of members of the Congress of Democrats, which was the old Communist Party whom in fact I was responsible for recruiting. They did sterling work in the Black Sash but they seemed to get iron in their soul. They were the kind of people who would be threatened by the possibility of gradual, piecemeal evolutionary change because that would not bring about the socialist millennium. Capitalism and apartheid were the same thing, and the biggest possible evil. I felt that they started to teach the ladies in their pearls, who kept their houses neat and tidy and gave dinner parties, a kind of rhetoric which those people went along with and did not understand.

In August 1982 the traditional editorial in *Sash* magazine was replaced with an article in which Jill Wentzel, who was editor at the time, expressed her concern with regard to the principles for which the Black Sash had always stood and the pressures to which these beliefs were currently being subjected: 'If there is any total onslaught in Southern Africa it is on human rights and liberties. Less obvious, but possibly more serious in the long term, is a reactive process that has built up over the years resulting in an overall disrespect for human rights even from government opponents, who, living in the atmosphere created by the government, have begun to be affected in subtle ways of which they are seldom aware.'

The article went on to point out that, while the Black Sash had tried to maintain respect for human rights and human dignity and for individual, creative thinking, it had to be acknowledged that the government had been more successful in establishing the habits of totalitarianism. Brutality seemed to teach brutality more effectively than it taught opposition to brutality, intolerance towards opposition created corresponding intolerance among the opposition, censorship and banning encouraged conflicting ideologies to anathematise each other rather than evolve creatively as a result of criticism and debate. Another undemocratic habit that developed in a totalitarian climate was apathy in the face of both fear and the failure of protest. The long failure of liberal protest had also caused a loss of faith in its values. The Black Sash had in fact at that point held a meeting in Johannesburg in June of that year to discuss what members could do to counter the feeling that the abuse of power was becoming so commonplace that people were simply becoming accustomed to it. It had decided that its members' only recourse was to carry on protesting and to make a particular effort to guard against their own apathy.

Jill Wentzel's concern was also, however, that the atmosphere of authoritarianism had pervaded dissident organisations, which increasingly demanded of their followers the same unquestioning obedience to their ideology and their strategies that Afrikaner Nationalism had demanded of its followers in order to establish itself: 'What is unhappy for us is that we have to acknowledge that this counter-rigidity seems to be the only weapon in the face of government intransigence and power and the votelessness of three-quarters of the government's opponents.' It was at a time when the government's proposals for a new constitution and tri-cameral parliament had been mooted which would trigger off heated debate about the merits or otherwise of participation, a debate that in fact would create a rift between the Black Sash and the PFP, the latter eventually opting to take its place in the new parliament. At that time it seemed to Jill Wentzel that the government had so successfully discredited the idea of universal suffrage that it had become the conventional wisdom to think in terms of solutions that did not include the vote. Radicals, it seemed, had become just as sceptical of its efficacy. Alternative 'solutions' included the boycotting of elections – a strategy which was in danger of being imposed on the 'oppressed masses' as part of a conforming affirmation of an alternative scheme of things which carried with it the desire to subject and compel others to suppress all individuality to the needs of the new order.

The Black Sash had long been used to confronting white

South Africa with the effects of apartheid. It had also undertaken solid, sacrificial hard work to further non-violent and
effective strategies of opposition. In all regions Black Sash
members were engaged in encouraging, exploring and teaching the law and social structures to people to enable them to
find effective ways of insisting on those rights they had and
finding strategies for gaining rights they did not have. The
question was now arising, however, as to whether the organisation was prepared to confront the liberation movement
with the possible effects of its ideology on ordinary people of
all races. At a time when economic sanctions and boycotts
were being called for, and the Black Sash was being called
upon to define its relationship with the United Democratic
Front and the rest of the liberation movement, was the Black
Sash prepared to examine critically the effects of the strategies it advocated on ordinary people? Did people really
believe that their best interests were served by boycotting
elections? Did they properly discuss the alternatives or were
they increasingly afraid to do so? Did the Freedom Charter
express the will of the people or seek to entrap the will of the
people so that one day they would be told: 'This is your will,
now you've got it and it must be consolidated within a one-
party state, so no more of the kind of elections that will
allow you to change your mind?'

'If we don't know the answers, or if we think we know
some of the answers, will we insist on the discipline of
continuously reassessing strategies?' Jill Wentzel enquired of
the organisation. 'Or will we through romanticism on the
part of some members and fear of opprobrium on the part of
others, fail to do so?' Were Black Sash members prepared to
face the disapproval of orthodox leftist opinion by acknowledging limitation and reality, or would they be afraid to
explore the unspectacular, imperfect yet possibly significant
advantages of piecemeal reform?

This article in *Sash* magazine in February 1984 was clearly
labelled as an individual article which did not represent Black
Sash thinking as a whole. An editorial in November 1984, in
which Jill Wentzel intended primarily to point out the risk of
a new dictatorship in an atmosphere of riot and intimidation,

was not. It intimated that one result of denying the vote to the majority of South Africa's citizens was that there were no popularly accepted structures for the expression of discontent. When, furthermore, leaders were not elected they were freed from responsibility to their constituencies and even from the necessity of having constituencies. When, in addition, in times of stress or especial discontent, such as when removals or rent increases were imminent, the government virtually proscribed all meetings – whether by direct banning, the withholding of permits or refusal of permission to use halls – then a situation was invited in which any determined group could order masses of people around by means of posters, leaflets and strong-arm tactics. That this sort of thing had not happened long ago was due to the phenomenal passion for justice and democracy of generation upon generation of black leaders, many of whom were members of the ANC. This democratic tradition continued in the structure of contemporary black organisations. Of especial interest to the Black Sash was the United Democratic Front's aim to give extra substance to the democratic discipline by dedicating itself to the principle of internal democracy within and between its affiliates.

But some disconcerting straws in the wind, set in motion by many disparate factors, need to be looked at and discussed very carefully, not only by the UDF, of course, but by all opposition organisations.

Firstly, there clearly are substantial numbers of people who want now to get on with their lives and schooling, who do not see what is being achieved by endless boycott and who do not seem to have the means to express themselves in a non-threatening environment. It is true that since the ban on indoor meetings has been lifted community discussions have begun to take place all over the country. A lot depends on the way these meetings are conducted in the next few months and whether all sections of each community feel unafraid to attend them. In this connection the kind of rhetoric which routinely invokes 'the wrath of the people',

together with statements that collaborators have only
themselves to blame for violent attacks upon them, do
not exactly create a suitable climate for frank and free
discussion.

This editorial provoked divided reactions in the organisation. There were those who raised objections to what was
seen as a 'thinly veiled' attack on the UDF. Mary Burton felt
constrained to put into writing some of the points raised in
'often heated discussion' in the Cape, in the course of which
it was acknowledged that the Black Sash must speak out
when violent tactics were used, but stressed that the organisation needed to document facts carefully and to identify
those responsible, 'or at least not to suggest that some
organisations might be responsible, especially if the leadership of, for example, the UDF and the Congress of South
African Students have explicitly rejected violence as a strategy, which we understand is the case'. Mary Burton also
pointed out that there were other Black Sash members who
were delighted with the editorial. The different responses
were, she wrote, all part of the on-going debate about how
best to bring about the changes all members agreed were
essential.

Central to that on-going debate was the issue of coercion
and violence, and Black Sash members' readiness if necessary
to risk jeopardising the 'bridgebuilding' and the 'credibility'
they had achieved among the black community by applying
the same critical standards to traditional friend as to foe. It
was a debate in which there were some who felt the real
issues were not being properly aired. Jill Wentzel remained
uneasy with the attitude she felt she was encountering in the
organisation that the structural violence of apartheid in some
way justified reactive violence, and that whites from the
vantage point of their comfortable privileged suburbs had no
right to stand in judgement on township people driven to
defensive violence by a violent and intransigent government,
which for all its talk of reform they knew had no intention of
making the changes that would really satisfy black
communities.

You had to make allowances because apartheid was so evil; the people would obviously develop counter strategies that were perhaps doubtful but you shouldn't criticise. You should be more understanding. Somewhere there was the idea that to be critical was not to be supportive, the idea that the violence used to enforce boycotts was excusable because of the violence of apartheid. I felt that the Black Sash ladies who had been so passionately for the ordinary man in the street, the person who seemed now to me to be suffering so vastly not only from the government but from the coercive strategy of the UDF, had now deserted him in favour of a leadership paid from abroad, who in fact were élitist.

No one seemed to want to stop and find out whether the mass of ordinary black citizens, who suffered most from the tactics of violent coercion, would agree that the violence of the townships was not to be criticised, and yet men like Archbishop Tutu were pleading, 'Why must we use the very same methods as the system in dealing with those who displease us? Why don't we use methods of which we will be proud in years to come when our liberation is attained?' I would raise these questions at Black Sash meetings and a lot of people would come and congratulate me at tea but they would never support me during the meetings.

Another leading Black Sash member who felt strongly that the Black Sash should speak out loudly and clearly against the violence that was being perpetrated by some blacks was Joyce Harris, a self-professed 'political animal' who, having been a member of the United Party, joined the Black Sash in 1955. Not only did she hold office as its national president from 1978–82, she was also vice-president for many years and at one stage editor of *Sash* magazine. With hindsight she would explain some members' reticence in terms of the fact that

in a way we had almost been speaking on behalf of black people over all the years when they could not, or

weren't organised enough to, or for whatever reason had
not. When they did start speaking and acting on their
own behalf and sometimes we found ourselves at odds
with the different strategies they were adopting, it was a
difficult adjustment to make to move from criticising
the government, as we had done so vociferously over all
those years, to criticising those on whose behalf we had
been fighting.

To this might be added the suggestion that, however fierce
the security police might have been in the 'sixties and
'seventies, and even when colleagues suffered greatly at their
hands for doing nothing much, it was considerably more
comfortable to feel on the side of good versus a collection of
gangsters, and that one was morally backed not only by a
warm cocoon of friends but also by public recognition. It was
much more difficult to put oneself on what was instantly
perceived to be the wrong side by confronting what was
happening within and on behalf of 'the oppressed', whose
activities were generally sanctified.

There were in any case those who did not feel that criticism
of the spiral of violence occurring in the townships was
appropriate. In the spring of 1985 a black journalist, Jon
Qwelane, wrote an article in the *Star* entitled 'They are ready
to be killed when the headhunters call', in which he described
how he had found himself involuntarily cast in the role of a
'headhunter' in pursuit of an alleged enemy of the people in
the streets of Langa:

> I had no choice in the matter, just as many of the 100-
> odd crowd must have had none. If I had not joined the
> crowd my end would probably have come faster than
> that of the crowd's quarry.
>
> The crisp command, following a sharp tapping at the
> door was: 'All the menfolk must come out and join us.
> Only women must remain behind.'
>
> We moved down the street picking up more people on
> the way. Patience reigned as we waited for men and
> youths to leave their beds and get dressed. We were

hunting an enemy I have never seen, and probably never will. But mine was not to reason why, I was to do and very possibly die.

What exactly he would be required to do Jon Qwelane would never know. As it happened, the possibility of an encounter with the law forced disbandment of the crowd before he had done anything more than knock on doors, but his witnessing of the violent atmosphere of the township – and the fact that the attitude that violence perpetrated in the name of opposition to the government was excusable as a consequence of apartheid was being increasingly criticised – induced the editor of *Frontline*, a magazine responsible for opening up a number of taboo areas of dialogue, to print not only Jon Qwelane's article but also the response of two Black Sash members to it. One was Jill Wentzel. The other was Margaret Nash, a Cape member who in expressing her abhorrence of the violence of 'headhunting' nevertheless compared an epidemic of violence to one of a disease which will recur until the primary cause of infection has been eliminated:

I hate the violence of 'headhunting' and shrink from it. But I see it as part of the pathology, the sickness unto death, of a society that has for nearly 350 years been deformed by white supremacy and the power that flows from the barrel of a gun. And I hate even more the institutionalised violence of a so-called Christian government that has brutalised, dehumanised and manipulated black people to the point where this kind of headhunting becomes part of the pattern of resistance.

Because of that I reject the 'cheap grace' of middle-class moralists/beneficiaries of apartheid, who self-righteously demand that any person or group engaged in the struggle for justice and liberation must be 'even-handed' in their condemnation of political violence. Such demands and naive responses to them only intensify black cynicism and bitterness, therefore exacerbating the situation.

It was arguable that for a period of time at least the Black Sash was not impartial, that in the process of being uplifted by the warmth and appreciation they experienced at black funerals, for example, they failed to pay proper attention to the violence that was electrically there, hardly below the surface, the same violence that was also to be sensed emanating from the police standing by. In listening to the speeches exalting death and sacrifice they seemed to some to overlook for a while what the outcome of such rhetoric was, in condemning the actions of vigilantes to forget what it was that had brought them into existence in the first place. Perhaps there was another dimension to the story of dedicated white activists who basked in the welcome of cadres, while other humble men and women quivered in their homes, not uplifted, but praying that they would not fall foul of those same young cadres. Should the Black Sash really be viewing the fact that the Cradock youngsters had taken down the councillors' protective shutters with excitement as proof of non-violence and community spirit, as if oblivious to the original element of coercion? Jill Wentzel recalled a time when she telephoned Molly Blackburn about a young man and his father who were 'sent for' from a funeral vigil. The father was subsequently sent home while his son was hacked to death. Molly Blackburn had said yes, she knew all about it, she was collecting affidavits – about the police over-reaction subsequent to the hacking to death of the youngster. She never, it seemed, interviewed the father or questioned the killing with the congress of South African Students people from whom she took the affidavits.

Criticism came from Johannesburg members at that time, and has since been maintained by those outside the Black Sash who are sympathetic to Chief Buthelezi, chief minister of Kwa Zulu, that the organisation was not even-handed in its criticism of the violence that was occurring in Natal either. It was alleged that the Black Sash was over-zealous in its attacks on Inkatha, the Zulu-dominated organisation led by Chief Buthelezi, and on Chief Buthelezi's participation in the homeland structures. His readiness to 'take all the paths offered to him, short of independence', placed him at odds with Black Sash members who took the view that his doing so made him very much part of the process of the breaking-up of South African society. They felt that the argument of the early days – that in order to build a power base and to be able to operate in opposition it was necessary to make use of the government's structures – was no longer valid. The Black Sash had found itself aligned with Inkatha and the Kwa Zulu government in relation to the tri-cameral parliament, for Chief Buthelezi had stated that he found little in the new constitution to indicate that the government was committed to meaningful reform and that the establishment of separate parliaments for whites, coloureds and Indians, while excluding blacks would 'close the door on negotiations'. However, issues such as the deficiencies of the pension payment scheme in Kwa Zulu, which had come to light in the advice offices in the Natal Coastal region, had inevitably resulted in confrontation between the Black Sash and the Kwa Zulu administration. The Black Sash had also accused Chief Buthelezi and his government and Inkatha of using and provoking violence despite the fact that he purported to be an advocate of non-violent change in South Africa.

In November 1985 Jill Wentzel wrote a letter to 'Sheena Duncan and Committee' in which she referred to the fact that she was accused by other members of being in the grip of conspiracy paranoia. In responding to that accusation she outlined what she would do if she believed that the present system was so rotten that it could never reform itself and that revolution was the only answer. The hypothetical plan was disconcertingly similar to the one General Stadler outlined as a justification for monitoring Black Sash activity. It included:

(a) Working through liberal institutions, encouraging them, slowly, step by step, to do and say those things which would further the all-or-nothing ethic, propagating ideas which negated evolutionary change, establishing habits whereby such concepts as 'reform', eventually even 'negotiation', became discredited. Evidence of such a process, Jill Wentzel claimed, was revealed in Black Sash conference 'fact papers' and resolutions.

(b) Anathematising those people and institutions through which evolutionary change might occur. Among the examples she cited were the PFP and Chief Buthelezi, regarded by a contingent within the Black Sash, as well as by the ANC and the UDF, as guilty of 'working within the system'.

(c) Softening up attitudes to violence by propagating the doctrine of defensive violence teamed up with the theological idea of the just war. This would be done slowly and carefully so that by the time the 'storm-troopers' really got going, liberals were paralysed with guilt, having had structural violence thrown at them in a concerted way over a long period of time.

> I would make sure [Jill Wentzel said] that the actions of the first few early revolutionary cadres were never condemned in specific terms, but rather in terms of overall and generalised condemnation of 'all violence from whatever quarter' on the good old 20:2 ratio (twenty sentences condemning the structural violence to two condemning the defensive violence). And, moreover, in the crucial stages, I would claim that coercive strategies were perpetrated only by 'criminal elements'.

As far as she was concerned, even if there was no group of people propagating such a programme, the Black Sash was doing all of these things, and others, which amounted to the creation of a 'climate in which the democratic habit wilts away in guilt and confusion – and the fascist climate begins'. She condemned the *Sash* magazine of August 1985 for the unbalanced way in which township terror was being represented.

It was a time when mothers were being made to watch while their sons were burnt to death and told that if they cried they too would be burned as 'enemies of the people'. Youngsters in Soweto were visiting houses and demanding that each household send a representative to the current funeral 'or else'. People suspected of breaking consumer boycotts by purchasing goods in Johannesburg were being made to eat the soap powder or the oil they brought back to the townships, children who wanted to go to school were prevented from doing so by other fourteen-year-old boys carrying petrol bombs. I heard such accounts inevitably perhaps from members of the SAP, but also from well-intentioned white employers whose 'boys' and maids were afraid to accept small gifts of food to take home to their families in case they were suspected of having bought them. At such a time a single-page article did appear in *Sash* magazine, but it was entitled 'Repression – the counter violence' and not unambiguous enough for some.

'The people who come to the advice office are the victims of repression by the apartheid system and the forces of law and order, but they are also sometimes victims of coercion by opposition forces,' it read by way of introduction to the example of Mr T., who had come to the Johannesburg advice office with head and hands horribly scarred and bound in medical supports. He had been quietly participating in a bus boycott in protest against increased fares and had decided himself to join with others in finding other means of transport to get to work. One morning, while travelling out of the townships, his taxi was stopped by police. All passengers were ordered out and on to a bus. Five blocks further on the bus was stopped by a picket. A petrol bomb was thrown in among the passengers. 'November 5 and 6' the article subsequently stated, 'were the days when there was a successful protest by thousands of people who stayed away from work. We have no doubt that most of those involved in the action did so willingly and of their own volition. However, there were also casualties . . .'

Was Black Sash members' compassion, their white guilt, rendering them vulnerable to the attraction of emotionally loaded words and phrases like 'people's power', the 'oppressed masses' and a romantic view of social change which failed to take cognisance of the fact that history had demonstrated that violent revolution was the most costly and cruel way of bringing about improved human life? Moral outrage had its more questionable aspects. It might well begin with a hatred of cruelty or poverty or injustice – this emphasised one's own humanity – but the next step was to seek whom to blame for the human suffering that was so hard to tolerate. The belief that all ills were caused by deliberate oppressive government action undoubtedly had a strong emotional appeal, and with the identification of the guilty party came the moral justification for anger, even for hatred, and the experience of very satisfying feelings of moral superiority and righteous indignation – the moral outrage which was the fuel that drove the politics of emotional expression.

Certainly the vocabulary was there in some, although by no means all quarters. So too was the emotion. By 1989, I witnessed among some Black Sash members I encountered a euphoric loyalty to the ANC and even the expressed readiness to assist in the armed struggle. I also witnessed the curious exhilaration at stories of police violence to which Jill Wentzel had referred in 1985. As a stranger perhaps not quite so bridled by guilt and all the emotions that being a white South African with a conscience entailed, leafing through the *Sash* magazines, resolutions and statements for the period when the violence debate was at its height, it was hard to appreciate the organisation's reluctance to condemn the horror of the necklacings as clearly and as frequently as it so consistently condemned the violence of the repressive state, hard to appreciate the complexities of finding a response to the call that was making itself heard from the black anti-apartheid organisations for the Black Sash to define its relationship to them.

There were other South Africans who, at the time, did not understand. In Johannesburg alone I met several former Black Sash members who had left the organisation primarily because they had not felt that it had come out clearly enough against the violence of the townships, and a criticism I would hear voiced on more than one occasion from otherwise sympathetic and admiring observers, including Denis Beckett, editor of *Frontline* magazine, was that the Black Sash was inclined to be uncritical of those involved in the sometimes bloody struggle, a tendency to believe that what was opposition was right, that those who had been in prison were necessarily the 'good guys'. Jill Wentzel, for personal reasons as much as for the reluctance she felt she encountered in the Black Sash to discuss the issues at stake, 'melted away' from it.

Finally, in March 1986, the national conference held in Durban 'approved certain elements to be expressed in a draft statement on violence to be circulated by headquarters to all regions for comment prior to finalisation'. In December of that year the national headquarters of the Black Sash, recently moved from Johannesburg to Cape Town, issued the following statement which had been approved by all regions:

> We live in a time when the struggle against the institutionalised violence of apartheid is rendering the townships ungovernable and bringing the country to the brink of civil war.
>
> During war, violence breeds violence, and there are atrocities on both sides; winning a 'war of liberation' does not necessarily result in a just peace. In an increasingly warlike situation, what is required of an organisation such as the Black Sash which is committed to justice and the rule of law and the use of non-violent methods in the attainment of these?
>
> Some of our members claim that, just as we have consistently condemned the structural violence of apartheid, now we should also condemn the 'liberatory violence' of those who have taken up arms against apartheid: that unless we do so we shall be acting on the basis of expediency rather than on principle. Others are uneasy lest we stand in judgement on people caught in a desperate struggle for survival and self-defence.
>
> All of us feel deep revulsion and horror at spectacles of violence such as the necklacing of 'informers' and the exultant youths surrounding the victims; also deep alarm at the seemingly arbitrary and anarchic forms of violence that are intensifying the miseries of township life, to the point where people caught in the crossfire are fleeing like refugees to rural areas or to hiding-places in the suburbs. And all of us want such things not to

happen, jut as we want an end to apartheid oppression,
which is provoking and fuelling such violence.

It is difficult to contribute effectively to the ending of
those and all other kinds of political violence and to the
establishing of a just peace. And it is the latter task –
learning to contribute effectively to the struggle for a
society based on justice and the rule of law – that is the
real challenge. To that task we commit ourselves.

In 1989 I put to Mary Burton, to whose wisdom and
diplomatic skills as national president many members attributed the overall unity of the Black Sash despite the wide
spectrum of views reflected in its membership, the accusation that there was a tendency in the organisation as a
whole to assume that to oppose the government was automatically to be on the side of the angels, to be pro-government was automatically to be a 'bad guy'. In quietly reflective
tones she admitted that Black Sash members probably were
vulnerable to criticism of being blanketly anti-government:

> I think when we get an invitation to attend a meeting
> which sounds as if it might be government-financed or
> have links with some of the regional local authorities,
> we are immediately on the defensive and suspicious of
> their motives. I think that is a reality. Probably just
> because of having been in opposition to the government
> for so many years, it may be quite difficult for us to
> accept the *bona fides* of new spokesmen and new
> representatives.

As for the idea that if a person had been in prison he was
all right, that was not really true. Black Sash members
frequently agonised over the rights and wrongs of their
monitoring the court when someone who had clearly been
part of Umkhonto we Sizwe and had placed bombs was being
tried. Similarly, with regard to funeral attendance, they had
spent a long time in a state of uncertainty early in 1989 over
whether they should attend the funeral of two young people
who were blown up by a bomb whilst involved in violent

action, and were clearly viewed by many of the community organisations as national heroes. Some Black Sash women had gone to the funeral not because they viewed the deceased as heroes, but because they had seen the incident as one more instance of the tragic death of young people, probably for misguided reasons. One of the questions that occasion had raised was whether it was any worse to go to the funeral of people committed to overthrowing the government through violence than to attend their trials. 'We see our presence in both cases as a *witnessing* one rather than a supportive one, but I think you have to recognise that it is construed in different ways by different people.' Certainly the kind of thanks and the welcome Black Sash members received from the black communities was because in a general way at least they were perceived as being supportive.

I thought of General Stadler and others of his colleagues who had been apparently unable to comprehend why members of an organisation which they acknowledged to be collectively in favour of bringing about change by non-revolutionary means stood with their banners at rallies and gatherings at which the ANC had a pronounced presence and individuals known to advocate violence were speaking. I had been shown a picture of such a rally in Cape Town in which members of the Black Sash were present. 'I ask myself that question,' a brigadier had said. 'Why are the Black Sash banners displayed at that rally?' It was known that members of the Black Sash had been to Lusaka to talk to leading members of the ANC. There were no objections to that. Talking to such people was their democratic right. The police recognised that. Despite their interest in individuals who were 'part and parcel of the revolutionary onslaught', General Stadler also recognised that the Black Sash was not an organisation which as a whole subscribed to violence, but why did members stand with their banners in apparent support of those who did?

His allegations that the Black Sash was vulnerable to being the albeit unwitting instrument of an ANC/SACP revolutionary programme or hidden agenda was one with which Mary Burton was familiar:

I think one recognises that the ANC and probably other groups have military strategies, but I don't think the attempt to bundle all other opposition groups that work against apartheid under the same umbrella would bear very close scrutiny. It's very useful propaganda because it turns everybody who questions the action of the state into part of that revolutionary band, and it has often been said that the Black Sash is naive and foolish and doesn't understand what is really going on. We are compromised by the fact that we very often say the same things as the revolutionary movements, in spite of all the comments we make about the processes that we would use to work through.

By 1989 Mary Burton no longer felt that the organisation's stance in relation to black violence was in question.

I don't think that the people in Sash who are very opposed to violence feel that their voices are not heard any longer, that the organisation has gone too far in support of the revolutionary movement. And I don't know if that means we have taken a step backwards. I think it's just that we've got a little braver. I think that at that time when everything was so turbulent and people were so clearly not on the side of the authorities, that in fact there was a lack of courage in speaking out, partly I think because everything was so confused and people did not know who the 'good guys' were and who the 'bad guys' were. I think now we have come through that traumatic period strengthened so that we do have the courage to say what we think.

Ultimately, as in the case of accusations that the Black Sash singled out Kwa Zulu for attack and was quicker to speak out against the violence perpetrated by Inkatha than by members of the UDF, the response of the organisation's leadership was to insist upon its members ensuring the complete accuracy of information monitored before any accusations were made in any direction. The Black Sash acknowledged that it had difficulties in its dealings with Chief Buthelezi because in its experience, whereas the UDF leadership did not like people claiming to be their members using violence against others and actually tried to stop it, the allegation that Inkatha encouraged vigilante groups was taken by Chief Buthelezi as a personal affront.

By 1989, according to the *Weekly Mail*, violence in the Pietermaritzburg area had claimed more than 1,300 lives in the previous two years. In 1988 alone 680 people were killed, probably as many as 3,000 homes were destroyed and 30,000 people were displaced. Black Sash contact with local communities indicated that, although this violence could not be attributed to any one single cause, it was when local grievances and problems merged into broader conflicts that the mix became explosive. One such issue was undeniably the deep political/ideological division between those holding a UDF or Congress of South African Trade Unions position and Inkatha. 'Inkatha's periodic membership drives,' stated one report, 'and resistance to them, have frequently precipitated contained tension into uncontained violence.'

Many commentators also believed that the state was playing a different role in the Natal conflict from elsewhere in the country, that while the police, sometimes assisted by vigilantes, had randomly crushed eruptions of violence elsewhere, they had largely allowed the violence in Natal to take its course when initiated by Inkatha and taken punitive action only against non-Inkatha groups. If this was true, deduced the Black Sash, there could be no solution without exposing and challenging the state's role in the Natal conflict. In devising future strategies there would be a great need for meticulous and factual monitoring of the situation. Mary Burton, in her 1989 presidential address, emphasised that the work of opposing violations of human rights required qualities of fearless impartiality. The Black Sash's non-aligned status as a small independent organisation could lend weight to future testimony.

In 1989 Joyce Harris also spoke of how several years of

struggle within the organisation had brought about a considerable amount of reappraisal. Her own position had been
clearly that 'lawlessness remains lawlessness whomever it is
committed by and for whatever reason and no matter how
understandable it may be', and that if the Black Sash started
applying judgements only in one direction and not in another
it would become rudderless, lose direction, even turn into an
acceptable wing of the struggle to overthrow the government
by violent means; in the process it would cease to be a
political pressure group for which the principles of human
rights and liberties were the guiding lights. By 1989 she felt
that the Black Sash had come to a clearer sense of its own
identity. It had realised that it was a human rights organisation with its own autonomy, but in the interim the diversity
of views within it had caused it to look at itself again, long
and hard.

Chapter Nine

Alignment

A significant factor in the Black Sash's slowness to speak out in condemnation of the growing incidence of violent action in the resistance to apartheid was undoubtedly its initial nervousness about engendering disharmony with other opposition organisations at a time when, within those organisations, the creation of an atmosphere of unity and the presentation of a united front against the government took precedence over the airing of differing views. With the wisdom of 1990 the Black Sash would readily recognise that President De Klerk's decision to unban the ANC and other organisations and to release Nelson Mandela must be seen as a response to that same unified resistance and to the international pressure which had grown from it. By then also, however, the Black Sash had witnessed the vindication of its own decision, in defining its relationships with other anti-apartheid bodies, to temper its desire to demonstrate commitment to unity with and support for the organisations which represented the majority of the people, with an insistence on its right to speak freely and to voice dissent.

Some years prior to the raising of the question of affiliation to the UDF at the 1984 national conference, the resolution was put on the conference agenda that the Black Sash should affiliate to the Institute of Race Relations, with which it had a long-standing close working relationship. The South African Institute of Race Relations had been founded in 1939 – significantly, nine years before the Nationalist Government had come into being – when a number of academics had felt that the situation in South Africa was deteriorating. They had decided that research should be undertaken in areas where this was most evident, and that the results of that research should be published and sent to people who could do something about it. Although not an activist organisation the Institute thus had much in common with the Black Sash, and in Cape Town in 1978 the link was strengthened by the sharing of premises in Mowbray. Nevertheless, the resolution had been defeated on the basis of the Black Sash's need to retain its independence.

With the formation of the UDF in 1983, however, the issue of that need for independence appears to have become a somewhat cloudy one. The idea of united action on the part of an alliance of organisations reflecting many different threads of political thinking was very welcome. The UDF was calling for a national convention, which was a call the Black Sash had been making for years. In resolutions of its national conference and, on a regional level, in statements and demonstrations, it had repeatedly called for a meeting of representatives of all the people in the country, gathering together on an equal basis to thrash out a mutually acceptable constitution for the future. The Black Sash also agreed with the UDF's preconditions for that convention: namely that political prisoners must be released, that there must be free return of all exiles and organisations' representatives and that all the banned organisations must be unbanned before it would be possible for any process such as a national convention to be entered into. The Black Sash further shared the UDF's opposition to the so-called Koornhof Bills – the Orderly Movement and Settlement of Persons Bill which it condemned as a new 'pass law', the Black Community Development Bill* and the Black Local Authorities Bill.†

Initially it had felt itself likely to be at variance with the

---

* The Black Communities Development Act of 1984 would empower the Minister of Constitutional Development and Planning to dis-establish a town or a portion of a town wherever it appeared to him that the conditions under which the inhabitants were living were such that the health or safety of the public or any group of persons might otherwise be endangered. The department could demolish any structure erected, without compensation.

† The Black Local Authorities Act of 1982 empowered a black town council and the minister to make by-laws relating to the control of slums in black local authority areas.

'broad democratic alliance' being formed to oppose the government's constitutional proposals and the legislation arising from them, on the grounds that participating organisations were likely to be required to endorse the Freedom Charter first adopted by the Congress Alliance, formed in 1955 to unite all the principal organisations fighting apartheid. By 1990 the Black Sash, to the embarrassment of some members, had still not taken the Freedom Charter to the organisation as a whole for discussion and a vote. As one regional chairperson explained, in 1983, when the issue of the Freedom Charter became a pressing one in the context of the relationship with the UDF, the Black Sash had not yet completed the process of stepping up internal democracy which it initiated that year. The response of the broad membership to the Charter could not be predicted.

> In those days there were likely to be strong reactions to the idea of nationalisation of industry and the idea of the land being redivided among those who worked it. I remember one member at one meeting announcing heatedly that she wasn't going to share her garden with anybody. People in general were not *au fait* with the Charter because whenever it was published in a book the book was banned, although in practice several versions of it were in circulation, which only added to the confusion.

A statement from the Black Sash annual conference in 1983 drew attention to the lack of clarity as to which of the various versions would ultimately be used for a final decision relating to the UDF, and went on to state that in the original version delegates to conference had expressed no difficulties with the four main introductory statements of principle, but that some clauses were not clear and not acceptable to all members of the Black Sash. It was in fact the economic clauses that had posed a problem. There was consensus that there were gross economic injustices in South African society, but delegates were divided with regard to the solutions proposed, which they found not to be perspicuous. Thereafter the question of the Freedom Charter was rather put to one side, although the economic issues would crystallise into a debate within the organisation over the relative merits of a socialist versus a free-enterprise economy, and eventually into the question of the acceptability of a mixed economy. 'Now the mixed-economy line from the ANC is something that Sash can welcome,' it would be explained in 1989. By then the chances of the Freedom Charter being endorsed by a substantial majority of the Black Sash were high, but in a sense by then the moment had passed the organisation by.

In the event, the UDF did not adopt the Freedom Charter as its manifesto, in part precisely because some UDF groups had reservations about the socialist slant or the lack of clarity of some of the Charter's economic clauses; partly because as an organisation it did not wish to claim to be 'a substitute movement to accredited people's liberation movements'. Nevertheless, the UDF's inaugural declaration had strong overtones of the 1955 programme:

> Freedom-loving people of South Africa say with one
> voice to the whole world that we cherish the vision of a
> united democratic South Africa based on the will of the
> people, and will strive for the unity of all our people
> through united action against the evils of apartheid and
> economic and all other forms of exploitation, and in our
> march to a free and just South Africa we are going to be
> guided by these noble ideals. We stand for the creation
> of a true democracy in which all South Africans will
> participate in the government of our country. We stand
> for a single, non-racial, unfragmented South Africa, free
> of bantustans and group areas.

The Black Sash's own statement from the international conference of the previous year on P.W. Botha's constitutional proposals had announced that: 'The Black Sash believes in a common citizenship in a unitary society, with political representation for all through universal franchise.' It was not surprising, then, that many members of the Black Sash greeted the UDF declaration with open arms, so much so that at the time of the new organisation's formation the Natal Coastal region of the Black Sash did actually affiliate to it. When in Johannesburg, in March 1984, the national conference was asked both to ratify that decision and to consider the resolution that the Black Sash 'work actively towards affiliation with the UDF', delegates, after much debate, approved the statement:

> The Black Sash wholeheartedly endorses the declaration of the UDF in its opposition to the new constitution and Koornhof Bills, and welcomes its formation as an event of great political significance. The 1984 conference of the Black Sash has decided not to seek affiliation with the UDF, but to seek full cooperation with it, observer status for its general councils, and participation in its campaigns wherever and whenever possible.

The national conference ratified the decision that Natal Coastal region had taken to affiliate at the time with the UDF, but the organisation's constitution required that the resolution to affiliate be carried at national conference by a two-thirds majority. In fact a straw vote had indicated that the conference was almost evenly divided. Objections had come from two different quarters within the Black Sash: from members who were already closely connected with the trade unions and were inclined to see the UDF as a bourgeois organisation, and also from the conservative membership. A third concern was that the UDF's very democratic structures would exercise a delaying tactic on Black Sash activity. Sheena Duncan, who was very much in favour of affiliation at the time but would subsequently have occasion to be glad that the Black Sash had not actually entered into such a relationship, congratulated delegates on the way in which the debate had been conducted 'with restraint and reason and tolerance'. Next day, however, Ann Colvin, a Natal member, read a statement to the conference, expressing her anger and her feeling that the Black Sash had made an ignoble decision and had nothing whatsoever to be proud of.

On the stoep of her Johannesburg home – the kind of home

to which members of the SAP referred, not without evident envy, as an illustration of the hypocrisy of privileged whites professing to care for the dispossessed – in the autumn of 1989 Sheena Duncan, who shares her garden with a number of squatters, elaborated a little on why she could now see the wisdom of that conference decision. She was well aware of the concerns of some that the Black Sash was vulnerable to Marxist manipulation. In fact, it was she who with fair-mindedness had first drawn my attention to Jill Wentzel's anxieties, but she had never shared them to the same degree. Experience had shown her that when Marxist young women came to join the Black Sash they ceased quite quickly to be Marxists in any radical way: 'I think it's working with people. You suddenly realise that all your doctrinaire theories about society don't exactly match what people want. You may be working with communities threatened with removal and you find that the freehold title to their land is actually the most important thing they have.' Her revised attitude to affiliation with the UDF was based on a recognition that the Black Sash needed to remain independent to criticise where it felt necessary: 'When you are a small organisation and you are affiliated to a much larger one you are in a position where, if they say something you don't like, you have to resign and that is a rather dramatic and terrible thing. Being so small, we also could not expect to influence any decisions we felt to be wrong.'

By the end of 1985 it was already becoming apparent that the unity of thought between the Black Sash as an organisation and the UDF, even in relation to something about which they had felt as certain as the national convention, could not be taken for granted. Dr Van Zyl Slabbert, the then leader of the Progressive Federal Party, had proposed the formation of a Convention Alliance to pressurise for and promote the idea of a national convention. He had specifically rejected the idea that any convention could take place under conditions of a State of Emergency: 'I am simply saying that those in favour of it [a national convention] should come together and demonstrate their commitment to getting rid of

apartheid completely and substituting it with one constitution with one citizenship in one individual country.' He had
also said: 'A Convention Alliance does not mean that all who
participate in it share the same policy, or belong to the same
party, or necessarily have the same detailed plan for South
Africa. In other words it does not seek to compromise its
members or its supporters in terms of policy, principles,
programme of action, or leaders of their individual organisations and movements.'

Black Sash members like Joyce Harris and Sheena Duncan,
at least, were receptive to the idea of an alliance which
constituted a means to an end and not an end in itself. Such
an initiative should not, they felt, be rejected out of hand on
the grounds that the government had not agreed to preconditions such as the lifting of the State of Emergency and
the release of imprisoned ANC leaders. The proposed alliance
was simply offering potential impetus for the convention
movement. The arguing and the hard bargaining could take
place once a convention had actually been achieved. Joyce
Harris told members in an article in *Sash* magazine in
November 1985:

> We all need to stop attacking and start communicating,
> to listen to each other and hear what is being said; to
> show evidence of our good intentions and learn to trust
> each other; and somehow to get through the agony and
> violence and hurt that is all around us and go forward
> together into a future that holds peace, stability and
> fulfilment for all of us. The National Convention
> Movement might be the vehicle for achieving this.

Yet the UDF, and, it should be said, a proportion of the Black
Sash also, remained resolutely opposed to the initiative to
launch a National Convention Alliance, insisting that it was
meaningless to push for a national convention while the
basic preconditions had not been met, and the Alliance was
never actually formed.

There would in fact prove to be a major policy difference
between the UDF (which would not work within parliament

or participate in any of the government and state structures, believing them to be illegitimate because they were based on white minority rule) and the Black Sash (which had always seen it as necessary through the advice offices to deal with officials and take problems to local authorities, and which, as a voters' organisation, had despite growing disillusionment worked for change through parliament). A Black Sash resolution taken at the time of President Botha's November 1983 referendum on his proposed parliamentary reforms actually committed members, in the event of the outcome being in favour of the tri-cameral parliament, to non-participation in the new system. The resolution became a point of contention with members who were PFP supporters and with Helen Suzman, who was faced with the question of how, after years of campaigning for reforms which would break the mould of white-dominated politics and open the way to a system of government in which all race groups could have meaningful participation, liberal opposition should confront a constitution which admitted coloureds and Indians but totally excluded blacks; eventually she took her place in the new parliament.

The Black Sash resolution was subsequently amended to allow for individual freedom of choice, and the dilemma of whether or not to participate, for example, in the 1987 elections for the white parliament would remain a complex one for many members, especially when non-participation by liberal whites as a result of a campaign to boycott the elections proved to be a contributory factor in ousting the PFP as the official opposition party and replacing it with the right-wing Conservative Party.

An equally complex issue of debate was that of sanctions, unequivocally advocated by the UDF. The Black Sash, unable to reach any common ground on the issue, would not make any statement on sanctions. There were those among its members who believed that the end of apartheid could be achieved by a process of evolutionary change which would not destroy the economy but lead rather to greater employment and prosperity for all. There were others who believed that unless the South African government was forced by economic and political pressures to reverse its policies there would be such war and devastation that irreparable harm would be done not only to the economy but to the whole fabric of South African society. The ramifications of these arguments were explored at length and with refinement, but those who served as representatives of the Black Sash confined themselves carefully to reflecting the complexity of diverse opinions even when the failure to advocate sanctions placed them out of step with anti-apartheid groups both in and outside South Africa. Sheena Duncan, who personally would support the call for comprehensive mandatory sanctions if she felt the political will was really there but who, ever realistic, advocated instead strategic effective sanctions, found herself threatened with censorship by one member of an anti-apartheid group in Australia if she expressed such a view in Sydney: 'I wasn't to be allowed to say such a thing. It was out of line with what the ANC was saying.' She remained undeterred by those inclined to see the ANC as the sole authentic voice of the South African people.

Increasingly, despite the fact that from its inception the UDF had stated that it was committed to a non-violent struggle against apartheid, the government accused it of promoting violence in the townships, of being a 'front' for the South African Communist Party and the internal wing of the African National Congress. There was no doubt in General Stadler's mind that the UDF and subsequently the Mass Democratic Movement formed part of the 'internal dimension' of the ANC's revolutionary plan. Certain restrictions had therefore to be placed on the UDF. As of February 1988 the UDF would be permitted a bank account and offices, but it would not be allowed to engage in any activity without the consent of the minister. As far as the Black Sash was concerned, the UDF was not seen as the internal wing of the ANC, but it was seen as having a strong direction in the Congress tradition. If, then, the Black Sash were to affiliate to what some would argue should be a freely operating political party in South Africa, it would be in contravention with the Black Sash's tradition as a non-party-political organisation. As it transpired, the unaffiliated Black Sash, despite

its full cooperation in a massive campaign against the tricameral election of 1984 and others to which the UDF were
also actively committed, remained exempt from the kind of
restrictions imposed on the UDF. Other organisations affiliated to the UDF escaped such curbs but there can be little
doubt, that, had the Black Sash elected to affiliate, its relative
space to manoeuvre could well have been placed in jeopardy.

Black Sash membership had a tendency to swell when
some instance of mounting repression constituted the 'last
straw' for whites who had hitherto remained uninvolved.
Nevertheless, with a membership which mounted during the
1985-6 period to some 2,500 and then settled on just over
2,000 women, it remained a relatively small body whose
efficacy depended to a large extent on cooperation with
others. Frequently that cooperation took the form of an
alliance which was issue-related and therefore to a greater or
lesser degree temporary. It was generally a case of either the
Black Sash or some other group suggesting that by acting
together a particular problem could be dealt with more
effectively.

At the Black Sash Conference of 1983, in response to the
provisions of the 1983 Defence Amendment Act then before
parliament, which determined that the board for religious
objectors could recognise only a religious pacifist as a conscientious objector, delegates passed a resolution on conscription and conscientious objection. It was an issue of primary
concern to whites for it was only whites who were subject to
compulsory conscription. The Black Sash believed that the
conflict in South Africa was predominantly a political rather
than a military one. It also believed that when the South
African army was called upon to fight those whom the
government was telling them were Cubans, Russians and the
organised forces of the South-West African People's Organisation (SWAPO) in Angola and Namibia – the 'terrorists from
abroad' – the requirement to fight was in reality based purely
on a political conflict in Southern Africa which divided the
people of that country against one another. In such circumstances it was imperative that individuals were granted the
freedom of conscience to decide whether they wished to

engage in that armed conflict. Where a minority government had power, it was doubly important that the merit and morality of what it stood for should be good enough to attract volunteers into the military forces. There were many young men who did not fall into the category of full religious pacifists who none the less objected to military service on moral grounds or grounds of conscience.

Prior to 1983 the Black Sash had worked for the recognition of more comprehensive grounds for conscientious objection. The Defence Amendment Act of 1983 brought disappointment. The organisation therefore decided that the way forward was to call for the system of compulsory military conscription to be ended. Moreover, it was felt that focusing on conscription and working towards its abolition were constructive and legal ways of promoting the whole issue of conscience and the unjust war:

> During World War II the South African government respected the conscience of individuals and there was no conscription. The country is even more seriously divided now that it was then.
>
> South Africa is illegally occupying Namibia and this is cause for many in conscience to refuse military service. When South Africa withdraws from Namibia there would be no need for a massive military establishment unless there has been a political failure to respond to the desires of the citizens, and that army will be engaged in a civil war, which is good cause for many to refuse military service. In such a civil war, if the state has to rely on conscription to man its army, the war is already lost.
>
> Therefore the Black Sash demands that the South African government abolish all conscription for military service. We maintain that there is no total onslaught against the people of South Africa and the total strategy demanded of us is not the military defence of a minority government but the total all-out effort of all South Africa's people to bring about democratic government

and the relief of the poverty and deprivation suffered by the majority.

In the recollection of Noël Robb, after the Black Sash had passed this resolution it was not entirely certain what to do about it. It was not felt to be appropriate to incite people to refuse to be conscripted when the consequence of such a refusal – which must be taken, not by the Black Sash women, but by the young men directly concerned – was six years imprisonment. The resolution was widely publicised, however, and in July 1983 the annual conference of Conscientious Objectors Support Groups, which had been formed to support young men who had gone to detention barracks or prison because in conscience they could not obey their call-up, took up the resolution and also decided to campaign on the issue of conscription. The issue was discussed with the Churches and other organisations, and the End Conscription Campaign was formed – a cooperative grouping of some eighteen organisations brought together by a common belief in the harmful effects of compulsory military conscription and increased militarisation of South African society, and the belief that the South African Defence Forces were active in upholding injustice in that society. The intention of this coalition was to educate constituent organisations and the community at large as a necessary part of the campaign against enforced conscription which it was designed to coordinate. That campaign included 'focuses' on the situation in Namibia. Poster demonstrations, press conferences, vigils for those who had died, public meetings and leaflet distributions were organised. Black Sash members attended and spoke at meetings and other activities arranged by the ECC. They wrote articles and letters to the press. In particular they made their support for the ECC known when the organisation was attacked by members of parliament or by government spokesmen.

Inevitably perhaps, that support gave rise in certain quarters to the allegation that the Black Sash's main objection to military conscription was based on a desire to prevent loyal South Africans from 'going to fight against the people who went out of the country', against the enemies of South Africa, namely the ANC, SWAPO and the SACP. When, in 1985, Sheena Duncan appeared at the 'Delmas' trial as a witness for the defence of members of the UDF, which had also given its support to the ECC, she was faced with precisely such a line of questioning. When asked: 'In your campaign, have you any objection to the army fighting terrorists, ANC terrorists?' her response was: 'I have always believed that the combating of terrorism should be more a task for the police, that it is a crime committed essentially within the country, a violent crime that is committed, and I have always been of the opinion that the police are the proper force to combat terrorism.' She herself was a total pacifist but if she were not she could see, she acknowledged, the justification for the army fighting a guerilla army or an invading force coming into the country from outside. All the same, she would not describe that force as terrorist because to do so seemed to her an inaccurate use of the English language. 'For me a terrorist is essentially someone who comes either alone or with a few others and commits an act which is not part of an army or a military engagement.' She had no objection to the army in South Africa being used to protect the country's borders or the people on those borders, but she would argue that if the political conflict with the ANC were resolved in a political way rather than a military one there would be no attack on people living in the border areas.

The current *de facto* position was, the prosecution insisted, that 'there are terrorists outside this country, ANC terrorists, PAC terrorists. They are coming into the country to kill people. The army is on the borders, protecting the people on the borders. Do you have any objection to the army being used for that?'

'I find it hard to answer your question,' the witness responded, 'the way you have phrased it, because I have no objection to the army being used on the borders to seek to prevent organised attack on the people on the borders or further in. But a terrorist is somebody who has entered the country in spite of the army and I believe that the police should be engaged in that action.' Did she regard the ANC, the SACP, SWAPO and Cubans fighting against our army as the enemy of South Africa? 'No, I do not regard the ANC, SWAPO or the SACP as the enemy of South Africa, nor do I regard the Cuban troops, as I understand from the little information at our disposal within South Africa, the Cuban troops are not there because they are enemies of South Africa. They are there to reinforce the government of Angola in its resistance to UNITA (the National Union for the Total Independence of Angola) in the civil war that is going on in that country.'

'And the fact that the ANC openly declare that they are busy with a revolution against South Africa, that has no meaning to you at all?' inquired the prosecution.

'As I understand it,' came the response, 'the ANC is not engaged in revolution against South Africa, it is engaged in revolution against the present governing system in South Africa. The ANC people are South Africans.'

One of the prosecution's key points in relation to the End Conscription Campaign at the Delmas trial was that it was because those supporting it did not see the ANC as the enemy of the South African people and the government that they objected to people being conscripted into the army and that the whole purpose of the campaign was to weaken the South African army. On this Sheena Duncan was adamant on behalf of the Black Sash as a whole. The Black Sash had not sought to weaken the South African army. The Black Sash had sought to maintain the principle of freedom of conscience.

The movement of the army into the townships in 1985 brought a dramatic growth in ECC membership. A growing number of young South Africans objected to fighting those whom they regarded as their own people in the black townships. New branches were formed in Afrikaans-speaking communities, but the ECC's national impact and the reported low morale in the army intensified the authorities' reaction, and when the national State of Emergency was imposed in June 1986 thirty ECC members were jailed and its meetings were banned in the Eastern and Western Cape. Under the Emergency, however, its member organisations and the Black Sash in particular was often able to carry forward ECC work where the ECC itself could not. The long-term future of the campaign might well, it was recognised, depend on the extent to which these organisations were able to take up the issues of militarisation independently of the ECC. By 1989 the Black Sash was still seeking to maintain its principle of freedom of conscience in relation to conscription.

The 'Free the Children Campaign' was another example of an alliance of a relatively temporary nature. Early in 1986 the Black Sash national conference had received many serious reports on the plight of the country's children. At that time Minister Louis Le Grange's figures, which, as the Black Sash pointed out, did not take into account those children killed by the SADF, acknowledged the detention under the State of Emergency of 2,106 juveniles and the death of 209 children killed in police action. Black Sash experience in the Port Elizabeth advice office and elsewhere revealed that children from as young as seven up to the age of eighteen made up a large proportion of the victims of the current state of unrest. Detained, imprisoned, shot, abused, tortured, they were treated no differently from adults despite their youth and a body of laws promulgated especially for the protection of children.

Black Sash members were prepared to acknowledge that not all the children abused and maltreated by the security forces consisting of the army, the police, the Security Police and the Administration boards and Community Councils police were necessarily innocent of a wide range of misdeeds and crimes. They were compelled to concede that stones were thrown, arson was committed, people were necklaced and coerced with varying degrees of violence to participate in boycotts, work stoppages or to join the 'comrades'. They were nevertheless unflinching in their denunciation of the brutal treatment to which children were subjected by the authorities as utterly reprehensible and counter-productive.

Children have become politicised at an earlier and
earlier age [wrote Joyce Harris in a memorandum

published by the Black Sash in April 1986], and the
question needs to be asked, 'What is to be done about
them?' What is to be done with children who use hand
grenades or dance around the dying bodies of people
they have set alight? What is to be done when authority
has lost all credibility and respect for the law has been
destroyed by the very people trying to implement it?
What is to be done when violence is seen as the only
strategy left to people whose peaceful appeals have
fallen on deaf ears? . . . It is difficult to see what
rehabilitative processes, if any, will be effective in
undoing all the damage presently being done, especially
to young people. The obvious and first thing to be done
is to demolish the policy of apartheid and all its
structures. However, this is extremely unlikely, given
the stated government stance. Therefore the necessity
still exists for the government to do something about
the brutality with which it is enforced and countered.
Unfortunately it is directing all its energies at
attempting to control the violence of the victims.

Young people who had been tortured and maltreated, as
numerous statements from juveniles claimed, were likely to
nurse bitterness, hatred and contempt for the authorities, the
law and the due legal process, which gave them no protection
whatsoever but left them totally at the mercy of cruel and
irresponsible members of the security forces. When security
forces were granted indemnity, when whatever they did
appeared to receive the tacit approval of their masters, and
when they themselves showed so little respect for the law
that they were prepared to abuse their powers, their victims
could not be expected to respect the law either. The South
African Police Force undoubtedly had a difficult task to
perform but, together with the army, it required restraint and
fundamental retraining in attitudes and behaviour. The
responsibility for a generation of brutalised children was
placed firmly at their door. What kind of society needed to be
protected from its own children? Only one in which the

government and its agents could no longer govern normally because they did not enjoy the consent of the governed.

The 1986 national conference asked all regions to arrange a 'focus on children', to include such activities as monitoring the courts, the press and any publications relating to incidents involving children; developing a profile of needs and resources to do with the well-being of children in the various regions with a view to self-education within the Black Sash; and also to exposing the prevailing conditions of the majority of children to the public and especially to the white community. The average age in South Africa in 1986 was seventeen. The United Nations Declaration on the Rights of the Child, and the Catholic Child Welfare Council of England and Wales, had stipulated that these children had certain rights: the right, for example to special protection and opportunities and facilities to develop physically, mentally, morally, spiritually and socially in a healthy and normal manner and in conditions of freedom and dignity. The Black Sash made direct approaches to institutions which explicitly concerned themselves with moral and spiritual values (churches, synagogues, temples and mosques) and ask them to cooperate and reinforce the focus in ways appropriate to themselves. Members also approached university extra-mural studies or education departments and child guidance units.

In late October 1986, a year of focusing on children, the plight of the hundreds of children believed to be in detention seemed to call for particular attention. A campaign for their release was suggested. Figures were at that stage sketchy. Of the 22,000 people estimated to have been detained under the State of Emergency declared in June, at least 40 per cent were believed by the Black Sash to be children as defined by the Children's Act, in other words under the age of eighteen. A small committee was promptly formed and a wide range of organisations was invited to a working meeting. Educators, doctors, lawyers, the clergy and social workers expressed their concern about the impact of detention on children, their families and the community at large. By December, twenty-seven organisations, including partially state-funded bodies such as the Child Welfare Society, were lending support to the campaign, and a 'Free the Children Alliance' had been formed.

A Black Sash member had the idea of producing Christmas cards to spread the 'Free the Children' message. Some 70,000 rolled off the presses, together with bumper and envelope stickers. Natal Coastal region personalised the campaign by producing balloons bearing the name of a child known to be in detention and the words 'Free this child'. The endorsement of prominent people both in and outside South Africa was enlisted. Among others, Helen Suzman and Helen Joseph supported a public meeting in Johannesburg. 'Free the Children' campaigns were launched in France by Madame Mitterand and in Sweden by Mrs Lisbeth Palme. On 10 December, Human Rights Day, about four hundred parents of detainees were brought together for a party intended either to celebrate the release of child detainees, if the government had found the compassion to release them, or otherwise to mourn and renew efforts on their behalf. A glimmer of hope came in the form of the news that twenty-one children aged between ten and seventeen had been released. When, however, the prospects of further releases seemed remote, and in fact another sixty-six names of children, of whom the Detainees Parent Support Committee had been unaware, were added to the list of those detained, Black Sash members tried to deliver food and balloons to the prisons where children were being held – to Modder Bee prison on the East Rand, Diepkloof prison near Johannesburg and Krugersdoorp and Westville prisons in Natal.

Looking back on the 'Free the Children' campaign, Sheena Duncan regards it as having been on the whole successful: 'It was a short-term alliance which succeeded in its aims in the end, although the other day there was a report that two fourteen-year-olds are in detention at the moment, which I haven't been able to follow up yet. Nevertheless, at that time hundreds of children were being detained, and that is no longer happening because together you build up internal and international pressure on a particular issue.'

*

A similar strategy was used in 1988 in relation to a drive to abolish capital punishment in South Africa. The Black Sash's opposition to capital punishment was long-standing. As a human rights organisation, it took the view that the deliberate, planned killing of any human being was indefensible. Such killing had a brutalising effect on society as a whole. It debased those who carried out the execution, those who witnessed it and all those who made up the society which authorised it. As far as the Black Sash was concerned, there was no satisfactory evidence that it was effective as a deterrent and there was always the possibility, however small, of judicial error, which in the case of the death sentence was irreversible. 1988, the fortieth anniversary of the United Nations' adoption of the Universal Declaration of Human Rights, was a year which the Black Sash devoted to a special focus on human rights. During that year it seemed particularly appropriate to reassert that the right to life was the ultimate human right, a right which no other person should be legally empowered to remove.

It also seemed appropriate because by 1988 other individuals and organisations which had not previously paid much attention to the issue of capital punishment were beginning to do so. The fact that South African courts imposed the death sentence more often than any other country laying claim to a 'Western'-style judicial system, that the death penalty was mandatory for murder where a court found that there were no extenuating circumstances, and that those sentenced to death had no automatic right of appeal, might have long been of concern to the Black Sash but hitherto little interest had been shown in the issue by many blacks. As one early member of the Black Sash put it, 'The attitude of most blacks tended to be that if a person had killed, then he or she deserved to be killed also.' Nor was the attitude of the greater part of the coloured or white community startlingly different. The prevailing view was that the death penalty had its place in a society's legal system as the ultimate penalty for those who calculatedly and deliberately took the lives of others.

In 1969 Helen Suzman had called for a Judicial Commission of Inquiry to establish whether or not the abolition of capital punishment was considered desirable, only to meet with the response from the then Minister of Justice that there was negligible public demand for abolition. A Society for the Abolition of the Death Penalty in South Africa had been active during the late 'sixties and early 'seventies under the leadership of the late law professor Barend Van Niekerk, but by 1974 it had become moribund. Various political groups had launched isolated campaigns to save African National Congress guerrillas from the gallows. On the whole, however, the decade leading up to 1988 had seen no widespread opposition to the death penalty.

Yet in that same decade, 1,100 people were hanged in South Africa. In the first seven weeks of 1988 alone 14 people were executed. By May of that year 50 people had reportedly gone to the gallows and 274 were waiting their turn on Death Row. By June, 71 people had been hanged in circumstances that a former Minister of Justice considered 'too gruesome' to reveal in an answer to a parliamentary question. What by 1988 was attracting more widespread attention than previously, however, was not these grisly circumstances but the fact that 53 people being held on Death Row at the end of 1987 had been sentenced for actions arising out of 'politically motivated crimes'. They were people sentenced to death for murders committed during the nationwide political unrest between 1984 and 1986. As Black Sash court monitors knew from close observation, an increasing number of people charged with murder and sentenced to death were men proud to make no secret of their membership of Umkhonto we Sizwe, men whom a substantial body of opinion regarded as freedom fighters, members of an army which, although official white South Africa did not recognise it as such, should be covered by the Geneva convention relating to war crimes.

The Black Sash recognised the need to make it clear that its own oppositon to the death penalty applied in all circumstances, not only to sentences arising out of 'politically motivated' crimes. It determined, however, to use the additional impetus brought on by the increasing political aspects of some of the offences to build up public pressure on the government to appoint a judicial commission of inquiry into the death penalty and declare a moratorium on all hangings until the commission had released its findings. Central to its campaign was the intention to take its own members and the public in general beyond the analytical debate and the clinical abstractions which allowed people not to feel a sense of joint responsibility for what was being done in dark corners in their name. People began to think differently only when they knew what the death penalty meant in practice.

The *Sash* issue following the 1988 national conference was already revealing some of the facts to be faced about the process behind the conveniently detached term 'capital punishment'. It revealed that after sentencing people were put in cells on Death Row to wait for weeks, months and sometimes years for their actual execution. Some people in these circumstances received no visits whatsoever. Some had no knowledge of whether or not any appeal or plea for clemency had been made. Sometimes this ignorance was due to the fact that many condemned prisoners had *pro deo* counsel, whose interest in the case was decidedly limited. Despite the recognition that 'there is no greater terror that can be inflicted on a person than knowing in advance the exact moment of one's death', a condemned prisoner usually received notice of his execution date seven days in advance. A couple of days before actual execution prisoners were taken to be weighed and measured – not, as was sometimes believed by the individuals concerned, in order to determine the size of their coffins but to enable the hangman to fix the noose properly. On the same day their clothes were given to their relatives. During the final and sometimes only visit from relatives, no physical contact was permitted. In South Africa seven people could be hanged simultaneously.

Few other details were known about the actual hangings. Independent visitors were not allowed on to Death Row. Consequently it was difficult to establish exactly what happened there, or even who was there, unless the family of a

condemned person approached a lawyer or some other concerned body, or the lawyer involved with a particular case
was able to elaborate. When in the 'eighties public interest in
the death penalty began to revive, the official provision of the
names of those about to die was stopped until after the
execution had taken place. Information was not released
until after the condemned person had been hanged, unless
the newspapers or Churches were informed by concerned
relatives. According to Beverley Runciman, chairperson of
the Cape Western region of the Black Sash, it was an effective
strategem. The fact that information only found its way into
the outside world by such means meant that the issue rather
disappeared from public consciousness.

Nevertheless, by February 1989, the Black Sash had managed to put together and publish a substantial research paper
entitled 'Inside South Africa's Death Factory', a title deriving
from a comparison drawn by Brian Currin, a member of
Lawyers for Human Rights, between Pretoria's Death Row
and the factory process and one which would be used again
for a television programme, subsequently broadcast in England, in which Sheena Duncan took part. 'Death Row,' Brian
Currin had said, 'is like a factory. I find the whole place has
been brutalised, dehumanised. It is a factory which produces
corpses. You know, you go in live and come out dead. To
produce that product a system is developed. The whole place
is serviced. They provide food. They make gardens. They give
notice of execution. They hang. And they bury.'

The research paper provided the statistics which placed
South Africa, despite its relatively small population of 27
million, among the world leaders as far as executions were
concerned. 'South Africa hanged 117 people last year,' it
announced; 76 were Africans, 38 were coloured and 3 were
whites ... These figures do not include executions in the
'independent homelands' – there are gallows at Rooigrond,
Bophutatswana; Middeldrift, Ciskei; Wellington, Transkei,
and Venda. The only known figures are the 94 people who
were hanged in the years 1980 to 1986.' The document also
included profiles of the people behind the statistics, case
histories of some of those executed and details of what the

process of hanging entailed. It reproduced an article from the Chris Barnard column printed originally in the *Rand Daily Mail* on 12 June 1978:

> Put a rope round a man's neck, tie the knot next to his ear, fasten his wrists behind his back and drop him a distance of just less than two metres.
> If you haven't botched it by miscalculating the length of the drop or the strength of the rope you'll achieve several things at once. The man's spinal cord will rupture at the point where it enters the skull, electrochemical discharges will send his limbs flailing in a grotesque dance, eyes and tongue will start from the facial apertures under the assault of the rope and his bowels and bladder may simultaneously void themselves to soil the legs and drip onto the floor – unless of course you are an efficient hangman who has thoughtfully fitted your subject with a nappy or rubber pants.

Armed with hard statistics and with the gruesome insights that, amongst others, a retired executioner could offer, the Black Sash encouraged its members to assist with the relaunch of the Society for the Abolition of the Death Penalty in South Africa. In 1988 the Black Sash had already embarked on its own campaign for the aboliton of capital punishment by stimulating public debate around the death sentence, considering the choice of this topic whenever members were invited to speak publicly, writing articles to the press and making use of media opportunities, bearing in mind always that in countries where drives to abolish the death penalty had been abolished the weight of public opinion had actually been in favour of retention. Where aboliton had occurred, the scales had been tipped by influential opinion-formers and political representatives. Its campaign would therefore be directed primarily at such people. The Black Sash asked the PFP to use one of its two private members' motions in the next parliamentary session to call for a Judicial Commission of Inquiry into Capital Punishment. On a very practical level, it asked lawyers throughout the country to notify the relatives of those condemned to death that the Churches could help to get them to Pretoria for visits if they could not afford the expense of the journey.

In 1989, with the revival of public interest arising out of the imposition of the death sentence for 'politically motivated' crimes, the Society for the Abolition of the Death Penalty in South Africa, which had petered out in 1974, was relaunched. In the Cape Western region the Black Sash Capital Punishment Interest Group took on practical chores associated with the relaunch, such as printing pamphlets and posters and arranging some aspects of the public meeting. It was not, however, a case of the Black Sash discontinuing its own campaign. The two were complementary, overlapping and mutually supportive. Subsequent to the relaunch, individual members of the Black Sash served on the regional committee of the Society. The national executive of the SADPSA included as its honorary secretary Beverley Runciman, the Black Sash Regional Chair for the Western Cape, and among its celebrated patrons was Sheena Duncan.

Individuals had always brought to the Black Sash their personal connections, for often Black Sash members were active members of other organisations. Beyond Sheena Duncan's strong personality, gift of eloquence and extensive knowledge of racist South African laws, acquired through more than two decades of voluntary work in the Johannesburg advice office, lay an enormously compassionate heart and a profound Christian faith. Sheena Duncan saw her political activity as a direct response to her belief in the love of God. She had served on the provincial synod. She had been chairman of the Johannesburg Diocesan Challenge Group, a diocesan programme for human relations, and active in the South African Council of Churches. Indeed, in July 1987 she had become its vice-president at a time when Bishop Manus Buthelezi was president and the Reverend Frank Chikane succeeded Dr Beyers Naude as general secretary. She had thus contributed in a powerful way to the link between the Black Sash and the Churches. At its most basic level that link was strengthened by the fact that in Johannesburg the advice office shared the same building as the SACC offices, which meant that visiting Church groups could be simultaneously introduced to the realities of the queues of black people seeking help. There were many in the Black Sash who were active in their respective Churches and there were many Churchmen who appreciated that fact.

'I am proud,' Archbishop Desmond Tutu told me in 1989 'that some of the leading lights of the Black Sash are members of my Church – Sheena Duncan, Di Bishop, Mary Burton – though I don't want to sound chauvinistic because there are many people of other faiths who are also in the Black Sash.' He spoke of their courage as white women willing to be vulnerable, of the passion of their commitment to human rights, of the way in which they had given a sense of dignity to people who thought they did not count. He also spoke of their astuteness: 'They have taught many of us quite a few lessons in thoroughness of preparation, in strategising, in having your facts straight.' Sheena Duncan had had a very important impact on the life and witness of the Church. She had been 'listened to very, very carefully'. Durban's Roman Catholic Archbishop, Denis Hurley was no less warm in his praise. The Black Sash had assembled together 'very impressive women of deep conviction and great dedication, of great breadth of view, very liberal, very humane, very human and many of them deeply religious'. For that reason he admired them very much. In March 1986, on the opening night of the Black Sash national conference in Durban, Archbishop Hurley and Dr Beyers Naude both formally became honorary members of the Black Sash.

Similarly, the fact that many Black Sash members were themselves involved in education as teachers at school or university level had meant that since the time when the organisation had first protested against the Bantu Education Act of 1953 a continuing interest in education and the enormous ramifications of manipulating ideology through the control of education had been sustained – although not perhaps to the extent to which, in the light of how many Black Sash members held academic and teaching posts, the potential lobby might suggest. When Judith Hawarden, chair-person for the Transvaal region, joined the Black Sash in the late 'seventies, it was only natural that as someone who worked with black students at the University of the Witwa-tersrand in her capacity as Assistant Director of the Aca-demic Support Programme, her 'portfolio' should become education. In the years from 1983 onwards there was a visible crisis in black education. The matriculation results for 1983 were appalling. Only 48.1 per cent of students passed, a fact which led parents, students and community leaders to agree that the standard of education, never good, had seriously deteriorated and a crisis situation had developed.

Early in 1984 a private working group of educationists from different organisations in Soweto concluded that problems arose fundamentally from inequality in education, from the fact, for example, that at that time seven times more was being spent on a white child than on a black child per year, that pupil–teacher ratios were 43:1 in black schools and 18:1 in white schools, that 73 per cent of teachers in black schools were unqualified. Shortly after schools opened in 1984, pupils at a school in Atteridgeville near Pretoria refused to attend classes unless ninety students were readmitted. Five other schools in the area joined in the boycott. At the same time the transfer of Matthew Goniwe to Graaff-Reinet occasioned the boycott in the Eastern Cape. Age-limit restrictions caused pupils at a school in Soweto to be expelled, giving rise to other boycotts. Shortly afterwards, boycotts began in Alex-andra Township and Tembisa. By the beginning of April, according to the South African Institute of Race Relations, 13,107 pupils at twenty-four schools were boycotting classes. Police action and violent confrontation inevitably followed. Children were shot and detained. Schools were burned down. By October, 220,000 pupils were boycotting classes and lectures countrywide. No real teaching was taking place and the prevailing philosophy among black pupils became 'liber-ation now; education later'.

Shortly after September 1984, Judith Hawarden and a group of other Black Sash members went to Sharpeville and spoke separately to groups of children, parents and teachers. The distrust between teachers and pupils was so great that it was impossible to induce either side to talk in front of the other. The teachers of Afrikaans were terrified. They must keep their jobs because they had to earn a living, but for doing so, they were seen by their pupils as 'sell-outs', part of the system of oppression. In a highly volatile situation the Black Sash discovered a role for itself of providing support when it was called for and, once again, of gathering and disseminating information. The paper which Judith Hawarden prepared each year for the national conference found its way into the press. Embassy people and other visitors from abroad were made aware of the realities of the educational situation, which did not always tally with the messages of improvement which the government was spreading. The fact was exposed that, whilst the number of black pupils passing their matriculation had subsequently increased, the quality of that matriculation made such an apparent improvement meaningless.

Another of the Black Sash's objectives was to provide a supportive and informative environment in which members could talk about their current anxieties and their apprehensions with regard to the future, and learn more about specific subjects. Education was one such subject. Education was also an area in which members simply as parents could bring pressure to bear. In the Western Cape Sue Philcox, active in the field of education as much, if not more in her capacity as a member of EDASA (Education for an Aware South Africa) as in her capacity as a Black Sash member, pointed to the fact that in the mid-'eighties education interest groups had been formed, although poorly supported, mainly because full-time teachers simply could not afford to give the time necessary to real involvement. So much in relation to the future of South Africa hinged upon bringing together children of all races into the same schools at pre-primary level, and Black Sash members in their capacity as responsible white parents could have some influence on white education and the process of indoctrinating ideas of white supremacy: 'We keep on reminding Sash parents that they can actually work on school committees, in PTAs, influence their schools, push and direct,' said Sue Philcox. A statement from the 1988 national conference urged Black Sash members to involve themselves actively in schools, universities and colleges, in parent–teacher associations, school boards, school committees and university councils. It also suggested that they support progressive teachers. On the whole, however, it came down to the implementation of individual principles. Some individuals responded but not, again, always as unambivalently as the organisation might have hoped. Even Black Sash mothers faced with the possibility that, in the first instance at least their own child's education might suffer, tended to abandon their political ideals.

The Black Sash's commitment to self-education had meant that from the very earliest days leading South Africans had been invited to address the organisation's members. Relationships had developed with people like Alan Paton, author of *Cry the Beloved Country*, against whose banning the Black Sash had protested; with Raymond Louw, editor of the *Rand Daily Mail* from 1966 to 1977, who 'held high the torch of Press freedom at a time when the English press, and particularly the *Rand Daily Mail* was under constant threat from the government'; and with a multitude of others. Black Sash national presidents and other members had travelled abroad both to spread the word about conditions in South Africa and to learn from the experience of other countries. In the autumn of 1983, on a trip to Britain in response to an invitation to a YWCA Conference on Human Rights and to Holland for a programme organised by a women's church organisation, Sheena Duncan made twenty-nine speeches and took part in twenty-one interviews, four radio and two television broadcasts in the space of twenty days. In June 1984 the Swedish government invited her as national president of the Black Sash to visit Sweden in order to inform their Foreign Affairs Ministry on recent developments in apartheid legislation. From mid-March to mid-April 1989 her successor, Mary Burton, travelled to the United States on a visit with the theme of 'Pluralism in the USA' organised by the United States Information Service.

In 1989 the first official delegation of eight Black Sash

members attended a conference with the ANC in Lusaka at the invitation of the Five Freedoms Forum, to the creation of which Sheena Duncan had energetically contributed. The central goal of the Forum was to harness the resources of the organisations concerned in a series of on-going campaigns to assist whites in South Africa to become part of the transition to a democratic, non-racial society. The range of member organisations – which included the Johannesburg Democratic Action Committee, the Detainees' Parents Support Committee, the Detainees' Support Committee, Jews for Social Justice, the National Union of South African Students, the Young Christian Students, the Justice and Peace Commission of the Catholic Church, the Academic Staff Association of the University of the Witwatersrand, Women for Peace and the Progressive Federal Party – gives some intimation of the scope in South Africa for joint action and involvement.

Inevitably the question of funding created another complication in Black Sash relationships. When in 1974 the Fund-Raising Act was passed the Black Sash opted not to seek registration as a fund-raising organisation because of the offical scrutiny such registration entailed, which meant that it was not able to obtain money from the South African public. Prior to that it had had a list of donors, many of whom were husbands of members and/or leaders in the business community, who could be depended upon to provide contributions of between ten and a hundred Rand a year. When the Fund-Raising Act was passed a new category of membership, that of associate members, was established, which entitled men to the privilege of continuing to give the Black Sash money. They were allowed to attend certain meetings. They were allowed to speak at meetings, but they were not allowed to vote. In effect they were granted taxation without representation. Not surprisingly perhaps, not many donors elected to become associate members. Even husbands who were willing quietly to contribute were often reluctant to become formally associated. The Black Sash was consequently thrown back entirely on its own membership for fund-raising.

It was when the need actually to employ people arose – to

work, for example, in the rural areas of the Transvaal – that the organisation started having to look further afield for possible sources of finance. Although money could not be taken from the public there were certain bodies whom practice more than anything else defined as not being 'the public', among them trust foundations and embassies. An 'Advice Office Trust Fund' was set up, which would administer all the money which came into the Black Sash. The regions continued to raise money for their own administration through membership subscriptions and morning markets; bazaars; sales of cakes, books and rummage; and other similar events. By 1989, however, the Black Sash employed just under forty people throughout the country, and in the process of making a difficult transition from being an entirely voluntary body to one facing up to the need for paid and professional service, found itself administering an annual budget of close to a million Rand.

The fact that many anti-apartheid organisations suspected of being part of the revolutionary programme in South Africa were financially supported from overseas, that countries such as Sweden, Norway, Denmark and the Netherlands were known to have a direct input to the ANC, meant that the sources of such funding were of interest to South Africa's security police. In the case of the Black Sash some of the money came from foreign embassies (principally British, American, French and Spanish), from the Ford Foundation and from one or two other big international foundations. There were those within the Black Sash who were ill at ease with the idea of the greater portion of the funding coming from abroad through embassies and foreign foundations, those who felt it shameful that it was necessary to look to organisations outside South Africa to fund the work, and others who were unhappy about the Black Sash taking, for instance, 'American money' when the same money was being used to finance UNITA in Angola and various other CIA projects.

Offset against this standpoint was the harsh reality that without foreign funding the scope of Black Sash work would be substantially reduced, and the view that there was in any case no such thing as 'clean money', that the organisation should not become too ensnared in other ideological issues provided it was satisfied that the money was being given for the purposes for which the Black Sash was using it and that there were no unacceptable strings attached to it. Some of their funders were, Mary Burton acknowledged, among the organisation's most important partners, especially where work was undertaken on a contract basis in which the money was supplied in exchange for Black Sash expertise, personnel and administration. The external balance was good for the Black Sash in that it challenged members to define the value of their work. The question of from whom the Black Sash would or would not take money remained, however, a subject for debate in which the question of independence to maintain its integrity was paramount. 'I have never come across a situation in Sash,' Jill Nicholson, one of the organisation's trustees, stressed, 'where we've been asked to do anything particular or say anything particular by our funders, and I certainly think we would drop them immediately if that kind of pressure was put on us.'

Bearing in mind the professed desire to ensure this integrity, relationships, both national and international, had thus been established at all kinds of levels. On my visits there, one of the greatest tragedies of South African society seemed to me that all relationships, even the most personal, apparently contained the embryo of some 'hidden agenda' and consequently the potential for all the suspicion and inhibition that went with it. Black Sash members were by no means exempt from such realities. Far from being blithely carried along by individuals' enthusiasm for shared causes – as, more and more, the Black Sash's resources and energy were being directed towards joint campaigns with other organisations in the belief that the pooling of strength with others who shared their ideals would result in an overall effort greater than the sum of the parts – the Black Sash picked its way through the minefield of potential alliances with a degree of cautious self-examination which gave rise to complaints from its own members that the organisation was indulging in too much 'navel-gazing'.

By the time, in 1987, the issue of affiliation arose in connection with the Five Freedoms Forum, the Black Sash seemed to be clearer, at least in its own mind, with regard to what its stance should be: the Black Sash should always retain its identity, joint work should be directed towards a clear objective and be consistent with its aims and methods. After long discussions, the Five Freedoms Forum came up with the concept of subscribing organisations. Individual organisations would subscribe to the aims and objects of the Forum, and if they no longer felt happy with them they would simple cease to subscribe. It was an arrangement which did not involve the dramatic submission of a letter of resignation, and was felt to work quite well.

With the Black Sash itself the capacity to encompass diversity of opinion was believed to be part of the organisation's strength. Differences were always, according to Sheena Duncan, 'handled in a very good process of open debate'. The 'great affiliation debate' thus continued, and in the course of it the question would inevitably continue to arise as to how far failure to affiliate would be regarded by other organisations involved in the liberation struggle as an indecisive 'cop-out', a lack of commitment and a reluctance on the part of the Black Sash to accept its share of the risks as well as the benefits of participation. The organisation had to consider how far to be influenced by these and other potential criticisms.

Chapter 10

Women organise

The question of affiliation became particularly pressing in relation to the relaunch of the Federation of South African Women (FEDSAW). The Federation of South African Women had never actually been banned. In the nine years following its formation in 1954 it had not only been the inspiration behind the largest mass gathering of women in South Africa's history to protest against the pass laws, it had also provided a platform from which women could assert their rights, challenge the pervasive patriarchy of the time and exercise their leadership so that they could 'march side by side with men on the road to freedom'. Although by its own admission, under the pressure of the requirements of the general struggle, it had not directed as much energy as it might otherwise have done into furthering women's rights, in its nine years of political activism it had held several national conferences, campaigned vigorously against the pass laws and drawn up a women's charter. It had then been decimated by state repression. With the detention, banning and house arrest of its leaders – women like Hilda Bernstein, who was also a member of the Communist Party; Ruth Mompati, who was active in the Women's League of the ANC before it was banned and who would subsequently become a member of the ANC's National Executive; and Helen Joseph, who became the first person in South Africa to be house-arrested – it had simply ceased to function. By 1987, however, plans were afoot to revive its still-glowing embers, and the Black Sash had been invited to take part in the process.

Although about 90 per cent of the women at the original 1954 launching conference were black, the Federation had always been eager to include white women. Membership was not, however, open to individuals. Women could only be members if they belonged to affiliated organisations, and in the 'fifties most organisations with white women members had been either apolitical or conservative and had been alienated by FEDSAW's links with the liberation movement and its opposition to white minority rule. The Black Sash vision of women's issues in those early years had hardly been one which saw them as necessarily integrated with the anti-apartheid struggle. Its approach had been rather in the vein of an article by Mrs Franklin D. Roosevelt entitled 'What women can achieve', which appeared in *Sash* magazine in May 1958: 'I think we as women must try to give women more confidence, to give them the feeling of the value of the work that they do.' The Black Sash had kept its distance from FEDSAW, nervous of an unduly close association with the political composition of its membership.

There was, therefore, a certain irony in the fact that when, as an aftermath to the 1976 Soweto riots, another women's organisation entitled Women for Peace was formed, representing another broad-based attempt to unite women across the entire political and colour spectrum, this time in the common cause of working for peace, the Black Sash found itself viewed with suspicion because of its political image. Although the two organisations were ostensibly working for the same end, and although the Black Sash had never been party-political, Joyce Harris (who in her private capacity occupied a position on the Executive Committee of Women for Peace) was reduced to resigning from it because of divided loyalties: 'There was suspicion of the so-called militancy of the Black Sash and of its political image, which saddened me, particularly at a time when it was essential for women to use their power politically.'

This 'militant' image of the Black Sash would continue to alienate it from a number of other women's organisations and societies. When in 1975 an exhibition involving forty-six women's societies was due to be held in Cape Town's Drill Hall to celebrate International Women's Year, the Black Sash was 'black-balled' because of its political associations. The

Black Sash exhibit would have consisted of a display of 'coloured housing, work that the organisation did and literature', but only one of the societies present at a preliminary meeting was prepared to support its inclusion. Its exclusion drew strong protest from the Cape Western Secretary of the Black Sash, who informed the *Cape Times* in no uncertain terms that 'it was a pity the only activities in which women in Cape Town appeared to be participating were needlework, cake-making and preserving'. Local feminists attacked the exhibition for its 'glorification of how society pretends women should be; pointing out that only a minority of women could now afford to spend time arranging flowers, baking cakes, keeping themselves beautiful, doing charity work and taking no part in politics. Nevertheless, the exclusion of the Black Sash was upheld on the grounds that its members were politically orientated and known as 'women standing with posters'.

The perception of the Black Sash within the Afrikaner-instigated women's organisation Kontak, according to Marietjie Myburgh, who before becoming a member of the Black Sash was a founder member of Kontak in East London, was once again one of militant women, marching or standing with posters. Kontak was an organisation started just before the 1976 uprising by a group of Afrikaans women who had realised that the only contact the average middle-class white woman had with people of other race groups was based on a madam-servant relationship, and who had endeavoured to bring women of different races together on a social basis for regular meetings and so break down some of the barriers between them. In a way, Marietjie Myburgh intimated, Kontak was drawing on the same constituency as Women for Peace, except that it was initiated by Afrikaner women. There was a feeling in Cape Town that Kontak directed its energies towards building links with the coloured community and tended to disregard blacks, but in some of the smaller, very conservative towns in South Africa Kontak itself was regarded as liberal and had to face problems of harassment. As far as Kontak was concerned, the Black Sash was an organisation for radical activists.

Part of the problem, Marietjie Myburgh would later acknowledge, was the ignorance born of lack of communication. Very few of her Afrikaner friends knew what the Black Sash really did: 'There is more prejudice among Afrikaans people against the Black Sash than others, although I think there is a problem even among English women. They are perceived as being radical activists and the Afrikaners specifically see them as Communist activists and the organisation definitely not as something you join.' One friend of hers was convinced that the Black Sash was a banned organisation. Others had a vague idea of women standing with placards and marching. Very few she encountered in East London knew about the work that was done in the advice offices. The solution must lie with greater contact between women across the community divides.

Contact between the Black Sash and FEDSAW had remained 'cordial' over the years and as, in 1987, meetings of various women's groups began to be organised with a view to a public re-launch of FEDSAW, the Black Sash, without making any membership commitment, became part of exploratory discussions.

A draft constitution outlined the aims and objectives of the revived Federation:

> We, the women of South Africa, recognise that we are racially oppressed, sexually discriminated against and economically exploited, and that apartheid holds us in chains. We therefore undertake to work towards the dismantling of apartheid and work towards establishing a non-racial, united, democratic South Africa. We further adopt the following aims and objectives:
> (a) (i) To bring the women of South Africa together to secure full equality of opportunity of all women, regardless of race, colour or creed.
> (ii) To remove social and legal discrimination and economic exploitation.
> (iii) To work for the protection and empowerment of the women and children of our land.
> (b) The Federation shall stand for:

(i) The removal of legal discrimination and the changing of laws and customs that deny women full equality.

(ii) Equal pay for equal work and equal opportunities for employment; the right of workers to belong to a trade union of their choice.

(iii) Better living conditions, including proper homes.

(iv) Compulsory free, non-racial and democratic education.

(v) Clinics and hospitals, maternity services, paid maternity leave and confinement allowances and child-care facilities for all working women.

(vi) The promotion of shared parenthood rather than just motherhood.

(vii) The right of all women to be free of the threat of rape, incest, sexual harassment and other forms of sexual abuse and wife-battering.

(viii) Democratic rights for women: the right to vote, to be elected to and fully participate in all political structures.

(ix) Cooperation with other organisations with similar aims in South Africa and throughout the world.

None of these avowed objectives, it may be imagined, would appear unduly controversial to the Black Sash. There were those outside the organisation who could understand why the Black Sash might not affiliate to the UDF, which was manifestly involved in radical politics, but who could see no reason why it should not affiliate as a women's organisation to FEDSAW and its programme based on a Women's Charter.

The concern with women's issues, the recognition of the need to secure women's rights, was in fact a growing consideration within the Black Sash. Quite apart from the subordination of women's rights to the more urgent struggle for racial equality, there had hitherto been other inhibiting influences on the concern with women's issues. Black women undoubtedly occupied one of the lowest rungs on

South Africa's social ladder. Until 1988, the law considered married African women as minors under the tutelage of their husbands. A wife could not own property in her own right, except for her clothing and a few personal possessions, and if she earned money or in any way acquired property this automatically became the property of her husband. She was also unable to make valid contracts without her husband's consent. The Black Sash experience by 1989 was still that when training programmes were set up for black communities to start their own advice offices there was a strong tendency not to send women for the courses. Black men had constantly to be reminded that women made up half the population, that they made good advice office workers and tended to remain in the job for much longer than their male counterparts.

Yet many black South African women themselves had for a long time felt that feminism was a concept alien to African traditions. Feminism was frequently dismissed as a white, Western, bourgeois movement, thus making it very difficult to take root in a country where progressive people tended to be preoccupied with the anti-apartheid struggle. There had also been a feeling among black women, which prevailed even during the years 1975–85 declared by the United Nations a 'Decade of Women', that the time was not yet right to challenge their menfolk with a form of feminism which appeared then to pose a threat to accepted ideas of masculinity. As one black woman would put it, 'The way our men have been emasculated by the pass laws – how can we add to their burden by challenging them on this?' Even the white female membership of the Black Sash in its struggle to focus on political issues, and what was at times inclined to be a knee-jerk response to more pressing needs, had not really grappled with women's issues in the way that it might otherwise have done.

By 1987, however, as reform and liberation and even a post-apartheid South Africa seemed to become less distant abstractions and more of an impending reality, there was increasing recognition among South Africa's women that discrimination and oppression must be resisted from whatever quarter they came, and no matter who the victims might be. The awareness was growing that liberation from colonial rule in other parts of Africa had not led to the emancipation of women. Instead, women had continued to bear the brunt of poverty and exploitation. They had continued to be denied justice and an equal right to participate in decision-making. The example of Zimbabwe was readily to hand. There, the active involvement of women in the guerrilla army had led to much talk of women having their full place in a new society, but female expectations had remained largely unfulfilled.

Influences from beyond the boundaries of South Africa had contributed to the renewed interest in seeking opportunities for women to organise themselves to work together towards common objectives. The effect of feminist pressures in the Western world, the growing knowledge of the role of women in development, especially in 'Third World' countries, the Decade of Women and the Nairobi conference held to mark the end of that decade had all had their role to play in influencing attitudes of and towards women. At the same time, inside South Africa recent history had contributed to a greater recognition of the part played by women in shaping society. As Mary Burton, who represented the Black Sash in the exploratory talks towards the revival of FEDSAW, wrote in the August 1987 *Sash* magazine:

> The strength of women's resistance to the pass laws is already legend; the lives of the mothers of the Soweto 1976 generation were irreversibly altered by that experience and loss. The examples of women like Ellen Khuzwayo (more popularly known as the 'Mother of Soweto' and author of *Call me Woman*) and Molly Blackburn, and many others, have given hope and a sense of purpose to thousands. Perhaps even more important than well-known role models have been the uncounted and countless community women who have formed part of the swelling river of resistance flowing through the country in reaction to the tri-cameral parliament. Women have participated in the formation and proliferation of civic associations and have played

an important part in mobilising and politicising their communities.

African women who, together with children and old people, had been referred to as 'superfluous appendages' by G. Froneman, a prominent Nationalist member of parliament who later became Deputy Minister of Justice, Mines and Planning, had eked out a pitiful living for themselves, their children and their elderly relatives from the infertile earth of the homelands when the money stopped coming from their husbands in the distant cities. Women had also been militant and innovative, and they had suffered for it. They had been restricted, detained and exiled. They had kept their families going while their men were treated in a similar fashion. They had seen their children suffer. Women had felt the effects of the States of Emergency deeply, at a time when violent conflict in the townships and turmoil in the schools were conditions of living from which no family was exempt. The famous declaration of Lilian Ngoyi, an early president of the Federation of South African Women, 'My womb is shaken when they speak of Bantu Education', had encapsulated the experience of many. And all this had given rise to a sense of urgency to unite women on the strength of the fact that their identity as women would provide them with a common bond to help transcend the many barriers and divisions that prevailed in South Africa.

The Black Sash was by no means untouched by the birth of feminism, any more than it was by other widespread social phenomena. During the rigours of the two States of Emergency in the 'eighties, which increased membership by some 500 to approximately 2,500 throughout South Africa, many people joined in a state of infuriation that because of the clamp down on the press and other media they were not hearing the full truth of what was happening. They joined out of a need for information and to become politically educated. It was not only that more recent membership tended to be made up of working women, a fact which in itself had required difficult adjustments for the organisation in terms of availability of time and energy, and which some by 1989 still felt had not been satisfactorily resolved. It also tended to be younger.

By the mid 'eighties, although the Black Sash was still not an organisation which appealed to those of student age, the average age of Sash members was considerably younger than it had been in the early years. It included single parents and divorcees. It still tended to consist on the whole of English-speaking liberals with some very real exceptions drawn from a traditionally conservative constituency. Often new members were not highly politicised individuals but rather people with a gut feeling about what was right and what was wrong, but they joined not, as had frequently been the case in the past, to indicate their moral support, receive the magazine and be better informed, but actually in order to be politically active, a fact which again was a source of new challenges for the Black Sash. To varying extents they were comfortable with the fact that other opposition organisations with whom they strove to maintain contact increasingly articulated the beliefs of the banned ANC. Some were very much at home with the language of the class war. Some were women undeterred by the negative connotations with which the word feminism had come to be imbued, by its association with the rejection of a whole set of values which many women found important: primarily the rejection of the traditional family structure. There was a small and quite vocal feminist grouping in all regions of the Black Sash. There were lesbians who found in the Black Sash one of the few homes available for people with lesbian political positions in a country where opposition organisations were politically directed against racialism. The Black Sash provided them with a means of entering mainline opposition and a platform which far exceeded its numerical size.

Jenny De Tolly, a graduate in architecture who joined the Black Sash in 1981 after eleven years spent in Toronto, and who in 1990 would succeed Mary Burton as national president of the Black Sash, was adamant that what one outsider had described as the 'influx of radical lesbians' had not posed a problem for the organisation. There were groupings in the

Black Sash who formed internal cliques but they had 'absolutely no effect on the work of the Sash'. The only real threats to the organisation were ones which allowed groupings which did not really represent a broadly canvassed opinion to take precedence. The guarantee against such an eventuality was the fact, that, whenever major issues arose, and affiliation was one such issue, every effort was made to 'go as deep down to grassroots as we can'. Groupings could only then become power groups if they had real supports. Lesbians, feminists and others might well try to affect the direction of the Black Sash, and if they had enough support the organisation could well change direction in the future just as it had undoubtedly changed direction in the past. As another member would point out, however, it was doubtful that the Black Sash would ever become a specifically feminist organisation because the transition would involve a fundamental change of ethos from fighting for other's rights to fighting for their own. In any case, groupings who brought a new perspective to the Black Sash debates were welcomed as valuable: 'What I have found very exhilarating is that they have come with different perceptions of life and how life should be made, which, given that we're moving into looking at very different models of family structures and all that kind of thing has been a tremendous challenge.'

As Karin Chubb stated in her 1989 national conference paper, working with FEDSAW would lend impetus to those challenges. Inevitably, the kind of experience opened up through association with a mass-based women's movement would confront Black Sash members with a different social reality. It would demonstrate in a very concrete way that, despite common areas of concern, the differences of starting point between, for example, a white Black Sash member staunchly opposed to the militarism of the apartheid society making a public stand against compulsory conscription, and a black mother who, whilst she might appreciate the stand taken by objectors, none the less felt obliged to support her own children's decision to joined the armed struggle, viewing them as patriots and heroes, were very real. More subtly, however, this issue would also challenge the Black Sash to an understanding of a new kind of feminism which was not so much in the liberal tradition which went back to the suffragette struggles; this brand of feminism had been reflected in a Charter for Women which in 1971 the Black Sash had itself circulated to all organisations and political parties. That Charter had confined its concern almost exclusively to the private sphere of women's existence, although the wider implications were implicitly there:

> Every woman has the right to choose her marriage partner.
> Every woman has the right to live with her husband throughout her married life.
> Every woman has the right to live with her children, to protect them and care for them.
> Every woman has the right to free education for her children.
> Every woman has the right to work, to the free choice of employment and to just and favourable conditions of work.
> Every woman has the right to live out her declining years with those who wish to care for her.
> Every woman has the right to these fundamental rights and freedoms, which shall not be violated by law or administrative action.

The Charter reflected the kind of feminism which some saw as failing sufficiently to challenge 'the exploitative aspects of the economic system within which it demands equal rights', rather than an inclusive type of feminism which linked women's issues with other political questions and concerns.

The fact that, in the guiding principles of the Federation of South African Women, the liberation of women from all forms of oppression was seen as an integral part of the transformation of South African society, and not as something to be addressed only in a post-apartheid South Africa, was significant. Karin Chubb, who served as a Black Sash representative with observer status to the Federation in the

Western Cape, saw as inherent in those principles a 'commit-ment to women's issues which can in due course serve as the basis for a common consciousness across the divisions of class and race'. She was an advocate of the type of feminism that derived from the socialist model, which she saw as the most inclusive in that it did not separate women's issues from other political concerns: 'Socialist feminism rejects the distinction between public and private spheres of existence, it aims to end not only women's oppression but all forms of exploitation, thus furthering the possibility of alliances with other groups engaged in combating varied forms of exploitation.'

Despite the intermittent raising of the question of male membership, the Black Sash had staunchly reserved full membership for women. There were still those who felt that the distinctive female nature and atmosphere of the organis-ation was something which should be preserved and that there was something particularly adamantine about female resistance and protest. 'Strike the woman, you strike a rock', the wording on one Black Sash poster commemorating Women's Day on 9 August 1987 had proclaimed. Archbishop Hurley, one of the organisation's appreciative honorary male members, had a rather softer vision of Black Sash ladies. He professed his admiration for what he saw as 'all the warmth and tenderness and sensitivity of women, so different some-times from pure theory that men like to elaborate'. There were people in and outside the Black Sash who felt that both the more pragmatic and the more sensitive qualities of its women should be cherished. There were also those within the Black Sash who, in an uncharacteristic display of insecur-ity, expressed the fear that if men were allowed to join they would take over the leadership of the organisation and, perhaps most significantly of all, those who felt that as women, they had space in which to function that was denied to men. At the same time, there were also those who felt that such a stance was in itself sexist, who were uneasy with a policy of accepting masculine support in all kinds of ways and yet denying men full membership.

Many women still experienced conflict in the home

because of their election to join the Black Sash. Some were dissuaded from joining in the first place; others were reduced to leaving. Some on the other hand were given very selfless support. Husbands of active Black Sash members were required at the very least to forego much of their wives' time and energy. Some gave positive practical assistance in the form of bailing their wives out, assisting with the production of posters, even, in one instance, purchasing the chain with which his wife could chain herself to the railings of parliament in Cape Town. Others, like Johann Myburgh, the minister in the Dutch Reformed Church who had lost his congregation because of his wife's involvement in the Black Sash but who still did not ask her to abandon the organisation, made enormous personal sacrifices and felt exasperated that they were excluded from some meetings and the right to vote. It was in any case doubtful that if the Black Sash did open its doors to men they would come flocking in large numbers to join, but hard that the dedicated few should be excluded should they actually wish to become full members. Nevertheless, the long-standing policy of female exclusivity prevailed.

As more Black Sash members began to explore the question of women's oppression and women's issues, it was perhaps inevitable that questions should arise in relation to the identity of a movement which, though consisting of women, was not really a women's movement as such. The challenge which Karin Chubb saw involvement with FEDSAW presenting to the Black Sash was that of using its considerable resources to educate both its own members and others about the role which women could play in the process of social transformation. 'The contribution which we could make now will contribute to the sort of future which we would like to see in this country,' she wrote in May 1989. 'As women we still have the space to do this – as long as we are prepared to engage in a process of self-education and remain open to change.' Gender oppression cut across lines of class and race and might prove to be more difficult to eradicate than class or race oppression. A broad tendency had been discerned by other Black Sash members during visits to Lusaka for ANC leaders to subscribe to the view that women should concern themselves with 'women's issues' – with the welfare of children, the problems of rape and other similar matters – while the men would deal with the broad political issues relating to a future South Africa. There was a feeling abroad that some women's organisations in South Africa were falling into the trap of not being involved in the 'macro issues'. By putting women's role firmly on the agenda of the liberation movement now, Karin Chubb felt, women could help to ensure the recognition and protection of their rights and freedom in a future South Africa.

It was not this challenge from which the Black Sash shied away. Yet once again it resisted affiliation, resolving instead to welcome the initiative to revive FEDSAW, encourage all regions and members to take an active part in seeking and strengthening contact with it and work in close association with it on projects and campaigns so that the 'process of building trust and friendship might become a reality in practice as well as in principle'. The Black Sash would also make it a concern to draw other women's organisations into the experience. When, in August 1987, the Cape Region of the Federation of South African Women was launched, a Black Sash representative expressed the organisation's support for the event in the distinctive language of the liberation struggle: 'We salute the women who have carried on the struggle in the past and salute the New Regional President and Vice-President. We wish FEDSAW long life and success in the struggle ahead and may we work together for the good of all women in our country. Viva FEDSAW.'

Nevertheless, notes circulated to Black Sash members as a starting point for discussion as to whether the Black Sash should change its constitution to allow affiliation with FEDSAW, and hence with other organisations who would be likely to request that the Black Sash affiliate once a precedent had been set, reflected longstanding concerns about the room which affiliation would or would not leave for later dissent on strategy or policy, about what autonomy/identity could be retained and the manner in which it would be possible to establish and maintain accountability and democratic procedure. If an organisation or federation to which the Black Sash was affiliated were convicted of a criminal or illegal activity, what would the Black Sash's liability be? Would the state be able to move against the Black Sash on the strength of its affiliations? Would affiliation involve alignments on one or other side of any of the 'great divides' in the black community, thereby 'legitimising' one faction or division at the expense of other legitimate factions or divisions? Should the Black Sash remain non-aligned in order to keep the middle-ground open so that it did not disappear? Was the Black Sash being pressurised to align with one of two poles (African nationalism and Afrikaner nationalism) in South African society, as though these were the only alternatives? Did the failute to affiliate, in any case, really imply a lack of commitment?

The great affiliation debate which was to be seriously considered at 'grassroots level' encompassed many questions, but ultimately, according to Sheena Duncan, the decision not to affiliate with FEDSAW rested upon Black Sash determination not to align itself with one particular political grouping. The FEDSAW leadership was articulating the policies of the ANC, and, whilst there were members of the Black Sash who had no qualms about calling themselves ANC, as an organisation, the Black Sash was beginning to envisage a time when the need might arise to be in a position, if necessary, to make its stand for human rights in relation to an ANC government.

12 November 1988 saw the first annual general meeting of the Western Cape Region of the Federation of South African Women. The Black Sash contingent, due to attend the meeting with observer status, assembled in a car park early that morning. For security reasons, the final location of the meeting was only then revealed. We reached our destination, a suburban church hall, at 9 a.m. Representatives from other women's organisations – Women's Movement for Peace, United Women's Congress, Rape Crisis, Belville Community Organisation – trickled in. The organisers, for the most part dressed in para-military uniform in the colours of the ANC –

black berets and skirts, green shirts and gold-coloured badges
and scarves – gave instructions that the explanation to be
given to any unexpected visitors was that this was an ecumenical church gathering. An hour and a half later the buses
bearing women from the townships, and evidently running
on proverbial African time, arrived. Mammas spilled out of
the coaches singing and dancing with unbridled exuberance
and apparent disregard for the need for secrecy, and toyitoyed
their way to the attendant rows of chairs.

The President of the Western Cape Region of FEDSAW,
Mamma Zihlangu, was to open the occasion with a presidential address, but she was subject to a restriction order now –
as indeed she had been in the 'fifties as a member of the ANC
Women's League. 'Our enemy's directions', it was explained
on her behalf, meant that she was unable to deliver her own
address. She therefore sat in dignified silence at a table facing
the assembled company of some 120 women while her speech
was read aloud for her. She would sit or toyitoy in that same
dignified silence throughout the meeting, which went on
until early evening; at the end of the meeting she had been
re-elected as an unquestionably popular if publically non-
vocal president.

> Women, I greet you in the name of our leaders who are
> behind bars [proclaimed her relayed address]. Oh yes,
> their bodies are in the cells, but not their spirit! Their
> spirit is here with us! And that is why I want to say:
> Viva the women in prison! . . . I wish to thank all our
> affiliates. I want to thank you for deciding to come and
> work with us. I want to thank you for your decision to
> build the unity of all women. Let all of us present here
> today commit ourselves to go forward with our
> Federation struggle. Decide, women! Come and join us!
> Our most important struggle work is to build strong
> unity.

For the Black Sash, who were evidently regarded by
FEDSAW as not quite 'decided' because of their failure to
affiliate, the meeting brought other slightly tense moments.

A visiting speaker from the council of the Federation in the Transvaal called for, among other things, the end of the State of Emergency, the unconditional release of Nelson Mandela, the free passage of exiles and in general the creation of conditions in South Africa in which 'progressive organis-ations' could negotiate from a position of strength. She gave overt expression to FEDSAW'S alignment with the ANC. Among the proposed bases for unity in FEDSAW were the commitment to working for the freedom of all women from all forms of oppression, exploitation and discrimination; to the promotion of women's rights; to having a structure which would guarantee its accountability to its membership; to a non-racial democratic South Africa; and also to the idea of a unitary state. Mary Burton, in giving the Black Sash's response to the last point, explained that the Black Sash would have difficulty with it, on the grounds that it was pre-empting a decision which should be a matter for democratic choice in the future. Although, in 1983, the Black Sash had made a statement concerning its own belief in a common citizenship in a unitary society with political representation for all through universal franchise, it did not feel it appropri-ate for any organisation to stipulate the format for the future South Africa. The reply of the visitor from the Transvaal left no room for democratic doubt: the ANC had stated that the future South Africa would be a unitary state and if the Black Sash read what the ANC had written they would know what to think.

Compared with many of the other contributors to the occasion, the Black Sash representatives appeared temperate and reserved, but this small but not insignificant confirma-tion of the organisation's apprehensions as far as dissent and democratic procedure were concerned raised hackles appar-ent to the close observer. Nevertheless, they got up at intervals to toyitoy with the rest of the women as individuals broke spontaneously into song and the whole room took up the cue: '*Senzenina, senzenina, Sono sethu ubumnyama, Sono sethu ubumnyama.*' ('What have we done? Our only sin is the blackness of our skin.') They seemed as at home with these inspirational interludes as they were with the term comrade as a mode both of being addressed and of addressing others. That day, as the sun shone through the generous glass of the church hall on to 120 closely confined women, I learned a new respect for the value of African song and dance as an effective means of taking the heat and tension out of situations on all kinds of levels.

Some time later I asked Mary Burton how comfortably the title of 'comrade' sat upon her shoulders. It had, she acknowledged, come as a slight shock at first because of its historical associations: 'I think perhaps we don't take it seriously enough. We regard it as a token of being included, accepted, rather than as denoting some egalitarian approach which we haven't really thought through properly.' Black Sash members were not the only people in South Africa who had not really digested the full implications of the term, and for that reason it was probably less of a problem than it might otherwise be. In practice, in South Africa's divided society it was often a way simply of overcoming the difficulties of calling her 'Mrs Burton' rather than by her first name when the hurdle of calling her 'Mary' might be quite a difficult one for a much younger black person in whom the inbred respect for an older person was still strong.

In the end, at the 1988 FEDSAW meeting, the visiting comrade from the Transvaal thanked the Black Sash for its show of cooperation, particularly with regard to the drawing up of profiles of women prisoners for a 'Women in Prison' campaign, and expressed the hope that this would serve as an example to other areas. The comment was not without secondary significance. In another part of the country the Black Sash's refusal to affiliate had provoked an angry reaction. In Cape Town at least the organisation's firm line had eventually been accepted by FEDSAW. In part this acceptance was due to the fact that anti-apartheid organisations in South Africa were focused on getting rid of apartheid, and in the light of that primary aim other differences had a tendency to pale into insignificance. Undoubtedly also, however, the Black Sash's proven track record had a role to play. Subsequent to that first annual general meeting of the Western Cape region of FEDSAW, I asked Cheryl Carolas, who was secretary at the time, whether she would be prepared to give me an external view of the Black Sash. She smiled and said she would be happy to, but such was the internal democracy of her organisation, like so many others aspiring to a 'non-racial democratic South Africa', that she could not possibly do so without first consulting her comrades. Those comrades present at the time got as far as agreeing that they would call a meeting of a substantial number of others who would be in a position to give a more representative viewpoint. They would telephone me when they were ready to share their collective assessment. Apparently they never reached that stage.

Among others engaged in the struggle who were prepared to talk, there were some who saw the Black Sash as liberals in the pejorative sense of being prepared to recognise and criticise what was immoral and unethical but not prepared to walk the last mile, not quite prepared to become involved to the extent that the 'oppressed people' would like them to be; but these critics were few and far between. For many members of black anti-apartheid organisations the Black Sash's record would be measured in terms of its readiness to stand up and be counted in situations which involved personal risk. Molly Blackburn had won widespread acclaim and trust because of her courage and determination to defend the underdog with little regard for her own safety. As one coloured headmaster who felt that Black Sash members were not seen by blacks as potential leaders in the liberation struggle because they were female, put it, 'Molly Blackburn was as good as any man.'

Chapter Eleven

Striking a rock

I believe that there is one small hope left in South
Africa at the present time [announced Sheena Duncan
in her presidential address to the Black Sash national
conference of March 1986], and that lies in those
political movements and black communities who have
withdrawn and are withdrawing their cooperation from
the apartheid state. The withdrawal of cooperation
entails civil disobedience. Civil disobedience is not to
be undertaken lightly but only in deep respect for the
idea of law. All societies need a framework of law in
which people can know what it is to be free. It is the
law which is necessary to uphold justice and democracy
and peace in free societies. Civil disobedience must not
be entered into when the law can offer redress. It is a
last resort. In South Africa the law does not offer redress
for the many gross violations of civil liberties and
human rights which are part of the laws of this country.

Her speech was subsequently printed in *Sash* of May 1986.
That issue was seized from the printers by the police.

The policy of the Black Sash as an organisation which
upheld the rule of law had hitherto been to act within it, to
such an extent that the allegation had even been levelled
against it that, with its absolute commitment to lawful and
peaceful protest, rather than being a burden to the government it had actually been used by it to persuade the white
electorate and the international community that protest was
tolerated in South Africa and that it was only militant,
extremist and revolutionary action that was rigorously

repressed. In the advice offices members had seen their task as that of explaining to people the law as it existed and the options available to them. The individuals concerned might well then choose to break the law, but it was no part of the Black Sash role to encourage them to do so. The organisation felt it had an obligation to test the limits of the law, but that was not civil disobedience. Laws in South Africa were often obscure in their language and, in the experience of the Black Sash, interpreted by the administration to mean much more than was justified by the actual wording and punctuation. Administrative decree often went far beyond what the law allowed, as had been shown repeatedly by successful challenges in the courts to Emergency Regulations promulgated in defiance of what the law actually said, as well as cases such as that of Tom Rikhoto in 1983, which had shown how officials had used technicalities to deprive people of their urban residence rights. Many aspects of the law had and still needed to be tested in this way.

Members had learned to be 'discreet' in the knowledge that their telephones were frequently tapped and their movements monitored. Coded messages had been used in the early days of the organisation. For example, it had been agreed that if a telephone message was received saying that 'Mary has been taken into hospital' it actually meant that Nelson Mandela had been arrested. One night Mary developed chronic appendicitis. The news of her rush to hospital was circulated and the whole contingency plan for Nelson Mandela's arrest was set in frenetic motion. But traditional Black Sash style was based, not so much on conspiratorial intrigue as on the assertion that 'We act openly as we have nothing to hide. We do nothing illegal.'

Sheena Duncan recalled not without some amusement one 'funny paranoid resource guy from England,' who had come round one night after dark with his hat pulled down and introduced himself, saying he wanted to talk to her. They had had their conversation and she escorted him to the door only to discover that he had left his car round the corner in case he had been followed. 'I told him that if he ever did that again he would not be welcome in my house. "Do you realise," I said, "that what you are doing is behaving in a way that immediately makes everyone suspicious about the people you are seeing. The next time you want to see me, make a proper appointment in the proper way".'

The Black Sash had persisted in seeking lawful non-violent strategies to achieve its ends. Until 1973 Black Sash women had stood in group protests against each new infringement of human rights with the same degree of determination and dignity as they had in first protesting against the Senate Act. When the Riotous Assembly Act of that year determined that more than one person standing together could constitute a riotous assembly they had stood for the last time for many years in a group protest outside parliament, protesting about the right to protest. Thereafter, they had stood alone. They had given up handing out leaflets or trying to disseminate information during stands; they had applied, as required, to the magistrates for permission to protest and submitted their carefully chosen slogans for advance inspection: 'Government may restrict protest but not the truth', 'We need police impartiality', 'No Apartheid', 'Women still say "No" to pass laws, 'To end violence, struggle for justice'. The organisation took to printing on the reverse of its placards a notice giving instructions what to do if approached by the police, and what to do and say if arrested. 'Protests must be single,' it directed. 'Protests must be silent – refuse to speak to anyone who approaches you.'

Stands became very organised. It became Black Sash practice for protesters standing alone to have a support person located within view, often in a parked car across the road, ready to divert unwelcome attention from well-intentioned drunks or less well-intentioned members of the public who had no reservations about informing protesters of how ridiculous they looked, or of how they wished such women would stop a bullet. If a member of the public tried to engage the person holding a placard in conversation it was the role of the back-up to draw that person away, so that the protester could not be accused of being involved in an illegal gathering. There had been rare occasions when Black Sash members had been arrested for being engaged in an illegal gathering because they spoke to each other, but if they reviled members of the public, even in response to extreme provocation, while they were protesting, or refused to behave in the way Black Sash members traditionally acted, they were considered unworthy of membership and the organisation, aware of the dangers of *agents provocateurs*, asked them to leave.

The question of the appropriateness or otherwise of the recourse to civil disobedience was not, however, a new one for the Black Sash in 1986. It was another issue on which members were not totally single-minded. Although bound by its constitution to non-violent methods of opposition, the organisation was not actually bound to lawful action. A decade prior to Sheena Duncan's speech on the subject, the Black Sash had defined its position in relation to civil disobedience or 'the considered and deliberate defiance of any unjust law as a strategy of non-violent resistance'. The Black Sash did not believe that it could bind its members to enter into civil disobedience. Such action, it was felt, must be a matter for individual choice and conscience. It recognised that there were good, sound practical reasons why individuals might be unable to take the risk of breaking the law at a particular time. The practical consequences for husbands and children, and for members' employment prospects, were very real. The Black Sash thus committed itself to supporting wholeheartedly any member who, in conscience, had made a decision to obey the law and simultaneously to giving its unquestioning support to members who, individually, or as a group, decided on a principled course of action which involved breaking it.

There had been several instances of such individual decisions. One Black Sash member had gone to prison for refusing to make a statement about a visit to Winnie Mandela; another had gone to prison rather than dismiss a domestic worker who could not be registered. Others had deliberately taken part in illegal gatherings and marches. Frustrated by the Black Sash readiness to wring its hands over the number of people dying in detention but what she saw as its reluctance actually to do anything more concrete about such tragedies, Beverley Runciman half jokingly declared her intention of chaining herself to the railings of parliament in Cape Town the next time it was heard that someone had died in custody. When word came through, one month before the imposition of the national State of Emergency in June 1986, that a twelve-year-old boy, Johannes Spogter, had been beaten to death in Sebokeng, she and another Black Sash member set about fulfilling her promise. They did so, however, as individuals and not officially as members of the organisation.

In the lavatories of the nearby cathedral they pinned pillowcases to their backs bearing the inscription, 'A child has died in police custody – we are horrified at his death.' Then they emerged, removed their coats to reveal the words on their backs and chained themselves to the railings surrounding parliament, just below a statue of Queen Victoria, with a chain which Dunstan Runciman, one of the most dedicated 'Black Sash husbands', had procured for them. They were frozen and terrified but remained there in silence, their heads bowed in mourning until, after half an hour, the police, clearly uncertain about how to deal with them, attempted to take them away.

A man shouted from the assembled crowd, 'You love people who throw hand-grenades and I'm going to throw a hand-grenade at you.' He threw what proved to be an egg at them, but for a moment they had taken him at his word and waited for the explosion. Both women were subsequently fined R50. So too was the man who had thrown the egg, against whom they had felt it their duty to bring charges. With hindsight the episode was not without its humorous aspects, but at the time the thought of the dead child had overridden all others in its horror: 'He was a little guy who had been on a march with his elder cousin as part of some protest in a small village in the Eastern Cape. At that time it was OK to march. People were marching all over the place. That was one of the reasons why they called a State of Emergency. On their way home they were pulled into a police cell and he was kicked to death.'

The two women's protest had considerable impact in terms of the publicity it attracted. Beverley Runciman was pregnant at the time. This fact, combined with the knowledge that the individual whose death they mourned was a twelve-year-old boy, augmented the publicity value of 'respectably' dressed white women prepared to take a public risk. The Black Sash saluted them and others who in conscience had made a decision to disobey the law, and as government decrees under the State of Emergency grew increasingly authoritarian the readiness to take that risk became more widespread even amongst the more cautious within the organisation.

The year from March 1985 to March 1986 was a year of mourning for the Black Sash, the year in which Matthew Goniwe, Brian Bishop and Molly Blackburn all met untimely deaths. There was a feeling that the hope for a harmonious future South Africa had been lost through the deaths of the best of the younger generation of black leaders. In the period from September 1984 to March 1986 the Institute of Race Relations estimated that 1,158 people had been killed. In 1985 at least eleven people died in police custody, or soon after detention or arrest for alleged political offences. At least 4,000 people were injured in a seventeen-month period. The Black Sash knew that these figures were incomplete. Too many people had disappeared without trace in circumstances which led their relatives to believe they must be dead. It was well known that many of the wounded would not go to clinics and hospitals for treatment for fear of instant arrest. Such people did not appear in official statistics.

The Black Sash conference of 1986, at which Sheena Duncan's historic advocacy of civil disobedience was made, heard report after report of repression and violence, of the countrywide use of vigilantes to terrorise black communities through murders, beatings, petrol-bomb and grenade attacks on the homes of leaders of community organisations formed to oppose apartheid and through the establishment of a rule of fear in townships, villages and rural communities. It heard of the obstruction experienced by the victims of vigilante assaults when they tried to lay charges with the police against their assailants. Reports of white vigilantes arming themselves and going on the attack against black people were

becoming more and more frequent. A Pretoria City Councillor had founded an organisation called the Movement for the
Liberation and Preservation of White South Africa. Membership of this organisation, which aimed to teach women and
children to shoot, fight fires and 'identify the enemy', was
open to anyone who 'put emphasis on race'. So much of what
was really happening remained unpublished because of
restrictions on reporting imposed in terms of the Police,
Prisons and Defence Acts and the clampdown on information
which was part and parcel of the State of Emergency. The
law prevented full and proper investigative reporting of
events. The Black Sash was having to balance what it saw on
SABC TV with its own knowledge of events, and neither
perspective led it to hope that South Africa was on its way to
democracy and justice.

As far as the Black Sash was concerned, despite talk of
reform, there had been no change towards the dismantling of
apartheid at this time. There had been some removal of race
barriers at a social level for those who were wealthy enough
to make use of expensive hotels, theatres and cinemas. There
had been a noticeable removal of race discrimination in
government-owned and privately owned buildings in the
major cities, and in shops, post offices, parks, sportsfields,
public places. These changes were welcome but, Sheena
Duncan argued, they had little to do with apartheid. There
had been significant improvements in laws relating to labour
relations, but these improvements did not really touch apartheid. Apartheid could not be 'reformed'. The administrative
procedures used to enforce it could, but there had been no
suggestion of removing the fundamental piece of legislation
on which the whole apartheid system was based. The 1950
Population Registration Act (Race Classification), which
demanded that everyone resident in South Africa must be
classified according to their race, still dictated a person's
entire existence – the state hospital or clinic in which he
could be born, where he would grow up, where he could go
to school, where he could live and where he could be buried.
Without it all other legislation dealing with parliamentary

government, homeland and local authorities, Regional Service Councils, health, education, welfare, pensions, housing, Group Areas, influx control, even the constitution itself would be rendered inoperable. That was what the 'dismantling of apartheid' would mean: the total repeal of an enormous body of law and its replacement with legislation which took no cognisance of the colour of a person's skin.

Instead, what was being offered was a new-look apartheid based on the principle of 'own affairs' government. 'Reform' had divided the duties of government into those areas of legislation which affected each race group individually and could therefore be dealt with by the group's particular chamber on its own, and into 'general affairs', those areas of legislation which affected all three race groups and would therefore have to be discussed by all three chambers. 'Own affairs' were deemed to be areas like social welfare, education, health matters including hospitals, clinics, medical services at schools, housing, community development, rent control, local government and water supplies. The white, coloured and Indian Houses of Parliament were now well into their second year of government and Sheena Duncan took the view that as a consequence apartheid, far from being broken down, was greatly extended in the administration of matters such as health and education. She cited the example of hospitals which used to be under the control of Provincial Administrations. They had always been segregated, but the transfer of control to the relevant racially defined House of Parliament was leading to a new and more rigid enforcement of that segregation. The Coronation Hospital in Johannesburg was a coloured 'own affair' and had now been instructed to refuse admission to patients of other race groups in preparation for its hand-over by the Province to the House of Representatives. In education, racially and ethnically defined departments proliferated, while power to decide on education policy for all of them and to allocate finance to them was centralised in the hands of the white ruling minority party. It was all very clever, subtle and sophisticated, but it was not leading to the dismantling of apartheid.

In a speech made on 31 January of that year, the State

President P.W. Botha had expressed his commitment to the sovereignty of law as the basis for the protection of the fundamental rights of individuals as well as groups and, to the belief that peace, freedom and democracy could not exist without law; that any future system had to conform to the requirements of civilised legal order and ensure access to the courts and equality before the law; and that dignity, life, liberty and property of all had to be protected, regardless of colour, race, creed or religion.

'The State President either does not understand the words his speech-writers put into his mouth', was the Black Sash president's response, 'or that is one of the most cynical statements ever made by the President of any nation.' It was the Black Sash's experience that 'his political clique' had long ago destroyed the sovereignty of law as the basis for the protection of the fundamental rights of individuals. It had denied assured access to the courts. There was no peace, freedom or democracy in South Africa. The dignity of his fellow citizens was violated every day. Life was not protected, nor was property, but rather laws made by white people in South Africa had wrenched from tens of thousands of black people the land they owned and used and the homes they occupied. There was no liberty in South Africa. Those who had the illusion that they were free merely enjoyed a privileged exemption from the bonds which tied all South Africans down, an exemption which was withdrawn the minute a person ceased to conform and to be obedient. Power was being maintained through the barrel of a gun. It was under such circumstances that some people were prepared to try and wrest that power from Mr Botha's political clique, also through the barrel of a gun.

Sheena Duncan was a staunch pacifist whose avowed aim was to find non-violent ways in which power could be transferred to the powerless, not out of any desire for the defeat or subjugation of the currently powerful, but in the true longing for a society in which equal distribution of powers would lead to peace and justice preserved in that creative tension which exists between conflicting interests of equal strength. She would not advocate the resort to violence, either as an individual or as national president of the Black Sash, but as the parameters of what was legal shrank dramatically she was prepared to give voice to the fact that she vested her hope for the avoidance of a future period of 'unimaginable terror' in civil disobedience, and thus to contribute to a major debate within the organisation as to whether it was appropriate for people who upheld the concept of the rule of law to break the law in order to oppose injustice.

Without law, it was fully acknowledged, human community became a chaotic, competitive battleground on which wars of survival were fought, in which the weak and the poor were destroyed and the strong and the wealthy became all-powerful and ruthless. If, however, the rule of law was to be respected, the laws must have the legitimacy that stemmed from the participation of all the citizenry in their formulation, and must protect rights as well as ensure that justice took its course. The history of legislation which allowed indefinite detention without trial and which denied people redress against the state was all too well known to Black Sash members, as were the laws governing the removal of land rights and ownership, freedom of movement, and freedom of speech and association. They had seen how court interdicts were often impossible to enforce because the enforcement agencies refused to obey the courts' injunctions. They had seen the state refuse to obey its own laws for its own political purposes.

On 16 April 1987 the *Star* reported a statement from the Department of Home Affairs summarising the current position on the issue of identity documents to black people. Among other things, the Department announced that the figure for applications for blacks included 253,986 'held back' pending negotiations with the Bophutatswana government on the reinstatement of South African citizenship. This was, Sheena Duncan pointed out, totally unlawful. The Restoration of South African Citizenship Act enacted on 1 July 1986 stipulated certain conditions which entitled people to regain the South African citizenship that had been taken away from them when their putative homeland became independent. The desires and opinions of the Bophutatswana government had nothing whatsoever to do with it. The state was in fact committing an act of civil disobedience.

An administrative disregard for the law had become the mark of the country's social order. Those who wished to use civil disobedience as a strategy for opposition to unjust laws and for forcing change but who wished to preserve the idea of law faced a difficult dilemma, for those same strategies of opposition could after all lead to its destruction. By August 1987 Sheena Duncan was nevertheless sure that civil disobedience would be in the forefront of opposition strategies in the months to come. Contrary to what the media was maintaining, she believed that the overwhelming majority of South Africans who were opposed to the present government and its policies, including the ANC, were anxious to limit and, where possible, prevent violence. When non-violent strategies of resistance had been made unlawful, civil disobedience became not only inevitable but, wherever there was no other effective means, obligatory. The prediction of this inevitability was, however, tempered with a warning for those Black Sash members who might take the deliberate decision to be disobedient: it was essential that they must be prepared to take the consequences.

In an attempt to prevent the organisation of the non-violent strategies of boycott and stayaway which had proved substantially effective, the Emergency Regulations had imposed a penalty for calling for civil disobedience of a maximum ten years' imprisonment or a fine of R20,000. For Black Sash members there were other possible consequences apart from domestic considerations of the effect on children and husbands of arrest, custody and public criticism. The acquisition of a criminal record could mean exclusion from teaching posts and other employment positions, or even sitting on school committees. It barred access to public service roles such as that of city councillor.

On 12 June 1986 Annica van Gylswyk, chairperson of the Black Sash Pretoria branch, was arrested in her own home in the early hours of the morning. She was kept in solitary confinement in Pretoria prison for several weeks and then taken to police cells, where she was interrogated. Born in

Sweden, towards the end of her overall six-week detention period, she was presented with two options: either to stay in detention under the 180-day regulation and face a court case thereafter, or to leave prison and take a plane to Sweden. She never knew the reason for her detention or the nature of the threatened charges. South Africa had been her home for thirty years but she opted, with great reluctance, to return to Sweden. There were many members of the Black Sash who did not hold South African passports, among them Mary Burton, who was born in Argentina and who declined on principle to apply for the South African passport for which she was eligible on the grounds that so many other South African citizens were denied that right. To hold a British passport, viewed by many South Africans as the ultimate safeguard, could also render people whose aspirations were to remain in South Africa to work for future justice, peace and democracy more susceptible to constraint in the form of repatriation.

In the course of 1988 Black Sash members in Pietermaritzburg and the Natal Midlands region held a number of group pickets with permission from the local chief magistrate to protest about the detention of those involved in local peace negotiations, the muzzling of the press, the banning of progressive organisations and the police force's apparent support of Inkatha in the township violence. Elsewhere, however, the right to assembly and to peaceful protest remained tightly curtailed. On 17 March 1988, none the less, twenty-nine women in black sashes stood side by side in silent protest close to the parliament building in Cape Town. The issue which had induced them to take this illegal action was the impending execution of six people convicted and sentenced to death for the murder of a councillor, Jacob Dlamieni, in Lekoa on 3 September 1984. The Sharpeville Six were not directly identified as his murderers but were convicted on the basis of 'common purpose' on the grounds that they were in a mob of a hundred people who, angered by rent increases, had stoned, hacked and burned the councillor to death. The case had gone to the Court of Appeal but the death sentence was not reduced. The prospect of the death sentence for so tenuous a charge had brought criticism both at home and abroad. A petition for clemency had been drawn up for submission to the State President. On 1 January 1988 Sheena Duncan had circulated to members of the Black Sash ideas for suggested action reflecting conciliatory tactics:

> At the moment most of the appeals to the State President have been public and 'political' in nature. Many foreign governments and overseas anti-apartheid organisations have made such appeals, as have organisations in South Africa. There is a group called the 'Save the patriots' campaign . . . This does not seem to be helpful in the circumstances. If the President does grant a reprieve from the gallows he will no doubt be accused by the CP [Conservative Party] of giving way to pressure. Their opportunity will come when parliament sits again at the beginning of next month and they are unlikely to let it go by. The State President's character is such that he will find it difficult to face up to such criticisms and mockery. It is therefore necessary to try to appeal to him privately and without releasing the contents of the appeals to the press. The lives of six people are at stake and it is horrifying that there may be error in this case.
>   It is suggested that people, either individually or with colleagues and friends, write their own appeals to the President, either at the Union Buildings, Pretoria 0001, or at Tuynhuis, Cape Town 8001. The grounds for such an appeal would be:
> 1. The possibility of error in this case. However small that possibility may be, the death sentence is irreversible.
> 2. The need for a process of reconciliation to begin in South Africa, and that mercy is the other side of the coin of justice, justice being essential to reconciliation.

Despite such efforts, by 17 March the six were still sched-uled to hang next morning. A Black Sash meeting was held in Cape Town, a special press release was sent out with information relating to the organisation's planned stand and embassies were invited to send representatives to monitor the occasion. When, at 1 p.m., the twenty-nine women took up their stand in traditional Sash demeanour with a large banner appealing for 'Clemency for Sharpeville Six' several embassy representatives came and stood beside them. The women were left to stand for just over twenty minutes, during which time some profess to have been terrified. It was only a week after water cannon had been turned on protesting clergy. According to one of the women involved, treatment of protesters depended very much on the police officer in charge: 'It might be somebody who goes mad, although it is difficult to go mad against twin sets and pearls. There is a value in strategic dressing.' As it transpired, they were given a six-minute warning to disperse and, when they failed to do so, the national president, Mary Burton, the then vice-president Jenny De Tolly, the Western Cape regional chair-person Beverley Runciman, Sue Van De Merwe (wife of the progressive Federal Party MP Tian Van De Merwe) and all the others involved were taken quietly away in a van and appeared before a court that same day. The state requested a postponement of the matter until 22 April for further investigation, and all the women were released without bail and warned to appear on that date. They were subsequently charged with attending an illegal gathering as defined by the Internal Security Act, Act 52 of 1973, found guilty and fined.

Following pressure from both in and outside South Africa, the Sharpeville Six were granted first a stay of execution and then had their death sentences replaced with prison terms of between eighteen and twenty-five years. It is hard to assess how significant a contribution the Black Sash's direct action made to this outcome. Certainly pictures of the protest found their way on to the pages of the international press, and as far as one person directly involved was concerned that in itself gave meaning to the stand they had taken. The value of their protest overseas had been to show that not all white South Africans supported what was happening in their country: 'Everybody thinks all the whites agree with what's going on. It is quite shocking when there is a group of women of all ages standing there saying, "We don't agree and we're not black and we're not clergy and we're not university students." ' Word also came back to the Black Sash from the black and coloured community that non-whites were quite overwhelmed that whites had been prepared to put themselves in a position of potential danger.

As far as the Cape Western Black Sash itself was concerned, the Sharpeville Six stand provoked a variety of reactions. The action had been felt to be wholly appropriate in the light of the Black Sash's on-going concerns. It had brought recognition that the time had come to explore the narrowing space available to the organisation in which to press its advantage from what was perceived to be a privileged position. It also, however, raised certain questions as to how well prepared those directly involved had been. There was a feeling that people had only inadequate knowledge of the possible consequences and of the correct procedure in the courtroom. In civil disobedience there should be no legal representation and no 'admission of guilt' fines. On this occasion both had been accepted. In future, further steps would be taken to ensure that those taking such action had a clearer mandate from the organisation and that they were adequately prepared and informed on the basis of a 'non-violent protest action checklist' and an information sheet which ensured that all practical details were covered, right down to whether a person involved as an activist had a car parked on a meter which required feeding or children and pets which her 'buddy' supporter would undertake to ensure were properly looked after.

By 1989 Sheena Duncan's 1987 prediction that civil disobedience would find its way to the forefront of opposition strategies proved to be prophetic. The South African Council of Churches, with a fresh appreciation of the freedom it enjoyed by comparison with political organisations, had declared its support for all those actively using civil disobedience as a strategy to 'force change in South Africa'. It had recommended that member Churches 'question their moral obligation to obey such laws as the Population Registration Act, the Group Areas Act, the Land Acts, the Education Acts and the Separate Amenities Acts'. It had encouraged employers to stop deducting PAYE tax from workers' wages on the grounds that the SACC upheld the principle that there should be no taxation without representation. It had called on blacks to reject conscription until there was universal franchise. It had stated unequivocally that it saw civil-disobedience strategies as a last resort before violence. During 1988–9 detained prisoners had been on hunger strike, for the first time in protest not against appalling prison conditions but against their incarceration itself. Some had been released but made subject to rigorous restriction orders. The Mass Democratic Movement, a new broad alliance with the Congress of South African Trade Unions and the United Democratic Front and its affiliates as a core, was formed, and in the weeks before the election on 6 September 1989 which would bring South Africa a new State President, it called for a boycott of the elections and the rejection of the 'tri-cameral fraud'.

A renewed spirit of political opposition sprang to life in the form of a Defiance Campaign organised by the MDM. As far as the SAP were concerned, the Defiance Campaign was yet another step in the mobilisation of the revolutionary process. Their information was that between 5 and 7 June 1989, a deputation of approximately thirty people, mainly officials of the UDF and the Congress of South African Trade Unions, held discussions with the ANC/SACP alliance in Lusaka, under the banner of the MDM. An official report on the ensuing discussions proposed that: 'A defiance campaign with a mass character needs to be waged to deepen our challenge to the regime.' As far as the liberation movement was concerned, this was the legitimate expression of the anger and frustration caused by the daily living conditions of millions of people, which arose initially as a reaction to the severe restrictions imposed on many of the detainees released in the wake of the hunger strike at the beginning of the year.

Discussions about how to oppose these restrictions led to a wider focus on restrictive laws in general. Leaflets were prepared detailing the facts and registering the bitterness felt by many about the ever-deepening problems of health, education, shelter, unemployment, crime, repression and fear. There was also widespread concern that the crisis situation in South Africa, created by internal resistance, external pressure and looming economic collapse, would bring about negotiations and settlements which ignored the views of the majority of the population who had borne the brunt of apartheid rule and the costs of resistance. There were fears that proper account would not be taken of organisations which had been banned and exiled, particularly the ANC. The Defiance Campaign was designed to bring these actors on to centre stage for participation in such negotiations. All over South Africa, people took the initiative in hospitals and on beaches, in churches and schools. They broke their restriction orders and they challenged the laws that governed the apartheid state, and they did it in the majority of instances with discipline and control.

Once more the Black Sash found itself having to define its own responsibility. At a public meeting held in an old Methodist church in a corner of Cape Town's Greenmarket Square, on 24 August 1989, Mary Burton, national president, stated emphatically that the Black Sash did not support the aggressive actions, the throwing of stones by angry people, that had sometimes occurred, any more than it supported police action which had on occasions led to violence. The Black Sash task, as she saw it, was not, however, to hide away from the violent reality of South African society but to do all it could to reassert the claim to the right of peaceful protest and assembly. Black Sash members did have doubts about the possible misuse and manipulation of the Defiance Campaign as a cover for those who wished for violence. Such anxieties needed to be acknowledged because there was a danger that they would otherwise paralyse Black Sash women who, rather than risk involvement, might well be inclined to retreat into a world in which perhaps they felt more comfortable: the world of ideas and debate. If, however, they allowed themselves to be paralysed, they would leave the terrain open to the very confrontation they dreaded: a confrontation between those who would no longer take oppression and those who would brook no resistance. There were strategies and techniques which could be learned by those who engaged in non-violent action which minimised the risks.

The question of its responsibility was, according to Mary Burton, a crucial one for the Black Sash:

> Do we need to throw our weight behind the organisations that represent the majority of the people to achieve their aims – because they are the majority? Will we be accused of being 'useful idiots' – the unwitting tools of the ANC, or of the working class, or of the communists? I believe the question for us is: Do we want to uphold and protect human rights? And if so how? We have a special responsibility to tell the truth without fear or favour.

Mary Burton herself would no longer be silenced by the Emergency Regulations, and she called on the editors of all the newspapers of South Africa to unshackle themselves to report events with only the proper restraint of wise and responsible journalism and no longer to deny their readers the full picture of what was being done. In the words of Professor Jakes Gerwel, Principal of the University of the Western Cape, the Defiance Campaign was 'an opportunity to rise in a disciplined and non-violent manner and indicate to a minority government that it does not rule with the consent of the people'. The Black Sash national president called upon her audience to grasp that opportunity.

The meeting in the Methodist church was a prelude for a protest stand on what was regarded as the basic human right to speak and protest.

> Since its inception [announced Beverley Runciman] the Black Sash has had a proud record of protest against injustice, exercising our right to demonstrate with posters and banners. This right has been whittled away over the years by the National Party government. We value this right very highly, not only for our own organisation, but for all in South Africa who have suffered from the denial of the right to be well informed and to speak out freely. It is for this reason that, although we are aware of the laws, we have decided to

hold a stand today to act in conformity with the
Defiance Campaign.

Greenmarket Square was about to become an 'unrest area'
and, under the State of Emergency, the world was not
supposed to see what happened.

In fact twenty-two women emerged from the church,
collected their placards at the door, donned their black sashes
and took up their positions in three ranks in the centre of the
cobblestone square. They stood in silence staring impassively
ahead with placards bearing the slogans: 'Defiance is the
right to protest . . . Free the press to tell the truth . . . Let's
learn from history.' As a crowd swiftly gathered, the police
gave the protesters eight minutes in which to disperse. When
they failed to do so, police took away the boards and then,
beginning with Mary Burton, led the women away, not to the
usual prison van but to a more comfortable small yellow bus
with padded seats, subsequently nicknamed by other anti-
apartheid activists 'The Black Sash Rolls Royce'. Something
about the rather homely appearance of the female protesters
touched the crowd of onlookers and they were driven away
to applause and cries of 'Viva Democracy' and 'Viva Black
Sash'. On that occasion they were treated with courtesy and
consideration at the police station, given iced water in glass
jugs and fingerprinted and photographed with great polite-
ness. They were quickly released on their own recognisance
and Mary Burton thanked the officer in charge for the manner
in which he had treated them in the course of their awkward
but cordial encounter.

Six days later, however, several Black Sash women who
had stood in Greenmarket Square took part in a women's
march organised by FEDSAW, in the course of which it had
originally been planned to deliver a letter protesting against
capital punishment to the British embassy, until the organisers, amongst whom the Black Sash did not number, discovered that the establishment in question was not actually
in Cape Town. The march was much more roughly handled.
The Black Sash members were arrested for the second time
in the space of a few days, together with a much bigger

grouping of black women. Back at the police station, Mary Burton found herself face to face with the same senior police officer. 'He was not pleased. Here we were again, causing all sorts of problems. The atmosphere was completely different. And I tried to see it from his point of view. Here he had treated us so nicely and we had gone out and done the same thing again. But there was definitely a difference also because we were a minority of white women among a much bigger group of black women, some of whom were admittedly aggressive towards the police.'

Black Sash members tended to respond in different ways to these close encounters with the police. For Sheena Duncan and some others there was a distinction to be drawn between the different branches of the police force: 'The riot squad are difficult people to reach because they are so violent, whereas with the uniformed people you can usually make some human connection by being polite and courteous.' Some could not see any form of police officer as a person trying to do his or her job and did not want to communicate any more than necessary, supplying only what information they were obliged to give. People were frightened of being tricked by an apparently reasonable attitude into saying more than they otherwise would. Others took the opportunity to spread the gospel of human rights. On one occasion a policewoman in the course of taking fingerprints asked Helen Zille, a highly articulate journalist who had joined the Black Sash because she felt it was on the cutting edge of the sound analysis which must precede political action, what it was that she had done to qualify for arrest. She responded in detail and the policewoman appeared to be very interested. Half the local Black Sash women thought it was a useful way to react. The other half were very cynical and considered it a complete waste of time. People, Mary Burton would acknowledge not without regret, were frightened to open themselves into behaving in a human way.

The Black Sash had for many years been in close touch with communities drastically affected by policing perceived and experienced as a brutal and aggressive arm of the Nationalist government. Its members had known both what it was to be on the receiving end of unwelcome attention and to look to the police for protection and receive a response with which they were far from satisfied. The advice office in Port Elizabeth was not the only one to have been placed under attack. On 21 August 1988 Khotso House, the building which the Johannesburg Black Sash advice office shared with the South African Council of Churches was destroyed by a bomb skilfully laid at the foot of the lift shaft so that the six floors imploded rather than exploded, thus avoiding any damage to neighbouring buildings. By the middle of October the police had not yet begun their investigation, apparently because it was still too dangerous to go into the basement.

At the end of June 1989 eight Black Sash members were among 114 people from around South Africa to take part in a conference organised by the Five Freedoms Forum, held in Lusaka and attended by eighty ANC members. They were by no means the first Black Sash members to meet the ANC in exile, but they were the first official Black Sash delegation to do so. The object of the exercise on this occasion was not simply to visit the ANC. The theme of the conference was the 'role of whites in a changing society'. Its aim was to develop understanding and clarity about delegates' own roles in future South African society. Topics debated ranged from those dealing with strategies, including negotiations, violence and sanctions, to those looking at possible future dispensations: socialism, nationalisation, free enterprise and models for South Africa's future constitutional structure. Also subject to discussion were the prospective potential roles of parliamentary and extra-parliamentary opposition, local government, business, the media and women.

Among the Black Sash delegates was Judy Chalmers. On her return to Port Elizabeth a 'report back' was planned to be held in a white 'upmarket' suburb because it was among the white community that it was felt the message would be of most relevance. Arrangements were also made for eight busloads of people to be brought in from the townships. Two days before the meeting was due to be held, however, at 5 a.m. there was a knock on the door to Judy Chalmers' home. 'Several security police proceeded to spend three hours searching my house,' she recounted later, 'going through every single thing. They took all my notes that were going to be used at the report-back meeting. I said "I have to have those notes for the public report-back meeting." They said "You can make application to get them back in time." The meeting was still held. Blacks spilled singing and dancing out of their buses; this, according to Judy Chalmers, had put some whites off. Nevertheless, well over 1,000 people squashed into a not very large hall and many more listened outside; but by November 1989 Judy Chalmers' notes had still not been returned.

Being watched was regarded as an almost inevitable conse-quence of Black Sash membership. Cherry Fisher recalls a visit from a neighbour who had been placed under some pressure by security police and also offered payment in return for keeping a watchful eye on the Fishers' home. Ironically, the approach had been made the morning after a talk had been given at the Fishers' house by Colin Bundy, a lecturer at the University of Cape Town, on 'Demystifying the ANC'. As it transpired, the neighbour in question had not wanted to resort to spying but the sensibilities of others were less highly developed. There were times, however, when the consequences of police action ranged far beyond the nuisance value of seized notes or the infringement of privacy. In the course of 1986 a number of Black Sash people were detained. Gill De Vlieg, the Black Sash photographer, was among twelve journalists held. The reason for detentions were not always clear. The apparently random nature with which several people in Grahamstown, who were members of the Black Sash but also members of other organisations, had been picked up served to increase the climate of fear and there were those who felt that this was the precise reason for the manner in which people were detained. The restric-tion orders imposed on them on their release precluded them from working for the Black Sash, so clearly the authorities did not like their Black Sash involvement but the lack of any apparent logic in detentions was part of the terror they inspired.

On 30 June 1988 Janet Small, the mild-mannered daughter

of white middle-class parents and hence, in South African terms, one of the least likely candidates for harsh treatment, was detained in Grahamstown whilst still in her mid-twenties. By the time she was released in Cape Town in September 1988 she was still not sure for what reasons she had been held. She had taken a degree in social work at Rhodes university in Grahamstown and whilst there had become involved with the National Union of South African Students, which had, she acknowledged, made her more 'politically aware'. At the beginning of 1987 she returned to Grahamstown in response to an advertisement for a Black Sash fieldworker/researcher to monitor repression and resistance as a paid employee working in conjunction with the advice office in the Eastern Cape. In Grahamstown she set up and maintained a small office and travelled to other isolated areas where there were no lawyers or support systems to which people could turn. In doing so she found herself not only maintaining records of incidents of repression, but also involved in referring people to lawyers and other resources, and assisting people with pension claims. She also helped people detained during 1985 and 1986 and released in 1987 to work through the psychological damage wrought by their experience and to find work or obtain unemployment benefits.

One of the avowed objectives of the declaration of the national State of Emergency in June 1986 had been to re-establish 'law and order' in the townships. The South African Police Force was relatively small. General Stadler drew attention to the fact that South Africa has less then two policemen per one thousand capita, whereas in Europe, I believe, it's between three and four per thousand, and in the USA it's about six per thousand. Our biggest problem is that you can look in the streets of Pretoria and wherever you go, you will hardly see a policeman.' The SAP, which modelled itself very much on the British police force, had, he pointed out, been trying to 'bring the bobby back on to the beat', but how was it to do that when training facilities were limited and the police had no money? Shortage of men and lack of funds had induced them in 1985 to enlist the help of the SADF to control the turbulence of the townships, a course of action which he would not otherwise have advocated. The same reasons had undoubtedly brought about the implementation of a new policing strategy. According to statistics published in *Now Everyone is Afraid* by the Catholic Institute for International Relations, on the imposition of the June 1986 State of Emergency an additional 16,000 *kitskonstabels* (special constables) and municipal police were added to the police force.

There had been a lesson for the SAP in what had happened at Sharpeville on 21 March 1960, one police officer told me: the fact that the police who fired on the crowd protesting against the requirement to carry passes had been exclusively white had created the erroneous impression that it had been a 'white on black' issue. It was because of considerations of this kind that, since 1978, the police had been actively recruiting other race groups. Nevertheless, the number of black applicants with the necessary matriculation results had never been high, the attractions of a good salary being frequently far outweighed by the social consequences of ostracism by the majority of their own black community. It was acknowledged, therefore, that the standards required of applicants had been lowered and the training they were given was basic.

Kitskonstabels were given six weeks' training and the municipal police, nicknamed 'Greenflies' because of their green uniforms, three months, and they were then deployed in areas where law and order was in pressing need of restoration. By July 1986 there were already 429 municipal police in nineteen black townships in the Eastern Cape. Municipal police were not a wing of the SAP. The SAP trained them and the commanding officer of the SAP in the area oversaw the operations of the unit, but they were employed by the local authorities and were directly responsible to them. Janet Small was involved in the Black Sash monitoring of the new municipal police's handling of petty crime, drunkenness, rent collection and other local issues which gave rise to a large number of allegations of thuggery and intimidation. The Black Sash received numerous complaints of brutal harassment of people who failed, for example, to pay rents particularly during rent boycotts, and the organisation was instrumental in taking a substantial number of allegations of assault and claims for damages to court. Janet Small was concerned with the documenting of such incidents, but so were others who remained undetained. In any case the SAP was prepared to recognise that, whilst for the most part 'these people do a tremendous job', there had been problems with what had been essentially an experiment.

The arrival of security police in Janet Small's office took her completely by surprise. She was told to pack a bag and taken to prison almost immediately. Because there were no other white women in detention, and because the prison authorities were very strict about racial segregation, she found herself in solitary confinement for three months. She saw warders, her parents took on the financial burden of flying from Cape Town to Port Elizabeth once a week to see her, since only her immediate family were permitted to visit her, and she was allowed books, but for her the isolation was the worst aspect of her confinement. 'It's very hard to sustain yourself when you're completely alone.' On her release she was, by her own account, 'very nervous, a bit depressed, quite anxious. You really crave human contact, cry a lot. Even just to converse about something utterly mundane like the weather with the warder made me feel better. I had never realised before how much those sort of things are important to one.' The other most difficult aspect of imprisonment had been the uncertainty as to how long the experience would last. She had been frightened of cracking up, falling apart completely. She was placed on anti-depressants while she was in detention. Those intervening for her release had argued that she was having difficulty coping with being in solitary confinement, and so two psychiatrists had been brought to see her and she had eventually been released on mental health grounds.

The experience had not made her any less committed to her work. Rather, she saw in it a constructive aspect: now she really knew what it was like to be detained, although she was painfully conscious that she had been treated better than any black detainee. At a time when so-called 'petty apartheid' was not as it used to be, when benches were no longer marked 'whites only', in prison all pretences to such enlightenment, it seemed to her, were just stripped away: 'If you're white you get treated one way. If you're black you're treated in a completely different manner.' Naive though it might seem, the flagrant practice of racism had come as a great shock to her. As a white detainee she had a bed, a mattress, sheets and blankets. Black prisoners were given thin mats and blankets only. The quality of meals for whites was much better than for blacks, who talked of rotten food with worms in it. Prison officials were quite different in their attitude to people of different races.

The reason for her detention given by Adriaan Vlok, Minister of Law and Order, after she had been detained for three months was that she had been involved in setting up a Marxist/Leninist reading group and was part of a group of radicals in the Eastern Cape which undermined local government and set up alternative structures. It was also stated that she was involved in trying to disrupt municipal elections. 'I don't recognise myself from that description, quite honestly,' was her response. 'When my parents asked, they were told my involvement with Sash was a front for other activities.' On her release she was given a restriction order, which was not unusual in itself but which she found particularly difficult because it restricted her, not to the house where she had been living in Grahamstown but to Cape Town and her parents' home, where she must be each night between the hours of 6 p.m. and 5 a.m. She was not allowed to work for the Black Sash. She was not supposed to speak to journalists or write for publication. Nor was she allowed to attend any anti-government meetings, or to attack or criticise the government or government acts, or to call for the boycott of the municipal elections.

By the autumn of 1989 President De Klerk had released eight long-term political prisoners. Peace marches were taking place all over South Africa, for the most part without undue police interference. Sheena Duncan discerned a certain confusion in the police force:

I think the police are feeling a bit bewildered about
what's going on. For years they were in total control and
now people are marching through the streets and the
government seems determined to allow them to do so.
People who have spent years in one mould, who have
been taught that the Black Sash is neo-communist, for
example, must find it quite hard to adjust, especially in
the light of the way people are handling the marches.

One week before arrival in Johannesburg, during an anti-
conscription march in Cape Town young men had handed
yellow flowers to soldiers standing on guard outside the
castle. In Grahamstown in the Eastern Cape a march led by
church dignitaries, prominent academics and members of the
Black Sash had ceremonially handed in at the police station
a petition calling for an end to apartheid and the State of
Emergency and the release of detainees. In return the police
had actually presented marchers with two bouquets of
flowers. The marchers then carried the flowers through
Grahamstown and laid the bouquets on the ANC flag.

Curious disruptions to a never-quite-accepted order were
taking place in South Africa. Among the delegates to the
three-day Lusaka conference in June-July 1989, organised by
the Five Freedoms Forum, was an ex-security policeman from
East London. He had thought long and hard before going but
once there had adopted a very open attitude. Finally, towards
the end of the conference he had stood up and said what a
tremendous experience it had been for him. He had anticipated rejection and anger and had found instead acceptance
and a warm welcome for his changed views. Such a welcome,
the more cynical would argue, could come more readily from
exiles. Furthermore, there were those, in the Eastern Cape
particularly, who still felt that De Klerk's 'ease off' message
had not yet reached places as far removed from Pretoria as
Bedford and Adelaide and Fort Beaufort. Anti-apartheid groups
were manifestly viewing promises of change with suspicion.
For too long they had heard the language of reform used to
disguise even tighter restrictions. They still remembered
what in practice the 'Abolition' of Passes and Consolidation

of Documents Act had meant. Two months after Beverley Runciman had sung *Nkosi sikelei iAfrika* at the conclusion of the Five Freedoms Forum conference in Lusaka, harbouring a private longing to be singing those same words ('God bless Africa. Let the voice of the people be heard.') in the City Hall in Cape Town, hundreds of thousands of people marched up Adderley Street in Cape Town, draped the ANC flag over the balcony of City Hall and sang the African national anthem – not inside the building, but outside it. This time the tide of change did seem inexorable, but as the mood of cautious optimism mounted there were still harsh realities which could not be overlooked.

The survival instinct is one of the strongest of human instincts, as Archbishop Hurley pointed out to me in Durban. Personal survival was very closely identified with the survival of an individual's society, his community and his culture. The social survival syndrome was strong in white South Africa, which felt itself to be grievously under threat, especially among the Afrikaner community, and 60 per cent of white South Africa was Afrikaans-speaking. During the Anglo-Boer war of 1899 the Afrikaners had been effectively defeated within a year. All their major towns had been captured, but they had kept up their guerilla warfare for another two years. On the level of Christian hope Archbishop Hurley kept on praying for the miracle of peaceful change. On the level of human assessment he was far from optimistic: 'Mr De Klerk says nice things about reform and negotiation but negotiation means two things. For the black liberation movement it means negotiating how to take over power; for the Afrikaner it means praying, arguing and discussing to preserve the essentials of white power, because to lose power is to lose control, to lose identity, possibly to lose the guarantee of survival.'

To give up power in South Africa would also mean giving up the 87 per cent of the land surface owned by whites, primarily by farmers and farming conglomerates who were not going to be easily parted from land their forefathers had accumulated and worked, and who would be all too quick to claim that black people could not farm on the large scale of modern business conglomerates. As for actual government, the capacity to govern depended largely on a highly efficient, traditionally well-established civil service. The white civil service in South Africa was entrenched. It certainly would not welcome working under a black government while blacks, although they did not lack the ability to fill their positions, still lacked the experience and the training. Those who were educated, the Archbishop pointed out, had not on the whole received a very technical education: 'They are mainly academic and the men have gone on to be lawyers and the women to be nurses and teachers, but there are hardly any engineers, hardly any accountants.' None of the professions that would be required to run an efficient civil service were yet filled by Africans.

The Black Sash was, as far as the Archbishop was concerned, like the Churches, working in the hardest field in which to educate people: the field of moral attitudes. It was hard to measure the impact and the effect of moral education on society. The three major Churches – Anglican, Methodist and Catholic – were fairly sizeable but they still had not achieved very much as yet. Sadly, he presumed that the influence of the Black Sash on society outside its own membership was still rather small. As I listened to this venerable man struggling to hold on to his Christian vision of hope, the thought inevitably came that the days of protest and confrontational politics, at least in relation to a Nationalist government, might yet be numbered. The question then arose as to whether the Black Sash women, who had at times but not in general been the victims, and who had over the years prided themselves on being at the forefront of change as far as the white community was concerned, might not be in a better position than most to make a move towards not only breaking down what was wrong but also laying the foundations for what was right in a future South Africa.

On the morning of 4 November 1989, *en route* to the march from Lingelihle township to Cradock, I drove with Janet Cherry through Ibhayi, a township outside Port Elizabeth which is home for some 900,000 black residents, to pick up three people who were to accompany us. The road, such as it was, was narrow. There was only room for single-file traffic. In the dim early-morning light a police vehicle was suddenly visible coming directly towards us. For a while both drivers held their course. Only at the very last minute did my companion swerve out of the way of the oncoming van into the even rougher verges of the road. My driver's subsequent comment betrayed the fact that, trivial though the incident was, it was highly charged with bitterness. Janet Cherry was the daughter of the Dean of Science at the University of Cape Town. Both he and her mother had played an active role in opposing apartheid. At the age of twenty-eight Janet was not only a member of the Port Elizabeth Black Sash, but also a leader of the End Conscription Campaign and the founder of the Eastern Cape Adult Learning Project, which had involved her teaching literacy skills to trade union members. In 1986, when the repression in the area had made it difficult for her to fulfil her role as a literacy coordinator, she had transformed her office into a community and detentions advice office.

Inevitably her activism had made her the focus of attention both from 'right wing' elements and from the security police. In 1981 she had been detained for a day after taking part in a protest for the rights of meat-workers. In August 1984 she had again been briefly detained on the eve of the coloured and Indian elections. In July 1985 she was held for a third time under Section 29 of the Internal Security Act and kept in solitary confinement for three weeks without charge. In March 1986, because she spoke fluent French, she had been chosen to represent the ECC at an SOS Racisme conference in France. Hours before her departure she had been arrested on a drugs charge despite her insistence that she had never touched drugs in her life. After two days she was released when police could find no evidence against her, fortuitously in time to travel to Paris and make her speech. On 22 August 1986 Janet had been detained by the security police while visiting Cape Town. She was subsequently transferred to Port Elizabeth and held in North End Prison there. For over two months of the 342 days of her incarceration she had found herself in solitary confinement.

Since moving to Port Elizabeth from Cape Town she had experienced a series of mysterious attacks with the apparent aim of driving her away. On at least ten occasions her car tyres had been slashed. Twice her car had been firebombed while parked outside her house or office. In July 1984 she had been hospitalised after a rock was thrown through her windscreen while she was driving. She had received numerous death threats, had been assaulted by white thugs and would hold little if any hope of police protection, if she could ever bring herself to turn to them. Instead, the security police had repeatedly raided her office and her home. Her reaction to the bright yellow vehicle we encountered in the early-morning hours in Ibhayi was all too understandable. It was as understandable as the euphoria evoked in some Black Sash quarters by the small gestures of recognition given by members of the black community to years of frequently unrewarded and sometimes very self-sacrificial effort, or as the satisfaction with which it was discovered that on the walls of one Grahamstown police cell, alongside such messages of comfort as 'Strength brother, it will not always be like this', one detainee had scrawled the words 'Viva Black Sash'.

In a polarised society the readiness to speak out even when there was personal risk involved, the resort to civil disobedience, the fact that some of its members had shared, even if at times in a moderated way, the experience of many blacks of harassment and detention, had placed the Black Sash, both in the eyes of a substantial number of blacks and in the eyes of the authorities, on the side of the 'struggle' and the ANC. That perception was reinforced in many cases by bonds of emotion. The fact that during the Five Freedoms Forum visit to Lusaka Oliver Tambo had had his photograph taken with the Black Sash delegates, or that during the welcome-home rally for the released political prisoners held in Johannesburg's vast stadium Walter Sisulu paid special tribute to the Black Sash, as indeed would Nelson Mandela on his release some months later, was enough to induce many of the otherwise carefully rational inhabitants of a world of political debate to displays of unusual emotion.

For Tish Haynes, who had spent much time and energy

transporting and providing accommodation for the families of prisoners held on Robben Island and in Pollsmoor, an invitation from the family of Andrew Mlangeni, one of the released prisoners, to stay in their home in Soweto before the rally was a more than deeply appreciated reward. Tish Haynes and her husband had welcomed his wife, June Mlangeni into their own family home on occasions and driven her from Cape Town to Pollsmoor on her thrice-yearly visits to her husband. The fact that on the day of his release in Johannesburg after twenty-six years of imprisonment, with the celebrations already underway, he came on the phone to say how grateful he was to them for the love, support and prayers they had given over the years, touched and cheered them deeply.

The hurt, the joy, the emotion were far from unnatural, but would they mean that the Black Sash would find itself unable, if appropriate, to relinquish the politics of confrontation – the kind of politics which determine that the first duty of an opposition is to oppose, which must at all costs deny that any real reforms are being made and which, in opposing everything, does not encourage negotiation, persuasion or compromise? And after so many years of opposition to the Nationalist government would the Black Sash be able to make not so much the intellectual as the emotional transition to fulfilling its role as a human rights organisation, if necessary in opposition to the very 'angels' whose side it had shared?

Chapter Twelve

Where to now?

By the end of 1989 leading members of the Black Sash were aware of many questions. They were conscious of the allegation from Nationalist quarters and even from certain sections of the liberal white community that the Black Sash, despite the failure of the pro-ANC group within it to achieve a vote for affiliation to the UDF, had in practice uncritically supported it. They were equally conscious of the criticism levelled at the Black Sash from the other end of the political spectrum, that because it had not aligned itself uncompromisingly with the ANC it had shown itself in some way to be unwilling to walk 'the last mile'. 'I sometimes feel', Mary Burton acknowledged, 'that we walk along the top of a wall, and sometimes we fall off on the one side and sometimes we fall off on the other, and as long as we fall off the same number of times on each that's about the best we can do.'

As someone who admitted to experiencing a 'sort of split mind' for much of the time, who was conscious of the pull between the warmth and enthusiasm and love offered by the black communities and the nagging doubts about some of the methods of the liberation struggle, between the knowledge that her own lifestyle in fact separated her from those she served and the recognition that for her as for many Black Sash women, temperamentally and for a multitude of other reasons, an alternative was simply not feasible, she was well aware in 1989 that the Black Sash was going to have to face some difficult transitions. Not least of those for people with a long Western tradition, a long commitment to human rights and the belief in the 'rightness' of their own views, was the lesson that what was right in their vision was not necessarily right as far as other people were concerned. Many liberals in South Africa embraced the right of everybody to have his or her say, but in fact what they really wanted was for everyone to agree with them. Conceding the right of others to have their point of view was very difficult. It had been one of the points of debate in the Black Sash when the organisation had subscribed to the right of everyone to have a vote. If everyone then voted for socialism, did that mean socialism was right? The truly liberal course of action was to accept that this was the case, however hard that might be for some, and Mary Burton felt that the Black Sash was fortunate to be part of the process of learning to do that: 'It's quite uncomfortable but whites and privileged people generally are going to have to learn to do it, so we might as well get used to it.'

Within the broad context of the learning of this lesson came the recognition that the organisation could well find itself caught up in a multitude of adjustments. The Black Sash had defined itself as a human rights organisation, but human rights could not all be had by everyone at the same time. The human rights of the dispossessed majority in South Africa would inevitably impinge upon the very carefully held and long-protected rights of those in possession of many things. In the case of the need for land reform, one of the difficult questions was how to marry the rights of black people to have access to land in places where they actually wanted to live, close to their families and close to places where they could make a living, with the perceived rights of whites to protect the value of their property. For years influx control, the Group Areas Act, the Land Acts, homeland government, the Squatting Act and all their allied legislation had been used as a means to control and exclude blacks from the cities. The dismantling of that process would now necessarily entail the sacrifice of what whites regarded as their inalienable rights.

In December 1987 a court case following the forced removal of squatters who had previously been unofficially allowed to occupy farmers' land in Noordhoek on the Southern Peninsula had allowed them access back on to that land. Some local white residents had accepted the decision but the

Noordhoek residents' association was fiercely opposed to it.
Even in a relatively liberal city like Cape Town there were
many who believed, with the sanction of long-standing
government legislation, that cities belonged to white people,
that the land was white and that influx control was a
justifiable necessity. One member of the Noordhoek residents'
association had said quite openly, 'We are totally opposed to
them coming here. They will reduce the value of our property
and we believed when we bought this land that we had the
absolute right to the accrued value of our property.'

'Say that in Europe or North America,' Jenny De Tolly
pointed out, 'and of course it is recognised that you have the
right to lobby not to have a nuclear power station on your
doorstep.' It was not going to be easy for people fed not only
on a political ideology, but also on the religious notion that
God had placed them in a certain position to enjoy certain
privileges, to accept the need for sacrifices on their part.
There was, however, a legacy to redress in which the rights
of the majority even to the most basic necessities of life had
been denied for so long that the potential decreased value of
white property was likely to be one of the lesser sacrifices
whites were going to have to face. 'We might have to be like
black people, grateful for a home and a job, and I think it's
important for people like me in Sash, who come from an
economic and educational background which makes us considerably less threatened than the railway worker who is
likely to lose his job, to realise that people are not willingly
going to say, "Of course, he can have my job and of course I
don't mind whatever the other threats are in our lives."'

One of the reasons why some white South Africans found
the Black Sash women threatening was undoubtedly because
they were seen as a group of people who worked apparently
against their own self-interests. Black Sash members had for
many years been working for the rights of people other than
themselves. Nevertheless, the organisation was fully aware
that the time was coming when it could find itself having to
stand up for the same or a different set of human rights in
relation to a new regime, and that in the process of doing so
it could find itself as unpopular with that regime as it was

with the present government. Already in 1989 in its dealings with the liberation movements – and Jenny De Tolly was at pains to emphasise the plurality of those movements 'because the ANC is not the only one' – the Black Sash had raised questions with regard, for instance, to the freedom of the press: 'You say to them, "Is that right going to be there after liberation?" and they say "There is a real necessity for us to have control of the press at that point in time because it will eliminate this or that problem," so the mental flips we have to take may well be quite interesting.'

By the autumn of 1989 the Black Sash was conscious of having to take those 'mental flips' rapidly and in considerable numbers. For so long its members had stood out on the streets alone in single-person protests. Now suddenly they were allowed to do so in groups and were allowed to do so anywhere. What then had they been doing all those years during which they had braved the missiles and the verbal assaults of hostile pedestrians and drivers informing them that they belonged in the kitchen and did not know what they were talking about. Now that, suddenly, that form of protest had become acceptable, what should they do in the future?

The Black Sash realised that its protest role was gradually being eroded as the government dispensed with many of the more obvious legislative controls, as the control of movement and the implementation of the Group Areas Act slowly disintegrated, but many of those laws had been laws around which it had been relatively easy to organise. So now the organisation was having to look very carefully at its future direction, and the new position in which it found itself was not one of unruffled comfort. Many of its members clearly had enormous emotional needs to do good for the underprivileged. In the past ten years, however, the dispossessed and the underprivileged had to a large extent regained their own voice. As an organisation the Black Sash more than welcomed that development but it did mean also that its role in speaking out and lobbying on behalf of others was greatly diminished. In many respects the Black Sash role had been reduced, and that role for some members was an important part of their lives – so much so that those members of the

Black Sash who for a variety of reasons found themselves living outside South Africa missed acutely the camaraderie and the cut and thrust of Black Sash life. 'What I'm saying,' the organisation's most recent national president, Jenny De Tolly, would acknowledge, 'is that you have to be constantly on your toes, reassessing honestly who you are and where you can play your part.' Beyond the question, 'Where to now?' lay the disturbing but, again, fully recognised possibility that the Black Sash, or at least its work, had almost had a stake in apartheid.

The Black Sash had, however, already proved itself capable of making the necessary adjustments to exterior change. With the abolition of the pass laws there had been those who thought that the role of the advice offices would be substantially diminished. Instead they had had to cope with the confusions associated with the issue of the new identity documents. The greater freedom of movement thereafter among the black population had focused attention on the problems of homelessness and urbanisation, quite apart from the problems relating to pensions, insurance, unemployment and poverty. In Cape Town, where the numbers of applicants to the Black Sash advice office in relation to the workers available were not so large as to necessitate its concentration solely on the people who came to it, the office had discovered an additional role in encouraging communities to develop their own advice offices.

When in the mid 'eighties it became apparent that 80 per cent of the employable people in Khayelitsha were unemployed and could not afford the fare for the twenty-five-mile bus ride to the Mowbray advice office, the Black Sash had embarked on a joint venture with people from the township to establish an advice office which would enable the community to redress its own wrongs. Whereas previously the organisation would simply have hired premises and moved in, in this instance they set up regular meetings and a steering committee, and the advice office in Khayelitsha eventually opened. The Black Sash began a training programme for rural people. It would provide the knowledge and the people themselves would decide how they wanted their office run.

More recently the organisation had been approached by other groups initiating advice offices to assist with training. That process in itself had required a major adjustment.

The way forward was beset with frustrations for an organisation with essentially Western ideas of efficiency. There were problems with language, problems about communicating with people who did not have telephones, a postal service or even fixed addresses. There were the ever-present complexities of 'African time', the sheer lack of fundamental skills, and, perhaps most undermining of all, the difficulties of motivating people all too understandably caught up in the struggle for simple survival to adopt a broader and more long-term vision. The temptation just to get on with the job rather than allow others to learn through their mistakes was always there, but the Black Sash had reached the conviction that that learning process was invaluable for those who must assume a new role in a new South Africa. During the 1989 elections faction fighting had broken out in Khayelitsha and the advice office there had become a centre where statements were taken, assaults recorded and people brought into contact with doctors and lawyers. The crisis had brought additional motivation to the project. The Black Sash still sat on the steering committee and was called upon frequently in that capacity. Twice a week workers and volunteers from Cape Town also made their way out to the Khayelitsha office, but the project was making progress towards greater independence.

On 2 February 1990, at the opening of parliament, F. W. De Klerk announced major steps towards breaking the political logjam: the unbanning and unrestricting of organisations and individuals, the amendment of Emergency Regulations, the release of some political prisoners including Nelson Mandela, and the suspension of executions. Reports to the 1990 Black Sash national conference held one month later, however, suggested that if indeed the organisation did have a 'stake' in apartheid it was as yet far from lost. Grand apartheid as it existed in the form of the homelands policy was still very much alive. The people of Peelton had won a momentous victory. The presence of, eventually, over eight hundred refugees in the middle of white King Williams Town, combined with a concerted high-profile campaign by service organisations against the South African government's inactivity, and increasingly vociferous threats of action by the MDM, had compelled the government to act.

The new-style Nationalist politics ruled out the threat of any eviction of the refugees. The intention of Leon Wessels, Deputy Minister of Foreign Affairs, had clearly been to find a compromise. For the people of the community of Peelton the bottom line had been the immediate removal of Ciskei police and administration of the area, even if actual re-incorporation took its slow course through parliament; but the Ciskeian chief, Lennox Sebe, had refused even to consider a compromise and snubbed Leon Wessels on his second visit by refusing to be available for a meeting. The deputy minister, faced with the choice between appearing indecisive and uncompromising while the community seized land anyway, and the prestige of resolving the crisis by actually granting them land, had announced on 28 November 1989 that the community was to be offered a piece of land within the King Williams Town municipal boundaries as a temporary settlement. Although the struggles of the Peelton people would continue in relation to the form and facilities of their temporary resettlement, it was, according to Larry Field, the fieldworker for the area, a particularly significant victory. Other communities might have previously had their incorporation overturned, but these had been legal victories. Peelton, deprived of similar legal recourse by the Borders of Particular States Extension Amendment Act, represented a decisive political reversal of the state's incorporation policy.

Elsewhere, however, the picture was not so optimistic. Despite rumblings of discontent from the Transkei at the forced incorporation of South Africans into its boundaries, despite the proven unviability of the homelands and despite the vast toll of human suffering, this more subtle form of forced removal was, in the experience of the Black Sash, still going on. In the Transvaal alone the Transvaal Rural Action Committee was involved with the problems of some forty communities. In the course of taking statements during a wave of repression following resistance to the incorporation of Braklaagte and Leeuwfontein into Bophutatswana, a TRAC fieldworker had been detained along with thirty-four others and held overnight in the police station. On 13 July 1989 TRAC and the Black Sash had been declared unlawful organisations in terms of Bophutatswana's Internal Security Act. TRAC maintained that it had openly and legally attempted to intercede with the government on behalf of the beleaguered Leeuwfontein residents and had repeatedly warned it of the disastrous consequences of an enforced incorporation, but the organisation was said to be 'operating behind closed doors' and implicitly accused of instigating the violence and unrest which had occurred.

The year 1989 had also seen yet another court case on behalf of the Mogopa villagers. During the previous year a small group of elderly people had moved back to the land to tend their ancestral graves. Despairing of a negotiated settlement, they had decided to remain there but in March 1989 were served with an eviction order. This was contested in court on the basis that the Mogopa people were not trespassing but in fact owned the land because the expropriation had been illegal. The case had been lost but an application had subsequently been made for leave to appeal. That leave had been granted and the tearful but jubilant people of Mogopa had trooped out of the courtroom and held an impromptu service of thanksgiving. In her last parliamentary speech before her retirement, Helen Suzman made a plea for the return of Mogopa as 'an act of grace' by the De Klerk government, but by March 1990 the outcome was as yet undisclosed.

As the State of Emergency went on, court monitoring continued to provide an insight firmly grounded in the political reality of the day, and throughout most of 1989 the cases Black Sash monitors had witnessed in the courts appeared to run counter to the government's apparently progressive moves. There had been, among others, the case of V. Handula, a drama student who in early December 1988 had been arrested and interrogated. He was subsequently charged with being in possession of banned literature on the strength of his wearing a SWAPO T-shirt. This was at a time when South Africa had agreed to the implementation of the United Nations plan for Namibian independence, yet Handula had had to go through seven court appearances before on 26 April the charges were finally dropped.

In July 1989, the same month in which Nelson Mandela met P.W. Botha at the Tuynhuis for tea, a period when the general impression was being created of a more relaxed and open attitude towards the ANC, a university student, Xolile Jaxa, was sentenced to eighteen months in prison with nine months suspended for being in possession of a speech by Oliver Tambo. A case in Athlone in September 1989 involved seven restrictees charged with breaking their restriction orders. Yet at the same time ANC leaders were being released without restriction. After several appearances, the charges against the restrictees were dropped. The restriction orders remained in force, however, until 2 February 1990.

> This ambiguous type of situation [Ros Bush pointed out] simply breeds further contempt for the law, and so the lifting of these restrictions, as a result of the announcements on Friday, 2 February 1990 was a relief but long overdue. However, similar ambiguous situations, which make a mockery of the law, will continue to abound for as long as the government's actions and the laws still on the statute books continue to be inconsistent with the announcements of reform.

By the end of 1989 the outcome of certain cases had started to indicate that the courts were taking cognisance of the changing political climate. The trial of Linda Tsotsi and Veliswa Mhlauli, both facing a main charge of terrorism, was a case in point. After intensive negotiation with the prosecutor the defence team lodged 'admissions' by the accused. On the basis of these admissions both were convicted: Linda Tsotsi on charges of receiving military training outside the country from Umkhonto we Sizwe and for recruiting members for the ANC; Veliswa Mhlauli on four counts of harbouring members of the ANC. In mitigation of sentence, the defence council gave details of the apartheid-ravaged lives of the two women. Several references were made to the recent change of attitude of the government, in particular to the protest marches which had been allowed to take place, and it was pointed out that had such opportunities for expressing grievances existed before, the two women might have adopted a different course of action. The accused stood their ground in the reiteration of their beliefs embodied in the Freedom Charter, but they were each given a five-year suspended sentence. Earlier in the year similar offences had met with effective prison sentences of three years or more.

In the Black Sash's monitoring of the courts in the year leading up to March 1990, evidence had also been heard containing allegations which verified what it referred to as 'the current exposure of excessive and unjustified use of force by the police'. General Stadler had emphasised the difficult circumstances under which police had to work in South Africa:

> I think 80 per cent of our policemen are under twenty-five years of age. We get a policeman, anybody's son. He goes to college and receives his basic training, which I think is very good, and then all of a sudden he's a policeman to whom everybody looks up as a protector of law and order. And the poor man is confronted with a situation, knowing that some of his colleagues have died in similar circumstances, and he is required to make a split decision which much older policemen would find difficult – whether to attack or run. And he can't run.

The General had also expressed his confidence in the police complaints procedure in South Africa: 'If a policeman intentionally oversteps the mark – whether white or black, it doesn't matter, I've said to the public: "Please come forward. We want to know about it . . ." And I can assure you that in each and every incident where a person has been killed by police or died in police custody of unnatural causes, then the law takes its course.'

For the Black Sash, however, the manner in which 'Police violence continued to evade any form of just retribution, even when the courts strongly condemned the police actions and behaviour', remained a source of grave concern. In September and October 1989 it had monitored a case arising out of the evidence of Police Lieutenant Gregory Rockman, who alleged that on 5 September 1989, during a demonstration at Mitchell's Plain, riot policemen with quirts and batons 'fell over each other's feet in their eagerness to attack like a pack of wild dogs'. Two riot police officers were charged with assault as a result of the brutal force applied by men under their orders. They had been found not guilty because they themselves had not actually inflicted the blows, which the magistrate nevertheless condemned as 'utterly reprehensible'. By March 1990 no further action had been taken in the courts in respect of this 'utterly reprehensible' behaviour.

In a private prosecution brought against thirteen security policemen involved in the 'Trojan Horse' killings, after three people died in October 1985 when police opened fire on a group which allegedly stoned a South African Transport Service truck in which they were hidden, the accused were acquitted of the charge of murder. They were found not guilty, more, it seemed to monitors, as a result of a legal technicality than as the logical consequence of the evidence. The prosecution had endeavoured to use the charge of 'common purpose' to convict all thirteen involved, but the case was found to be unproved. The judge referred to the response of the police as being 'clearly excessive'. 'There is a substantial body of evidence,' he said, 'which points to the existence of a sinister and illegal purpose' to the operation – that of a punitive expedition. In spite of this, he ruled that 'since the cornerstone of the prosecution case has not been proved (i.e. a moral certainty that each and every accused shared a prior common purpose to use excessive force), the accused are entitled to their acquittal'. To allow the police to get away with excessive behaviour with no more than a scolding was, Ros Bush reported to the 1990 conference, 'surely in effect a *carte blanche* for them to continue in such a way'.

The Black Sash had also monitored a number of terrorism

trials, claims against the Minister of Law and Order, and public-violence cases. It was recognised that some of these cases were long-standing. Nevertheless, the prevailing conditions for those convicted of public violence still gave cause for concern. Despite President De Klerk's announcements on 2 February 1990, freedom was definitely not around the corner for those convicted of public violence. Since no differentiation was made between politically motivated public violence and public violence of a purely criminal nature, those serving sentences for public violence were regarded as common-law prisoners and imprisoned with ordinary criminals. 'Questioned recently as to whether De Klerk's recent announcements would result in a reduction of political trials,' was the Black Sash's conclusion,' we were unfortunately unable to answer in the affirmative.' A review of the third week of February 1990 as compared to the same period in the previous year in fact indicated an increase in the number of trials, although the fact that many of the cases in question arose out of the repression of 1988 still allowed room for hope that they would not be succeeded by as many new ones. 'However, in the light of the large number of public violence and terrorism cases we followed last year there is a deep concern that the "criminalising" of cases of political origin is escalating. Government announcements of reform will be meaningless if they are not enacted by changed legislation and if they are not accompanied by a reinstatement of the rule of law.'

In Natal the advice office workers, field-workers and repression monitors were pointing to the fact that mounting hope was mingled with despair. The figures for the advice office in Durban demonstrated that the queues were growing longer and longer. A breakdown of new cases for 1989 revealed 1,455 cases concerning social pensions, 121 cases concerning pay disputes and unfair dismissals, 89 Unemployment Insurance Fund cases, 70 Workman's Compensation Act cases, 72 company and government work pension cases, 55 insurance cases, 29 maintenance and single-care grants, 28 housing and flood-relief problems, 68 'miscellaneous' and 1,949 'interviews'. What was not evident from such analysis was the effects of the violence. Most of Durban's unrest-related cases were recorded under the unemotive classification of 'interviews' but the advice office there, as in Pietermaritzburg, was an increasingly frequent witness to the consequences of the Natal conflict. Advice office workers had recorded the tragic stories of people's disrupted lives and homes to add to the litany of death and destruction in the 'repression monitoring' bulletins. Where possible they had referred people to an organisation which might pay for a funeral, provide a food parcel, supply clothing or blankets, or to a lawyer if legal assistance seemed feasible.

The shortage of alternative accommodation for refugees who had been compelled to flee their homes or whose homes had been destroyed had become a major problem, and in the weeks during which President De Klerk announced his sweeping reforms, the conflict, far from abating, had intensified.

Despite the scale of the hostilities, despite 201 fatalities in the townships around Durban during November and December and, according to John Aitchison at the Centre for Adult Education in Pietermaritzburg, the deaths of more people during the previous three years in Natal than during the previous twenty years in Northern Ireland, the region had not been declared as a disaster area. There had been no large-scale co-ordinated relief effort and the government had consistently refused to appoint an independent commission of inquiry. Black Sash monitoring implied that the protracted violence, far from being simply a matter of 'black on black' violence as the media was suggesting, or even of a UDF/Inkatha struggle for power, embraced a number of complicating factors: 'There is, for example, the state's support of Inkatha and therefore tacit condoning of the SAP's non-interference with and even active siding with Inkatha. Further complications are the desperate socio-economic conditions and the existence of lawless bands of unemployed, half-educated, disaffected, angry youths.'

Atrocities were being perpetrated on all sides. There had been a disturbing emergence of 'people's courts', looting and necklacing since December and, as far as the Black Sash was concerned, the collusion and complicity of the police made the re-establishment of law and order a formidable task.

I've never been an advocate of the conspiracy theory [stated Wendy Annecke, chairperson of the Natal Coastal Region], but how come racially inflammatory pamphlets appeared in the townships of Natal just a week after the unbannings and on the same weekend as Mandela was released? What does the escalation of the war in Natal since the unbannings indicate and, once again, to whose advantage is it that the war continues? . . . It feels as though the infrastructure in this region is rapidly disintegrating [she concluded]. Where and how should we intervene?

The message of advice offices throughout the country was that the problems of urbanisation, homelessness, unemployment, poor wages, inadequate education and hunger were becoming more pressing than ever. On Monday, 12 February 1990, the day on which Nelson Mandela came home to Johannesburg, the waiting-room in the advice office was full.. The constitution brought into effect in 1984 meant that South Africa had a vast bureaucracy divided into racial and ethnic administrative structures. It had fourteen legislative bodies: ten homelands making laws and regulations for the people living within their geographical borders, three race-based Houses of Parliament making laws and regulations for the 'own affairs' of the people of their particular race group, and the General Affairs process for making laws pertaining to black persons who lived outside the homelands and to regulate and control national affairs for everyone. This whole structure was further complicated by the fact that four provincial administrations had been given the power to administer certain affairs for some race groups in the provincial areas of jurisdiction.

All the major issues affecting the lives of the 'little people' who found their way into the advice offices, who were not among the crowds at the 'welcome home' rallies, who did not have television on which to watch the political debate –

their education, their housing, pensions, lands, health care –
all were governed in terms of this 'own affairs' system.
Dismantling it was going to be a mammoth task. There were,
moreover, thousands of bureaucrats and several hundred
legislators who had a vested interest in its continuance. This
cumbersome system, rooted in the Population Registration
Act, would make the task of doing away with apartheid
impossible until a new democratic constitution had been
agreed upon.

The poor and dispossessed in the advice offices were not
part of the current excitement but they were, Sheena Duncan
pointed out, the people who had the most vested interest in
democratic government, in the rule of law and a just and
equitable distribution of the great wealth of South Africa.
They needed to be assured of the right to shelter, education,
security, food and a just wage. There was a very long way to
go to the achievement of such assurances and the total
dismantling of apartheid from the measures the State President had taken in unbanning banned organisations and releas-
ing Nelson Mandela. The Black Sash was not denying the
existence of real moves towards reform, however. Nor was it,
even as it sought to define its future role, pursuing the path
of rigid confrontation. In her report to the 1990 national
conference Sheena Duncan acknowledged the unprecedented
signs of hope and the enormous steps taken by the State
President towards removing the obstacles to negotiation.
When, on the occasion of the thirty-fifth birthday celebrations of the Black Sash held over the weekend of 19-20
May, she was asked by a journalist of the *Sunday Star* about
her understanding of the organisation's future role, she
defined the change as the transition to one of promoting
rather than opposing: 'Though we have always tried to
promote justice, it was done by opposition; now it must be
seen as a creative activity.'

'There is a new vocabulary in the air,' a Grahamstown
newsletter had pointed out in October 1989. 'Maybe we have
to stop using confrontational words like "demand" and seek
less emotive language too?'

During her 1989 visit to the United States for a programme

with the theme 'pluralism in the United States', perhaps precisely because of the theme chosen for the trip Mary Burton had been particularly struck by the extent of the fragmentation of United States society along ethnic lines. She had met people and groups who defined themselves as black Americans, hispanic Americans, native Americans or 'Anglos'. She had encountered people who saw themselves as marginalised and discriminated against, in spite of legislation which existed to protect those who were victims of racism, oppression and exploitation. This had led her to appreciate more fully the difficulties of resolving conflict and competition for resources. It seemed to her that people emphasised their group identity as a means of mobilising themselves for action and pressure, but that this in turn made them vulnerable to manipulation and even made it easier for them to be excluded, as groups, from access to opportunity, power, influence and wealth. She had spent sleepless nights wondering what hope there might be for South Africa if the USA with all its might and resources had not found ways to resolve these problems. After her return she had come to believe with stronger conviction than ever that the best future lay in sharing resources, in strengthening democracy and non-racialism and in building unity, minimising conflict and division.

It was almost impossible to measure the achievements of the Black Sash over the thirty-five years of its existence. The organisation could count an impressive list of failures, for seldom, if ever, had its protests actually managed to stop the passage of legislation destructive to human rights. But perhaps its mere survival for thirty-five years in a political climate inimical to human rights and dissent was a not inconsiderable achievement in itself. The words of two long-standing Black Sash members pinpointed the process in which the organisation had been consistently engaged. 'We keep banging our head against a brick wall and hoping for a miracle,' one explained. The other's response was: 'Miracles don't happen. But the wall is crumbling and those ensconced behind it have lost faith in its protection. We have to find ways of picking out a bit of mortar here and removing a brick there.' How was it possible to assess the progress of such an undertaking, to know who read what the Black Sash women wrote, who listened to what they said? How was the process of 'conscientising' to be measured other than in terms of chance comments sometimes accidentally overheard that, had it not been for the Black Sash protests an individual would not have known about certain conditions, certain problems?

The respect its members had earned for themselves was manifest in a multitude of ways: in the warmth and deferential tones of the solemn comment: 'That's the Black Sash', as one young woman in East London arrived at a garage to take issue with the manager over the circumstances of the dismissal of one of his employees; in the admission of one whose Pan-African allegiances added to the stature of his compliment: 'Maybe my way of approaching certain issues would be different, but in my African tradition they are mothers and I hold them in very high esteem. Even if it has meant travelling three hundred kilometres, the Black Sash have been there. They have come to me and the suffering people.'

With AZAPO (the Azanian People's Organisation), which did not in general have much regard for the role of white liberals in the freedom struggle, the Black Sash had earned itself recognition as a 'useful resource'. According to a spokesman for the Cape Democrats, among the Mass Democratic Movement Black Sash members enjoyed enormous regard for 'their sincerity, their integrity and their willingness to participate in a very democratic way without pushing themselves'. There were still those who regarded them as biased and still those who felt that Black Sash women would be better occupied at the kitchen sink. In October 1989 Ken Owen, journalist and editor of *Business Day*, referred to the 'Protesting Mums of the Black Sash'. Helen Suzman, on the occasion of the twentieth anniversary of the Black Sash, had commented on how the quiet persistence of the Black Sash, its nagging, had had its effects over the years: 'There was a time, I remember, when the very mention of the Black Sash used to send the then Minister of Bantu Administration and

Development into a paroxysm of sibilant rage. He used to hiss "Black Sash" as if it were a nest of vipers. These days the reaction is less violent, far more resigned, indeed almost conciliatory. Concessions are sometimes made or at least promised.' What Black Sash women themselves would probably regard as the highest accolade of all, however, came more recently from a Nationalist junior cabinet minister. 'We hate them,' he said. 'They are our consciences.'

In 1987 the Black Sash was nominated by the Swedish party Folkpartiet, a member of Liberal International, for the Nobel Peace Prize. Perhaps never until the events of 1990 had that peace-making role been so crucially challenged, but by 1990 the organisation also had a wealth of experience on which to call. For some years now the Black Sash itself had reflected a unity, albeit sometimes strained, of different views, generations, political standpoints. It had managed to embrace not only those for whom credibility with the black communities was of crucial importance, but also those who, always assuming that the two were in some way mutually exclusive, would opt for moral integrity on the grounds that, as Noël Robb put it, 'I'm not sure that we have much credibility with the black communities anyway.' It had included women who felt that the organisation could no longer afford not to be a feminist organisation, and those who saw feminism as a threat to established family structures. It had held together those naturally drawn to the intellectual gratifications of the world of political debate and those more openly motivated by compassion in its full sense of 'suffering with'. It had also held together those who aligned themselves with the more traditional liberal values of the women who had initiated the organisation, and those whose vision was essentially that of the ANC.

There had been a lesson with regard to relationships with the ANC for the organisation as a whole in the November 1989 Namibia elections. Prior to those elections SWAPO had been recognised by the international community, both east and west, and by the Black Sash, as the sole and authentic voice of the Namibian people. In Namibia the independence which was about to be celebrated might never have happened

without the tremendous support given to SWAPO. Nevertheless, the elections had demonstrated that SWAPO was by no
means the only party with support in the fledgeling independent state. The attitude of many Black Sash members to the
ANC was characterised by the pragmatic recognition that the
ANC currently represented the black liberation sentiment in
South Africa, by a feeling that they must get to know it, work
with it, live with it because it was going to run South Africa.
That was not being used; it was simply recognising a politi-
cal/social fact. Nor did it rule out the recognition of other
voices. Mary Burton had no doubt that in the future many
Black Sash members would decide to belong to the ANC, but
those who had belonged to the Democratic Party would
undoubtedly continue to do so.

The language of *Sash* magazine, and indeed of the organisation as a whole, no longer reflected the high moral tone and
overt expression of Christian principle which it had done
during the 'fifties and 'sixties (although curiously enough,
quotations from *Alice's Adventures in Wonderland* were still
frequent and apposite). There were those in the organisation
now who would prefer to exclude from the dedication (otherwise unchanged except that it no longer expressed the reaffir-
mation to the 'contract of the Union') the last line: 'So help
us God, in Whose strength we trust.'

> Working-class organisations must be rebuilt to take
> forward the task of leading the mass struggle for food,
> shelter and democratic rights [wrote one Transvaal
> advice office researcher in assessing the challenge for
> the advice offices during the 1990s]. Advice offices have
> an important role to play as a source of continuity and
> access to resources. They need to analyse successes and
> failures in order to plan strategically. The challenge for
> the 1990s is to recognise that the bulk of advice office
> work is related to the attack on the working class by the
> state and big business, and to actively align advice office
> work with working-class organisations in their struggle.

Alongside the language of Marxism and the class war, however, alongside the warnings to the present government and

the criticisms, there was also within the Black Sash the message of healing, forgiveness and peace.

It was from a vantage point of its own unity in diversity then, that the national executive of the Black Sash endeavoured to understand the causes of the widespread violence which was shaking the country and augmenting the uncertainty of a transition period. It had identified a contest for power and control, attacks based on racist hostility, intimidation, punishment and revenge, and outright warfare between competing forces. In such a context the Black Sash continued to see its task as one of defending the rule of law and protecting the rights of the public against incursions by the state, but it also made a point of expressing the horror it had felt over the years at the killings of alleged collaborators and informers, whose actions, it stated clearly, it did not excuse. The most urgent task now was to find ways of building peace instead of conflict. 'How is this country to be healed?' a letter circulated to all members in May 1990 posed the question, and supplied the answer as the executive saw it:

1. All must share the responsibility. Causes and culprits must be identified, and the government must acknowledge its task as the ultimate provider of protection for all. This means that it is of the utmost importance that the police and the army are impartial servants of the public and are seen to be so.

2. The constitution-making process must be as speedy as possible, and as consultative and open as possible. Those who see no future for themselves unless they fight for it must be persuaded that there is a vehicle through which their aspirations can be met. The Bill of Rights is essential, but so is a real commitment to address the economic restructuring which must take place.

3. The help of those who have power to affect the outcome of events must be enlisted. It is inevitable that

the actions of the powerful business community, the
outside world, the unionised labour force, the religious
communities and other groupings within and outside
the country have an impact on events. It is perhaps not
surprising that those who fear the possibility of one
political grouping (for example the ANC) acquiring too
much power will therefore support an opposing party.
Of course this is entirely legitimate as long as the
competition remains at the level of political contest –
but when thousands of lives are at stake, and the fabric
of the society is being torn apart, sectarian interests
must take second place to a common commitment to
peace.

4. Part of the process of healing is the
acknowledgement of past wrongs. Retribution and
revenge are not conducive to reconstruction, but a new
edifice cannot be built on secrecy and guilt. The role of
independent commissions is vital in opening up to the
light all the evils which have taken place, so that old
ghosts can be laid to rest. South Africa will depend
heavily on the capacity of all its people to forgive, a
capacity which has often been generously demonstrated.
Knowledge of the truth, however, is the precursor to
forgiveness. (It is for this reason that the prompt
acknowledgement by the ANC of its responsibility for
any malpractice in its detention camps is to be
welcomed, and that its commitment and that of other
parties to continuing openness is a necessary
component of future peace.)

5. Those who are and have been combatants and
victims must be of primary concern. The country's
resources must be urgently directed towards a
programme of counselling, curing, educating and
training this battered generation – those within the
country and those who will return to it. This requires
the mobilisation of all who have skills to impart,
resources to share and the ability to provide

employment and occupation. It means using educators and counsellors, traditional and modern healers, religious leaders and people of influence in the economy. It also needs ordinary men and women who are willing to devote time, care and effort towards meeting this vital need.

The Black Sash was confident that it had some of these abilities. Its advice officers and field-workers could offer valuable services. Its commitment to human rights, to justice and to peace demanded that its members dedicated themselves to this work. It would not allow itself to be dismayed by the current conflict, nor to lose faith in the prospect of a future founded on justice and therefore conducive to peace.

In her presidential address to the 1990 conference, entitled ' "Fighting out of the Darkness" or moving gradually towards the light?', Mary Burton picked up precisely the point which Archbishop Hurley had made. The words of the first half of her title came from a member of a right-wing organisation who had told a journalist of the *Weekly Mail* in February of that year to remember 'that the Boers were the ones who invented guerilla warfare. It's still in the soul of our people, that fighting out of the darkness.' This was, she said, a sombre reminder of the legacy of anger, racism and bitterness which apartheid had bequeathed to South Africa – a legacy which would have to be reckoned with long after apartheid itself was truly dead. The white people who gathered at rallies to support the Afrikaner Weerstandsbeweging (the Afrikaner resistance movement) and who attacked black people and smashed property came from the same cauldron of hate as the disaffected black youth who took advantage of mass marches to vandalise and loot. The militant cadres of Umkhonto we Sizwe and the well-armed factions of the white extremists could equally pose a danger to the precarious process of negotiating the transformation of South African society into one united nation.

In such a context what was the role of the Black Sash to be? The aims of the Black Sash constitution left no doubt that the organisation was against apartheid. 'We know we are AGAINST injustice, exclusion and repression. We need to know also what we are FOR.' The Black Sash needed to look very carefully at what it meant by human rights. The right to free assembly; to freedom of speech and of the press; to freedom of movement; to protection from arbitrary arrest, detention or exile; to protection from torture; to a fair and public trial; to a nationality; to equality – these were the 'first-generation' rights which had been written into constitutions and bills of rights in many countries of the world, and indeed into the Universal Declaration of Human Rights. The drive towards these first-generation civil and political rights underpinned the work of the Black Sash, but the organisation's members also knew that social and economic deprivation was a denial of freedom. In a country like South Africa, where there was an enormous disparity between the rich and the poor, attention must be directed towards the 'second-generation' rights – to social security, to education and training, to work opportunities and to adequate and non-discriminatory wages and working conditions. Some of the solutions to these problems lay in the political realm and would form the basis of the changes which must come. The Black Sash's first task there would be to maintain the pressure to undo the bureaucratic and financial disaster of separate and very unequal government departments.

Then there was the question of land and housing: if there was to be any reality in the changes to come the Land Acts and the Group Areas would have to be repealed. Would new mechanisms be introduced? Who would have access to land for urban and agricultural development? And who would pay? The present government must not be allowed so to privatise the provision of housing and of services such as the South African Transport Services, nor so to tax basic foods, that these were denied to those who most needed affordable shelter, transport and food. A clearer understanding had to be developed of how the essential reforms were to be financed in a future society. The Black Sash must consider how to foster the growth in the economy which would lead to greater employment and generate the necessary funds to provide protection for the needy and redress the injustices and imbalances of the past. These socio-economic issues were the foundation stones on which the 'third-generation' rights – to opportunities for development, to a clean and healthy environment, and to peace – could be built.

These rights, Mary Burton intimated, could be written into a new constitution, in a Bill of Rights, in specific charters or by signing international conventions such as the Universal Declaration of Human Rights or the International Convention of the Rights of the Child. Such a formal commitment would be a great step forward for South Africa, but an even more important process was the inscription of those same rights deep in the minds of South Africans: 'Only by learning to place faith in them, to recognise that these are what protect and nurture the whole society, will we learn not to seek our security in group identity and ethnic divisiveness.'

As she concluded her term of office at the March 1990 conference Mary Burton expressed the view that the Black Sash would best serve this end and a future government representing the majority of South Africans if it could uphold the ideal of human rights regardless of party political constraints. It would do so most successfully if it reflected within its membership a broad spectrum of the total society, so that what held it together was neither colour, nor class, nor gender but common values. The organisation had not made adequate space within it for Afrikaans-speaking women who shared its political perspectives. She was conscious too of the criticisms levelled both in and outside South Africa at white South African women who claimed to work for equality and justice but who paid their domestic workers abysmal wages. The Black Sash response must be that many of its members did indeed occupy a privileged position as employers and that part of their effort to learn to live as equals with fellow South Africans required them to address employment practices, particularly their own. It was in this regard that, whilst remaining non-affiliated, they had much to derive from working closely with other women's organisations.

There was still a place in the collective task of changing South Africa for an organisation which at that particular point in South African history was made up mainly of women who were classified white and who were educationally and financially among the privileged class, and one area on which Mary Burton considered it should concentrate more was the need to make opportunities to talk to their critics in the white sector, to address the doubts, hostilities and fears encountered in their own peer group. Power was the potential corrupter of any government. There would always be a need for an organisation that worried about human rights and the dignity of the individual. Already there were fears among South Africa's coloured population, for example, that coloureds would find themselves in a worse position under a black nationalist government than under a white one.

The 1990 conference, far from reflecting a diminution of role, established a new 'Northern Transvaal Region' for the Black Sash, based in Pretoria, an area where white conservatism was at its strongest and the AWB had its roots, and gave the organisation a clear programme of work for the future. It tackled the internal problems arising out of the fact that many members were employed outside the organisation and therefore had little or no time to offer during formal working hours, the consequent need to employ workers to expand the work even further and finance and administer it properly. It reasserted its position on affiliation, alignment and alliances. With regard to redressing the injustices of economic disadvantage, lack of educational, training and employment opportunities and inadequate social services and welfare, it committed itself to the principle of redistribution but also in the short term to sharing the resources and skills it had achieved in its work, to working alongside communities and facilitating the voicing of their grievances and aims, and working with other service organisations on related issues. It also undertook to educate itself and the broader public in the complexities of redressing such injustices.

As far as human rights were concerned, a new dimension had entered into its commitment to the development of a human rights culture in South Africa with the recognition that the civil and political, the socio-economic and the developmental and environmental rights were inextricably interlinked. A focus on environmental issues had not previously been a major concern for the Black Sash but interest was clearly growing, together with an awareness that the protection of the ecology could clash with the real needs of a growing urban population. Among the contributions the organisation felt it could make to the spread of a human rights culture was the provision of resource material to stimulate study and debate.

With regard to women's issues, it was concluded that on a philosophical level the Black Sash should adopt a 'feminist ecological perspective', that on a political level it should continue to be a human rights organisation – with an added dimension of always asking how each area of its work affected women – and that on a practical level it should remain an organisation of women 'as an interim strategy for our empowerment'. Not insignificantly, the women's interest groups seemed to be moving towards a more mature vision, not so much of a feminism which was a laundry list of women's issues but of so-called eco-feminism which sought to address all oppression: the oppression of black people by whites, of the Third World by the First, of women by men, of children by adults, of the countryside by the cities, of the ecosystem by industry, of humanity's deeper self by consumerism. Eco-feminism was an increasingly nuanced diagnosis of the illness that afflicted both humanity and the earth and an attempt at creating a holistic cure seen as a movement towards a SHE (sane, humane, ecological) future as opposed to a HE (hyper-expansionist) future.

Finally, in relation to the dismantling of apartheid, it was agreed that the organisation would embark on a campaign against the 'own affairs' schedule to the 1983 constitution which lay at the root of the apartheid administration system. This campaign would build on the work already being done in the broad democratic movement in the form of the defiance campaign regarding hospitals, beaches and all public amenities; the demand for all schools for all people; the one city, open city campaigns; and the opposition to racially based local authorities. A Black Sash campaign could put these and other mass actions into the constitutional perspective and further the process of public education on constitutional systems and justice.

'It is very simple for the ANC to say that when they take over they will have a democracy, but what will the situation really be?' General Stadler had asked. 'It is very simple for the Conservative Party to say, "If we take over we'll double the police force," but the fact is that if either of them take over, they will have exactly the same problems as the government is having now . . . If the Black Sash could come up with a solution . . .' the General had implied that in that case he would hold the organisation in higher regard, but perhaps that was not its particular role, any more than it was its role to take strong positions and adhere to them or to walk what some would call 'the last mile'.

In a quieter moment, Mary Burton had confided:

In a time of turbulent change, it is probably important
for people to take strong sides and strong loyalties and
stick to them in an effort to acquire power for their
point of view, but I don't think that is our role. I think
our role is precisely to stay a little on the side lines and
to keep on raising uncomfortable questions and posing
difficult issues. And a lot of the time we will be brushed
aside by the events of our history, but I like to think
that in the end it will have been valuable to have been
making those points, raising those questions, reminding
people of the issues. I hope it won't all have been for
nothing. I don't believe it will.

The Freedom Charter

as adopted at the Congress of the People
on 26 June 1955

Preamble

We, the people of South Africa, declare for all our country and the world to know:

That South Africa belongs to all who live in it, black and white, and that no government can justly claim authority unless it is based on the will of the people;

That our people have been robbed of their birthright to land, liberty and peace by a form of government founded on injustice and inequality;

That our country will never be prosperous or free until all our people live in brotherhood, enjoying equal rights and opportunities;

That only a democratic state, based on the will of the people can secure to all their birthright without distinction of colour, race, sex or belief;

And therefore, we the people of South Africa, black and white, together equals, countrymen and brothers adopt this FREEDOM CHARTER. And we pledge ourselves to strive together, sparing nothing of our strength and courage, until the democratic changes here set out have been won.

The people shall govern!

Every man and woman shall have the right to vote for and stand as a candidate for all bodies which make laws.

All the people shall be entitled to take part in the administration of the country.

The rights of the people shall be the same regardless of race, colour or sex.

All bodies of minority rule, advisory boards, councils and authorities shall be replaced by democratic organs of self-government.

All national groups shall have equal rights!

There shall be equal status in the bodies of state, in the courts and in the schools for all national groups and races;

All national groups shall be protected by law against insults to their race and national pride;

All people shall have equal rights to use their own language and to develop their own folk culture and customs;

The preaching and practice of national, race or colour discrimination and contempt shall be a punishable crime;

All apartheid laws and practices shall be set aside.

The people shall share in the country's wealth!

The national wealth of our country, the heritage of all South Africans, shall be
  restored to the people;
The mineral wealth beneath the soil, the banks and monopoly industry shall be
  transferred to the ownership of the people as a whole;
All other industries and trade shall be controlled to assist the well-being of the
  people;
All people shall have equal rights to trade where they choose, to manufacture
  and to enter all trades, crafts and professions.

The land shall be shared among those who work it!

Restriction of land ownership on a racial basis shall be ended, and all the land re-
  divided amongst those who work it, to banish famine and land hunger;
The state shall help the peasants with implements, seed, tractors and dams to
  save the soil and assist the tillers;
Freedom of movement shall be guaranteed to all who work on the land;
All shall have the right to occupy land wherever they choose;
People shall not be robbed of their cattle, and forced labour and farm prisons
  shall be abolished.

All shall be equal before the law

No one shall be imprisoned, deported or restricted without fair trial;
No one shall be condemned by the order of any Government official;
The courts shall be representative of all the people;
Imprisonment shall be only for serious crimes against the people, and shall aim
  at re-education, not vengeance;
The police force and army shall be open to all on an equal basis and shall be the
  helpers and protectors of the people;
All laws which discriminate on the grounds of race, colour or belief shall be
  repealed.

All shall enjoy human rights!

The law shall guarantee to all their right to speak, to organise, to meet together,
  to publish, to preach, to worship and to educate their children;
The privacy of the house from police raids shall be protected by law;
All shall be free to travel without restriction from countryside to town, from
  province to province, and from South Africa abroad.
Pass laws, permits and all other laws restricting these freedoms shall be
  abolished.

There shall be work and security!

All who work shall be free to form trade unions, to elect their officers and to make
  wage agreements with their employers;
The state shall recognise the right and duty of all to work, and to draw full
  unemployment benefits;
Men and women of all races shall receive equal pay for equal work;
There shall be a forty-hour working week, a national minimum wage, paid annual

leave, and sick leave for all workers, and maternity leave on full pay for all working mothers;

Miners, domestic workers, farm workers and civil servants shall have the same rights as all others who work;

Child labour, compound labour, the tot system and contract labour shall be abolished.

The doors of learning and culture shall be opened!

The government shall discover, develop and encourage national talent for the enhancement of our cultural life;

All the cultural treasures of mankind shall be open to all, by free exchange of books, ideas and contact with other lands;

The aim of education shall be to teach the youth to love their people and their culture, to honour human brotherhood, liberty and peace;

Education shall be free, compulsory, universal and equal for all children;

Higher education and technical training shall be opened to all by means of state allowances and scholarships warded on the basis of merit;

Adult illiteracy shall be ended by a mass state education plan;

Teachers shall have all the rights of other citizens;

The colour bar in cultural life, in sport and in education shall be abolished.

There shall be houses, security and comfort!

All people shall have the right to live where they choose, to be decently housed, and to bring up their families in comfort and security;

Unused housing space to be made available to the people;

Rent and prices shall be lowered, food plentiful and no one shall go hungry;

A preventive health scheme shall be run by the state;

Free medical care and hospitalisation shall be provided for all, with special care for mothers and young children;

Slums shall be demolished and new suburbs built where all shall have transport, roads, lighting, playing fields, crèches and social centres;

The aged, the orphans, the disabled and the sick shall be cared for by the state;

Rest, leisure and recreation shall be the right of all;

Fenced locations and ghettoes shall be abolished and laws which break up families shall be repealed.

There shall be peace and friendship!

South Africa shall be a fully independent state, which repects the rights and sovereignty of all nations;

South Africa shall strive to maintain world peace and the settlement of all international disputes by negotiation not war;

Peace and friendship amongst all our people shall be secured by upholding the equal rights, opportunities and status of all;

The people of the protectorates Basutoland, Bechuanaland and Swaziland shall be free to decide for themselves their own future;

The right of all the peoples of Africa to independence and self-government shall be recognised, and shall be the basis of close cooperation.

Let all who love their people and their country now say, as we say here: THESE FREEDOMS WE WILL FIGHT FOR, SIDE BY SIDE, THROUGHOUT OUR LIVES UNTIL WE HAVE WON OUR LIBERTY.

The Iceberg Principle

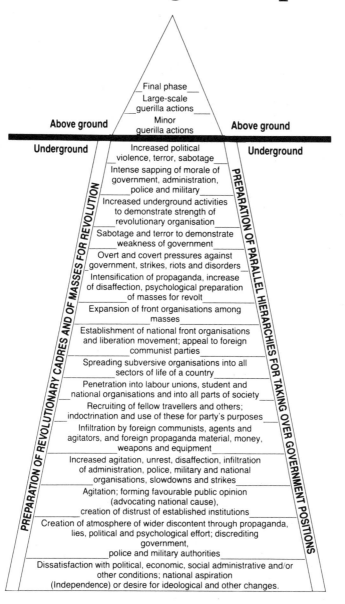

Appendix 3

Glossary

ANC	African National Congress
AWB	Afrikaner Weerstandsbeweging
AZAPO	Azanian People's Organisation
CAL	Cape Action League
CATAPAW	Cape Association to Abolish Passes for Women
COSAS	Congress of South African Students
COSATU	Congress of South African Trade Unions
CP	Conservative Party
CRADORA	Cradock Residents Association
CRADOYA	Cradock Youth Association
ECC	End Conscription Campaign
EDASA	Education for an Aware South Africa
FEDSAW	Federation of South African Women
MDM	Mass Democratic Movement
NICRO	National Institute for Crime Prevention and Rehabilitation of Offenders
NUSAS	National Union of South African Students
PAC	Pan African Congress
PFP	Progressive Federal Party
SACC	South African Council of Churches
SACP	South African Communist Party
SADF	South African Defence Forces
SAP	South African Police
SWAPO	South West African People's Organisation
TRAC	Transvaal Rural Action Committee
UDF	United Democratic Front
UNITA	National Union for the Total Independence of Angola
WPCC	Western Province Council of Churches

Index

Abolition of Influx Control Act (1986), 78, 100
Abolition of Passes and Coordination of Documents Act (1952), 51, 52–3, 61, 71, 100, 286–7
academic freedom, 73
Academic Staff Association of the University of the Witwatersrand, 237
affiliation, issue of, 209, 240, 241, 250, 254–5; with FEDSAW, 241, 254, 255, 258; with Institute of Race Relations, 209; with UDF, 209, 213–14, 292
African Resistance movement, 68–9
Africa Watch, 160
Afrikaans language, 25, 135
Afrikaner Weerstandsbeweging (AWB: Afrikaner Resistance Movement), 313, 316
Afrikaners (Boers), 5, 6, 25–6, 27, 163, 243–4, 287; Black Sash supporters among, 30–1, 35–6, 43, 60, 315; Broederbond, 5; Kontak women's organisation, 243; social survival syndrome, 287–8
AIDS among black population, 9
Aitchison, John, 304
Alexandra Township, 234
Amnesty International, 160
ANC (African National Congress), 9, 15, 17, 20, 47, 62, 64, 68, 98, 135, 146, 162, 183, 193, 200, 215, 217, 221–2, 238, 249, 295, 300, 309, 312, 318; acts of terrorism, 20, 136–8, 221; Arusha conference (1987), 137; banning of (1960), 20, 63, 64, 68, 69, 138, 139; and Black Sash, 202, 205–6, 217, 221, 255, 280, 290, 292, 309–10; and civil disobedience, 270, 275; Defiance Campaign (1989), 275–6; establishment of (1912), 43; FEDSAW's alignment with, 257; Five Freedoms Forum (1989), 237, 280; and 'internal dimension', 20, 136–8; leadership in Lusaka, 22; misuse of funds, 15; National
Executive, 241; 'people's war' revolutionary strategy, 20, 136–7; trial of ringleaders, 138; Umkhonto we Sizwe (military wing), 20, 22, 161, 204, 228, 300, 313; unbanning of, 209, 306; women's role according to, 253–4
ANC Women's League, 63–4, 241, 256
Andrew, Ken, 169
Anglican Church Mother's Union, 63
Anglo-Boer War (1899–22), 25, 26, 287
Angola, 135, 218, 222, 238
Annecke, Wendy, ix, 305
apartheid, 5–7, 266–7; Afrikaners' rationalisation of, 6; Defiance Campaign (1989), 275–8; dismantling of, 189, 262–7, 295–6, 297, 305–6, 317; English-speaking whites' moral condemnation of, 6; new-look, 267; 'petty', 284–5; and violence, 187–208, 209; see also homelands; pass laws; relocation
Appellate Division, 28
Arusha conference, ANC (1987), 137
Asians, 5, 81, 82, 100; see also Indians
Association for Rural Advancement, 106
Athlone advice office, Black Sash, 64–6, 68, 86, 149
Atteridgeville school, 234
AZAPO (Azanian People's Organisation), 98, 308; UDF feud with, 178

Baird, Zilla Harries, ix, 55
Bakwena tribe, 107
Bantu Education Act (1953), 49, 233
Bantu Homeland Citizenship Act (1970), 113
Bantu (Urban Areas) Consolidation Act (1945), 51–2, 71
Bantustans see homelands
Baragwanath Hospital, Soweto, 14
Beckett, Denis, 202
Beckett, George, 29, 31
Belville Community Organisation, 255
Berman, Mr Justice, 152–3

Bernstein, Hilda, 241
Bethanie, 108
Biko, Steve, 155, 156, 161
Bisho, Amatola Sun Casino, 120
Bishop, Brian, 165, 171, 180, 182, death
    and funeral of, 182–3, 184, 265
Bishop, Di, x, 164–7, 169, 170, 180–1,
    182, 185; trial of (1984), 170–1
Black Administration Act, 111
Black Communities Development Act
    (1984), 210 &n
Black Consciousness movement, 135,
    136, 156, 185
black funerals/cemeteries, 7–8, 127–8,
    178–9, 198, 200, 204–5
Black Local Authorities Act (1982), 210
    &n
Black Sash (originally: Women's Defence
    of the Constitution League), Advice
    Office Trust Fund, 238; advice offices,
    2–4, 7, 19, 64–6, 68, 69, 70, 71, 74–7,
    79, 82, 91, 98, 104, 118–19, 140, 147,
    148–9, 163–4, 187, 201, 261, 296,
    303–4, 305–6, 313; affiliation issue,
    209, 213–14, 240, 241, 250, 254–5,258;
    African schools issue, 126–7; and ANC,
    202, 205–6, 217, 221, 255, 280, 290,
    292, 309–10; associate members, 237;
    bail fund for African women, 66–7;
    'Black Sash' adopted as official name
    (1956), 49; Blackburn and Bishop trial,
    Cradock (1984), 170–1; campaign
    against forced removals and
    homelessness, 83–99, 101, 103, 105–12,
    188; campaign to abolish capital
    punishment, 227–32; Cape Town
    demonstration (1956), 38–42; Charter
    for Women (1971), 251; civil
    disobedience, 260–1, 263–5, 268–74,
    276–8, 290; 'Clemency for Sharpeville
    Six' protest, 272–4; 'Comment
    addressed to the Churches' (1982),
    115–16; community advice offices
    fostered by, 296–7; and conscientious
    objection, 218–19, 250; court-
    monitoring by, 129–35, 140–9, 151–3,
    204, 225, 299–303; Crossroads
    campaign, 86–97; deaths and funerals of
    Molly Blackburn and Brian Bishop,
    182–5; Declaration of Human Rights
    accepted by, 57; Defiance Campaign
    (1989), 276–8; detention of members,
    270–1, 281–2, 284–5, 289; and detention
    without trial, 154–60; in Eastern Cape,
    162–85; eco-feminism, 317; and
    education, 233–6; End Conscription
    Campaign, 218–23; environmental
    issues, 317; excluded from IWY
    exhibition (1975), 242–3; female
    exclusivity policy, 252–3; and FEDSAW,

241–2, 244–5, 247, 250, 251–2, 253, 254,
    255–9, 278–9; 'Fighting out of the
    Darkness' (Mary Burton's address to
    1990 conference), 313–15; first advice
    office opened in Athlone (1958), 64–6;
    Five Freedoms Forum (1989), 237, 240,
    280–1, 290; Free the Children
    Campaign, 223–6; and Freedom
    Charter, 192, 211, 212; fund-raising,
    237–9; Guguletu Funeral Gang case,
    149–51; Helen Suzman made honorary
    life member (1990), 79; homelands
    issue, 112–23; 'How is this country to
    be healed?' (letter to members, 1990),
    311–13; Internal Security Act, 138; and
    Institute of Race Relations, 209–10;
    Kontak, 243; Langa massacre (1985),
    174–6; lesbian members, 249–50; link
    between Churches and, 232–3; male
    membership, 252, 253; membership,
    17–18, 57–8, 218, 237, 249, 252–3;
    murder of Goniwe and friends, 177–9;
    and national convention, 210, 214–15;
    National Executive, 38; New Brighton
    trial of Molly Blackburn, 181–2;
    nominated for Nobel Peace Prize, 309;
    and pass laws, 54–5, 56, 61–7, 70–2,
    74–80, 188; petition calling for
    Strijdom's resignation, 31, 32–3; and
    PFP, 191, 216; police relations with,
    19–22, 68–9, 162, 278–82, 289–90;
    policy of upholding rule of law, 260–2,
    269; Port Elizabeth advice office set on
    fire, 19, 164; problems in the home for
    members of, 252–3; protest stands,
    262–3, 271–4, 295; and relaxation of
    legislative controls, 295–6, 293; Senate
    Bill protest, 28–32, 38–42; silent vigils,
    33–5; 59; Surplus People's Project, 81,
    82; support among Afrikaners for, 30–1,
    35–6, 43, 60, 315; telephone tapping,
    261; 35th birthday celebrations (1990),
    306; TRAC, 104–5, 107–13; trips
    abroad, 236–7; UDF'S relations with,
    139–40, 192, 209, 210–18, 221, 245,
    292; Uitenhage police station
    encounter (1985), 172–4; universal
    franchise supported by, 58–9; violence
    debate, 187–208; women's
    organisations' relations with, 242–5;
    women's issues (feminism), 18, 54,
    245–52, 253–4, 317; Workbench
    Centre, 119; 'You and the New Pass
    Laws' booklet, 114, 116
Black Sash see Sash
Black Sash national conferences, 210;
    1955, first conference, Port Elizabeth:
    38; 1956, Bloemfontein: 48–9; 1959: 73,
    145–6; 1983: 211, 218; 1984,
    Johannesburg: 110, 111, 209, 213; 1985,

30th conference, Port Elizabeth: 171, 172; 1986, Durban: 203, 223, 225, 233, 260, 265; 1988, Johannesburg: 98, 229, 236; 1989; 250; 1990; 297, 306, 313–15, 316
black townships, 7, 10–12, 13–15, 162; gang warfare, 147–8, 149–51; movement of South African army into, 222; necklacings, 9, 22; police control of, 282–4; schools boycotts/drop-outs, 137, 147, 148, 168, 234, 284; violence in, 22, 138, 169–70, 200–1, 202, 203, 217, 223, 271; *see also* individual townships
Blackburn, Dr Gavin, 182–3
Blackburn, Molly, 10, 162, 198, 247, 259; arrest and trial of, 170–1, 181–2; death and funeral (1985), 7–8, 23, 182–5, 265; Eastern Cape activities, 164–82 *passim*; 'Life among the evicted in "the fairest Cape"', 166
Blesi, Michael, 182
Bloemfontein, 35, 36, 43, 48–9
Blue Water Bay, 177, 178
Boesak, Rev. Dr Allan, 11, 109, 138, 183
Bongolethu, black township, 182
Bophutatswana, homeland, 5, 103, 107, 112, 117–18, 230, 269–70; Independence (1977), 113; incorporation of Braklaagte and Leeuwfontein into, 113; and of Pachsdraai, 107
Boraine, Alex, 183
Border Council of Churches, 121
Borders of Particular States Extension Act (1986), 112, 298
Bosazza, Jean, 28
Botha, President P. W., 79, 92–3, 114, 139, 176, 212, 216, 268; Nelson Mandela's meeting with, 300; 1983 referendum of, 216
boycotts and stayaways, 10n, 120, 192, 193, 195, 223, 270; consumer, 137, 200–1; election, 191, 192, 216, 275; rent, 137, 284; school, 137, 147, 148, 168, 234
Braklaagte, 113; incorporation into Bophutatswana of, 113
Brandvlei prison, 146
Broederbond 5
Broeksma, Mr Acting Justice, 76
Bundy, Colin, 281
Burton, Mary (President of Black Sash), 158–9, 194, 204, 205–6, 207, 236, 239, 247, 249, 257, 271, 273, 292–3, 310, 318; and Defiance Campaign, 276, 277, 278; 'Fighting out of the Darkness' (address to 1990 conference), 313–16; and police relations, 278, 279; US trip, 306–7
Bush, Ros, x, 149, 150–1, 300, 302

Buthelezi, Chief Gatsha, 74, 198–9, 200
Buthelezi, Bishop Manus, 232

Calata, Fort, 10, 169; murder and funeral of, 177–9
Campbell, Tilly, 55
Cape Action League, 98
Cape Coloured Voters Bill, 48
Cape Coloureds, 50; removal of voting rights, 24, 25, 26–32, 35, 44
Cape Democrats, 308
Cape Province, removal of non-white voting rights in, 25, 26, 27; *see also* Eastern Cape; Western Cape
Cape Provincial Council, 48, 164–5, 166, 169, 182
Cape Times, 40, 166, 170, 176, 181, 182, 243
Cape Town, 1–4, 18, 34, 50, 146, 182, 205, 243, 253, 258, 294; Black Sash advice offices in, 2–4, 7, 19, 64–6, 68, 75, 86, 91, 147–9, 296; Black Sash HQ moved to, 73, 203; Black Sash protests and demonstrations, 36, 38–42, 106, 271, 272–4, 276–7, 286, 287; Defiance Campaign in Greenmarket Square, 276–8; funeral of Brian Bishop, 184; law courts, 130–2, 134, 150; Legal Resources Centre, 77; population growth, 100; *see also* Athlone; Crossroads; Guguletu; Khayelitsha; Langa; Mowbray
Cape Western Black Sash, 230, 232, 243, 274
capital punishment (death sentence), 10, 153; campaign to abolish (1988), 227–32; and Sharpeville Six, 271–4; suspension of (1990), 297
Carolas, Cheryl, 258–9
casspirs (police armed vehicles), 11
CATAPAW (Cape Association to Abolish Passes for Women), 56, 62
Catholic Child Welfare Council of England and Wales, 225
Catholic Institute for International Relations, 283
Centre for Applied Legal Studies, University of Witwatersrand, 120
Chalmers, Judy, x, 162, 164, 169, 175, 177, 178, 182, 184, 185, 187; security police search house of, 280–1
Charter for Women (1971), 251
Charterists, 185; *see also* Freedom Charter
Cherry, Janet, x, 288–90
Chikane, Rev.Frank, 232
Chikane, Moses 'Moss', 139
Child Welfare Society, 224
children/juveniles: assaults and deaths of, 172–4, 223, 264–5; court cases, 143,

147, 148–51; in detention, 155, 180, 182, 223, 225–6, 234; Free the Children campaign, 223–6; gang warfare, 147–8, 149; Guguletu Funeral Gang case, 149–51; school boycotts, 137, 147, 148, 168, 234
Chinese in South Africa, 114
Christian National Education, 49
Chubb, Karin, 250, 251–2, 253, 254
Church of the Province of Southern Africa, 146
CIA, 238
Ciskei, homeland, 5, 86, 103, 112, 118, 119, 120–2, 128, 162, 230; conflict in, 120; incorporation of Peelton into (1988), 121–2, 123, 124, 297–8; Independence (1981), 114, 120–1; State of Emergency (1988), 121–2
citizens' action committee, 84
civil disobedience, 260–1, 263–5, 268–78, 290; Defiance Campaign (1989), 275–8; FEDSAW march in Cape Town, 278–9; penalties for calling for, 270; SACC's support for, 274–5; Sharpeville Six stand, 273–4
Civil Rights League, 165
civil service, white, 288
Claassens, Aninka, ix, 104, 110, 111, 112
Coleman, Audrey, 174, 178
Coloured Labour Preference Policy, 62, 63, 69, 87
coloured (or mixed) race, 5, 17, 67–8, 100, 114, 124, 243; free movement of, 50; House of Parliament, 199, 216, 267; municipal advice bureaux for, 68; relocation of, 81, 82; removal of voting rights (1955), 24, 25, 26–32, 35, 38–42, 44; in Western Cape, 62
Colvin, Ann, 213
Commonwealth, South Africa's withdrawal from, 61
Congress Alliance, 56–7, 211
Congress of Democrats, 190
Congress of South African Students, 194, 198
Congress of South African Trade Unions, 207; and Mass Democratic Movement, 275
Congress of the People, Freedom Charter adopted at (1955), 319–22
Connolly, Bob, cartoonist, 34
conscientious objectors, 218–19, 250
Conscientious Objectors Support Groups, 220
conscription, compulsory, 275; campaign to abolish, 218–23, 250, 286, 289
Conservative Party, 101, 216, 272, 318
Constitution (1910), 24–6, 59; clause 35 (franchise rights of Cape Coloureds), 24, 25; clause 137 (language rights), 25

Constitution, new (1983), 114, 116, 138, 168, 191, 199, 212, 216, 305–6; 'own affairs' schedule to, 267, 306, 317; UDF opposition to, 138–9
consumer boycotts, 137, 200–1
Convention Alliance, Slabbert's proposal for, 214–15
court cases (law courts), 129–35, 139–54, 273, 299–303; bail fund/system, 66, 67, 150–1; Black Sash monitoring of, 129–35, 140–5, 146–7, 148, 151–3, 160, 204, 225, 299–303; Craddock trial of Blackburn and Bishop (1984), 170–1; Delmas trial (1986), 117, 139–40; Guguletu Funeral Gang case, 149–51; and International Security Act, 137–8, 154; juvenile offenders, 143–4, 146–7, 148–51; New Brighton trial of Molly Blackburn, 182; pass laws, 66, 130, 140, 141; political/treason trials, 138, 139–40, 141, 151, 153, 170, 303; Port Elizabeth assault and defamation cases (1985), 174; prisoners' living conditions and families, 145–6; prosecutions against police, 302; public violence, 141–4, 149–51, 153, 303; remands, 143; 143; terrorism trials, 302–3; trial of ANC/SACP ringleaders, 138; trial of Mlauli and Tsotsi, 300–1; V. Handula case (1988), 299–300; *see also* capital punishment; detention; prisons
Court of Appeal, 27–8, 271
Covenanters, 36, 54
Cradock, x, 22, 168–71, 178, 185, 198; mass march from Lingelihle to (1989), 10–12, 167, 288; resignation of council (1985), 179; trial of Molly Blackburn and Di Bishop (1984), 170–1
CRADORA (Cradock Residents Association), 168, 169, 171, 178
CRADOYA (Cradock Youth Association), 168, 169, 171, 178
Crewe, Muriel, x, 141, 142, 144, 152–3
Criminal Law Amendment Act (1953), 49, 138
Criminal Procedure Amendment Act (1965), 154
Crossroads, 86–98, 99, 152; friction and violence between rival squatter groups, 90–1, 92, 95–8; and Khayelitsha, 92–3, 96, 97, 98–9, 101, 102; KTC satellite camp, 95, 96, 99; New, 91, 92, 95, 98
Cubans in Angola, 218, 221–2
Currin, Brian, 230

Daily Despatch, East London, 162
De Klerk, President Frederik, 9, 23, 209, 285, 286, 287, 297, 299, 303, 304, 306
De Tolly, Jenny President of Black Sash), x, 249, 273, 294, 295, 296

De Vlieg, Gill, 105, 110, 281
Death Row, 228, 229
'Death Row' (TV programme), 230
'Decade of Women, (1975–85), 246, 247
Defence Amendment Act (1983), 218, 219, 266
Defiance Campaign (MDM: 1989), 275–8
Delmas Trial (1986), 117, 139–40, 221–2
Democratic Party, 4, 310
denationalisation and homelands, 112–15, 121–3, 127–8, 269
Dependents' Conference, 146
Deportation Bill, 48
Detainees' Parents Support Committee, 155, 158, 226, 237
Detainees' Support Committee, 237
detention, 153–60; of Black Slash members, 270–1, 281–2, 284–5; 289; children in, 155, 180, 182, 223, 225–6; death in, 155–6; emergency detainees, 157; hunger strike of detainees (1988–9), 275; Section 29 detainees, 157; torture of detainees, 155; without trial, 154–60, 269; see also court cases; prisons
Diepkloof prison, 226
Dijkhorst, Mr Justice K. van, 140
Dlamieni, Jacob, murder of (1984), 271–2
Driefontein (Eastern Transvaal), 104, 105, 111
drought relief, 103
Du Plessis, V. Barend, 169
Duncan, Sheena (President of Black Sash, ix, 23, 55, 74, 79, 83–4, 117, 139, 156, 158, 183, 199, 213, 214, 215, 217, 221, 226, 230, 240, 255, 266, 267, 279, 285–6, 306; Christian faith of, 232–3; civil disobedience advocated by, 260, 263, 265, 268–9, 270, 274; 'Comment addressed to the Churches' (1982), 115–16; and Sharpeville Six appeal, 272; trips abroad, 236, 237; witness at Delmas Trial, 221–2; 'You and the New Pass Laws' compiled by, 114, 116
Duncan Village, black township, 124–6, 127–8
Durban, 9, 18, 36, 153, 287, 304; Black Sash in, 55, 74, 106, 233, 303–4; Black Sash national conference (1986), 203, 223, 225, 233
Dutch Reformed Church, 49, 162, 163, 253

East Cape Murder and Robbery Squad, 178
East London, 18, 34, 36, 124, 126, 243, 244, 286, 308; Black Sash in, 57, 74, 118–19, 162; Duncan Village, 124–6, 127–8; peace march in, 122

East Peelton, incorporated into Ciskei, 121–2, 123, 124; see also Peelton
Eastern Cape, 161–85, 187, 234, 264, 285; black political and union organisation in, 161–2; Black Sash in, 162–85; detention without trial, 153–4; ECC meetings banned in, 222; housing rentals, 167–8; municipal police, 283; police conduct, 162, 168, 169–70, 171, 172–82
Eastern Cape Adult Learning Project, 289
eco-feminism, 317
economic sanctions, 192, 216–17
education/schools, 189, 267, 305, 306, 317; African (Bantu), 126–7, 189, 233–6; Bantu Education Act (1953), 49; Black Sash's involvement in, 233–6; boycotts/drop-outs, 137, 147, 148, 168, 234; compulsory teaching in Afrikaans language, 135; Eastern Cape, 161, 167; Fort Hare black university, 161, 167; free white compulsory, 126; manipulating ideology through control of, 233; white Christian National Education, 49
Education Acts, 274
Education for an Aware South Africa (EDASA), 235
Eiselen, W. H., 62
Eiselen Line, 62
Ekuvukeni, relocation area, 104
elections: 1948: 26; 1953: 28, 54; 1958: 59; 1984: 218; 1989: 275, 297; boycotting of, 191, 192, 216, 275
End Conscription Campaign (ECC), 220–3, 289
English language, 25, 44
English-speaking whites, 5, 6, 25–6, 44
environmental issues, 317
Ezakheni, relocation area, 104

farming, black methods of, 9–10
Federation of South African Women (FEDSAW), 54, 56–7, 63, 248; aims and objectives, 244–5, 251, 257; Black Sash relations with, 241–2, 244–5, 250, 251–2, 253, 254, 255–9; first AGM of Western Cape Region (1988), 255–9; formation (1954), 241; relaunching (1987), 241, 244, 247, 254; women's march organised by, 278–9
feminism see women's rights
Field, Larry, 298
fingerprinting, 78, 279
Fisher, Cherry, ix, 131, 281
Five Freedoms Forum (Lusaka: 1989), 237, 240, 280–1 286–7, 290
flood-relief problems, 303
Foley, Ruth, 28, 29, 31, 37–8, 41, 73
forced removals see relocation

Ford foundation, 238
Fort Beaufort, 180–1, 286
Fort Hare, black university, 161, 167
'Forward to the 1990s' conference (1989), 22
Fouché, Lieutenant J. W., 173–5
Fourie, Commissioner, 133–4
franchise (voting rights): removal of non-white, 24–44 *passim* , 114; restricted to European women, 26; universal, 58–9, 191, 212
Franz, Anton, 22
Free Settlement Areas Act (1988), 101
Free the Children Campaign, 223–6
'Free the Children' message, 226
Freedom Charter (1955), 20, 192, 211, 212, 301, 319–22; *see also* Charterists
Friends of Crossroads, 90
Froneman, G., 248
Frontline magazine, 197, 202
fund-raising, 237–9; foreign, 238
Fund-Raising Act (1974), 237

Gage, Ngeni, 155
gang warefare, 147–8; Guguletu Funeral Gang case, 149–51
General Law Amendment Act (1964), 'ninety-day clause', 154
German Democratic Republic, 136
Gerwel, Professor Jakes, 277
Gijsbers, Brigadier, ix, 13–14, 15
Goniwe, Alex, x, 176, 178, 183
Goniwe family, 176–9
Goniwe, Matthew, 167–9, 170, 171, 234; murder and funeral of, 10, 176–9, 265
Goniwe, Mbulelo, 169
Goniwe, Nyami, 177
Graaff-Reinet, 167, 168, 234
Grahamstown, 18, 74, 106, 123, 128, 153, 162, 177, 281–2, 285, 286, 306
'Green Point' camp, 99
Group Area removals, 82, 113
Group Areas Act (1957), 50, 78, 164, 189, 293, 295
Group Areas Amendment Act (1988), 101, 274, 314
Guguletu, black township, 1–2, 76, 93; gang warfare in, 147–51
Guguletu Funeral Gang case, 149–51
Gylswyk, Annica van, detention of, 270–1

Handula, V., 299–300
Harris, Joyce, ix, 156, 195–6, 207–8, 215, 223–4, 242
Hawarden, Judith, ix, 234–5
Haynes, Tish, x, 146, 290–1
'headhunting', 196–7
Hertzog, James Barry Munck, 26, 38
High Court of Parliament, 28

High Court of Parliament Bill (1952), 28
homelands (bantustans), 51, 69–70, 81, 103, 112–23, 198, 293, 297–9; black labour commuting from, 82, 83; and denationalisation, 112–15, 116, 121–3, 127–8, 269; executions in, 230; foreign non-recognition of, 119; incorporation policy, 107, 112–13, 117–18, 120–1; pensions, 118–19; poverty, 115–16; relocation/resettlement, 81–2, 112–13, 117
homelessness, 81, 83, 84–5, 87, 100, 296, 305; *see also* relocation; squatters
hotel accommodation, 81, 82
House of Assembly, 24, 26, 27, 33
Houses of Parliament *see* House of Assembly; Senate; tricameral parliament
housing, 15, 81–3, 267, 303, 306, 314, 321; Crossroads, 86–98; Duncan Village, 124–5; home ownership, 101–2; increased rents, 103, 167–8; Khayelitsha, 92–3, 96, 97, 98–9, 101, 102; Lingelihle, 167–8, 171; Nationalist policy, 81–2, 83; *see also* squatting
Human Rights, UN Declaration of (1948), 57, 227, 314, 315
Human Rights Commission, 160
Human Rights Day (1986), 226
hunger strike of detainees, 275
Hurley, Denis, Archbishop of Durban, ix, 47, 233, 252, 287, 288, 313

Ibhayi, black township, 288–9
'iceberg principle', 21, 323
Identification Act (1986), 78
identity documents, issue of new, 269, 222, 296; *see also* pass laws
Immorality Amendment Act, 50–1
incorporation policy (into homelands), 107, 112–13, 121–3, 297–9
Indians, 114; House of Parliament of, 199, 216, 267; relocation of, 50, 81, 82; *see also* Coloureds
influx control, 50–4, 67, 68, 78, 81, 87, 101, 114, 115, 116, 267, 293, 294; *see also* pass laws; relocation
Inkatha, 74, 199, 206, 207, 271, 304; Black Sash's attacks on, 198–9
'Inside South Africa's Death Factory', 230–1
Institute for a Democratic Alternative for South Africa, 163
Institute of Race Relations, 146, 265
insurance, 117, 296, 303
Internal Security Act (1982), 137–8, 154, 273, 289, 299
International Convention of the Rights of the Child, 315

International Police Association, ix, 13
International Women's Year (1975), 242

Jacobs, Madoda, 169
Jan Smuts airport, Johannesburg, 34
Jansen, Dr, 32
Jaxa, Xolile, 300
Jews for Social Justice, 237
Johannesburg, 13, 18, 22, 24, 34, 35, 40, 42, 134, 191, 202, 226; Black Sash in, 28–32, 36–8, 48, 73, 74, 79, 104, 105, 162, 188, 198, 201, 203, 232–3, 280; Black Sash national conferences, 98, 213; Commissioners' Courts, 130; Coronation Hospital, 267; Khotso House destroyed by bomb (1988), 280; Legal Resources Centre, 77; Mandela returns home to (1990), 305; welcome-home rally for released prisoners, 290, 291; *see also* Soweto
Johannesburg Democratic Action Committee, 237
Johannesburg Diocesan Challenge Group, 232
Jones, Judge Nathaniel, 181
Joseph, Helen, 57, 226, 241; house arrest of, 241
Jordan, Pallo, 22
just war, theory of a, 188, 200
Justice and Peace Commission of the Catholic Church, 237
Justice and Reconciliation in South African Council of Churches, 22

Kannemeyer Commission of Inquiry (1985), 174–5, 176
Khayelitsha, township, 92–3, 96, 97, 98–9, 101, 102; community advice office, 296–7
Khuzwayo, Ellen, *Call me Woman*, 247
Kimberley, 103
King Williams Town, 119, 120, 121, 122, 123, 298
kitskonstabels (special constables), 283
Klerk, President *see* De Klerk
Kona, Norman, 172–3, 174
Kontak, Afrikaner women's organisation, 243
Koornhof, Dr Piet, 77, 89, 90, 91, 108, 109, 116
Koornhof Bills, 210, 213
Kruger, Jimmy, 156
Kruger National Park, Skukuza camp protest, 34
Krugersdorp prison, Natal, 226
KTC satellite camp, 95, 96, 99
Kwa Zulu, 74, 198, 199, 206
Kwanobuhle, black township, 162, 171–2, 175

labour, black: commuting from homelands, 82, 83; Eastern Cape, 161–2, 171; hostel accommodation for male migrants, 82; illegal squatters, 86, 90, 93, 115; skilled, 189; vs. white, 51; *see also* trade unions
Labour Relations Amendment Act, 10 &n
Lady Frere, 71–3, 76
Ladysmith, 104
Land Acts, 104, 105, 106–7, 274, 293, 314
land ownership/reform, 83, 85, 105–7, 287, 293–4, 306, 314, 320; *see also* incorporation; relocation
Langa, black township, 93, 162, 166, 196; jail, 145; law court, 130–1, 132–4; male migrant workers, 82; 'massacre' and Kannemeyer report (1985), 174–6; shootings and protest march (1960), 68
law, sovereignty/rule of, Black Sash's policy of upholding, 260–2, 269; P. W. Botha's commitment to, 268; *see also* civil disobedience
Law Society, *pro amico* rules of, 66–7
Lawyers for Human Rights, 128, 230
Le Grange, Louis, 139, 155, 168–9, 174, 176, 223
Leeuwfontein, incorporation into Bophutatswana, 299
legal aid, 66–7, 77, 130, 149–50
Legal Education and Action Project, University of Cape town, 157
Legal Resources Centre, 77, 96, 178
Lekota, Patrick 'Terror', 139
Lenkoe, James, 155
lesbians, 249–50
Lewin, Eleanor, 16, 55
Liberal Party, 188
Lingelihle, black township, 167, 169, 170, 178; mass march to Cradock from (1989), 10–12, 167, 288; murder and funeral of Goniwe and friends, 177–9; rent increases, 167–8, 171; Sam Xhalli Junior Secondary School, 167; unemployment, 171
looting, 304, 313
Louw, Eric, 34, 42–3
Louw, Raymond, 326
Lusaka: ANC leadership in, 22; Five Freedoms Forum in (1989), 237, 240, 280, 286–7, 290

Machakaneng, 113
Maclaren, Elizabeth, 28
Mafeking, Elizabeth, banishment of, 69
Makidwa, Nancy, 133
Malcomess, John, 168
Malindi, Mrs Lettie, x, 64–5, 147–8
Malindi, Zoli, 64
Mampe, Bellington, 155
Mandela, Nelson, 3, 9, 161, 257, 261;

found guilty of high treason (1963), 140; P. W. Botha's meeting with, 300; release of (1990), 23, 209, 290, 297,305, 306
Mandela, Winnie, 263; Soweto home of, 14–15
Marxism, 214, 310
Mass Democratic Movement (MDM), 217, 275, 308; Defiance Campaign, 275–8
mass stayaways *see* boycotts
Mbeki, Govan, 161
Mbunge, Fuzddi, 133
Mdantsana, Ciskei, 120, 121
Memani, Oliver, 90, 92
Meny-Gibert, Rosemary, ix, 7
Mgwali, Eastern Cape, 103, 111
Mhlaba, Raymond, 161
Middeldrift, homeland, 230
Mitchell's Plain demonstration, 302
Mitterand, Mme François, 226
mixed marriages, 57
Mkhonto, Sparrow, 10; murder and funeral of, 177–9
Mkize, Saul, 104, 111
Mlangeni, Andrew, 291
Mlangeni, June, 291
Mlauli, Veliswa, trial of, 300–1
Mlauli, Scelo, 10; murder and fungeral of, 177–9
Modder Bee prison, East Rand, 226
Modipane, Solomon, 155
Mogopa villagers, eviction of, 107–10, 111–12, 299
Molefe, Popo Simon, 139
Mompati, Ruth, 241
More, Jacob, headman, 107, 108, 120
Moutse people, 112
Movement for the Liberation and Preservation of White South Africa, 266
Mowbray (white suburb of Cape Town), 210, 296; Black Sash advice office, 2–4, 7, 19, 75, 86, 91, 149
Mozambique, Independence of (1975), 136
Mqanduli school, 167
municipal police ('greenflies'), 283
Myburgh, Johann, 163 253
Myburgh, Marietje, ix, 162, 163, 243, 244, 253

Nairobi Conference, UN (1985), 247
Namibia (South-West Africa), 218, 219, 220, 309–10; Independence of, 309–10; 1989 elections, 309, 310; UN plan for independence of, 300
Nash, Margaret, x, 97–8, 197
Nasionale Jeugbond (Nationalist youth group), 35
Natal, 25, 74, 104, 303–4; Coastal region,

213, 226, 305; conflict and violence in, 198, 207, 304–5; Midlands region, 271
National Committee Against Removals, 104
national convention alliance, 210, 214–15
National Council of Women, 56, 63, 146
National Institute for Crime Prevention and Rehabilitation of Offenders (NICRO), 165
National Medical and Dental Association, 172
National Party, 6, 8, 23, 26, 69; electoral victories, 26, 28, 54, 59
National Union of South African Students, 237, 282
Native Commissioners' Courts, 130, 132–4, 145
Native Land Act (1913), 104, 105, 106, 107
Native Laws Amendment Act (1937), 51
Native Representation Act (1936), 26, 43, 44
Native Trust and Land Act (1936, 106
Native (Urban Areas) Act (1923), 51
Naude, Rev. Dr Beyers, 5, 163, 232, 233
necklacings, necklace murders, 9, 22, 137, 155, 202, 203, 223, 304
Nel, Louis, 109
New Brighton, black township, high schools, 161; Magistrate's Court, 182
New Crossroads, 91, 92, 95, 98; *see also* Crossroads
Ngoyi, Lilian, 248
Ngudie, Solwandli, 155
Ngxobongwana, Johnson, 90, 92, 95, 97
Nicholson, Jill, ix, 239
Niekerk, Barend Van, 228
Nkosi Sikelei iAfrika (African nationalist anthem), 17
Nkqonkweni, East Peelton, 122
Noordhoek, squatters in, 293–4
Northern Transvaal Region Black Sash, 316
Now Everyone is Afraid, 283
Nyanga, black township, 93

Operation Hunger, 121, 127
Orange Free State, 25, 35, 82
Orange River Colony, 25
Orderly Movement and Settlement of Black Persons Act (1982), 114, 115–16, 210
'orderly urbanisation', 77–8, 80
Owen, Ken, 308
'own affairs' government, 267, 306, 317

Pachsdraai, 107, 108, 109–10
Palme, Mrs Lisbeth, 226
Pan-African Congress (PAC), 12, 68, 161, 162; banning of (1960), 68

Parliament *see* House of Assembly;
  Senate; tri-cameral
pass law courts, 130, 140, 141
pass laws, 52–5, 56, 61–80, 81, 116, 129,
  134, 188, 189, 247; abolition of (1986),
  135, 296; arrests of women under,
  66–7; number of convictions under, 77;
  passive resistance to, 68; Rekhoto case
  (1983), 77
Paton, Alan, *Cry the Beloved Country*,
  236
pay disputes, 303
peace marches, 285
Peelton, 120, 297–8; *see also* East Peelton
Penal Reform, 146
pensions, 117, 118–19, 199, 267, 296, 303,
  306; payouts, 187
people's courts, 9, 137, 304
people's power, revolutionary and radical
  rise of, 137
Petersen, Molly, 73
petty apartheid, 284–5
Philcox, Sue, x, 235–6
Pietermaritzburg, Black Sash in, 74, 106,
  153, 271, 304; Centre for Adult
  Education, 304; violence in, 207
Pikashe, Elizabeth, 75–6
police *see* South African Police
political prisoners, 10, 161; death
  sentence for 228–9, 232; release of, 9,
  23, 161, 209, 210, 285, 290–1, 297, 305;
  trials of, 138, 139–40, 141, 151, 153,
  170, 303
Pollsmoor prison, 143, 145, 146, 149, 150,
  151, 291
'poor whites', issue of, 51
Population Registration Act (Race
  Classification: 1950), 266, 274, 306
Port Elizabeth, 18, 34, 36, 74, 106, 118,
  155, 156, 176, 177, 178, 187, 280,
  289–90; Black Sash advice offices, 19,
  163–4, 180, 223; Black Sash national
  conferences, 38, 171, 172; Black sash
  membership, 162, 164; detention
  without trial in, 157–8; funeral of
  Molly Blackburn , 183–4; North End
  Prison, 289; organised black labour,
  161–2; police conduct, 172–4; Rooihell
  prison, 172; satellite townships, 162
Port Elizabeth Regional Court, 174
poverty, 14, 115–16, 118, 120, 121,
  124–6, 171, 220, 296, 305, 306
Power, Sue, ix, 119, 121, 123, 124, 125–6,
  127
President's Council, 114; *see also* Senate
Pretoria, 19; Black Sash in, 32–3, 36, 59,
  74, 270–1, 316
Prevention of Illegal Squatting Act (1951),
  78

Prevention of Illegal Squatting
  Amendment Act (1988), 100
prisoners, 153–4, 168; death sentence,
  227–32, 271–4; detention without trial,
  154–60 ; families of, 146; hunger
  strike, 275; juvenile, 172–4, 180, 182,
  223, 225–6; living conditions, 145–6 ;
  political, 9, 10, 23, 161, 210, 228, 285,
  290, 291, 297, 303; release of Mandela
  1990), 23, 209, 290, 297, 305, 306;
  solitary confinement, 154, 284, 289; *see
  also* detention; court cases
Progressive Federal Party (PFP), 10, 79,
  101, 156, 164, 165, 168, 171, 188, 200,
  214, 231, 237, 273; Black Sash and, 9,
  191, 216; replaced by Conservative
  Party as official opposition, 216
Progressive Party, 58, 73
Prohibition or Interdicts Bill, 48
public-violence offences, 141–4, 149–51,
  153, 303
Pybus, tercia, 28

Quail commission, 113
Qwa-Qwa, 112
Qwelane, Jon, 196–7

Rand Daily Mail, 34, 231, 236
Rape Crisis, 255
reference books, Africans', 52–4, 61–2,
  68, 71, 74, 129, 133; campaign of
  passive resistance to (1960), 68; *see also*
  pass laws
referendum, 139; on creation of Republic
  (1961), 61; on parliamentary reforms
  (1983), 216
relocation (forced removals), 81–2, 84–5,
  93–5, 96, 103, 104, 105–13, 117, 188;
  Black Sash week of protest against
  (1983), 105–6; compensation for, 82;
  see also incorporation; influx control;
  'voluntary removals'
rent(s), 167–8, 171, 193; boycott, 137,
  284; relief, 169
Republic of South Africa, formation of
  (1961), 61, 66
restriction orders, 285; breaking of, 300
revolution, 20–1, 162, 188, 199, 222;
  'iceberg' principle, 21, 323; US research
  into, 20; vs. evolution, 21, 199–200,
  216
Rhodes University, Grahamstown, 29,
  282
Rikhoto, Mehlolo Tom, 77
Riotous Assembly Act (1973), 262
Robb, Noel, x, 3–4, 28–9, 44–5, 56, 57,
  58, 69, 76, 86, 88, 91, 92, 97, 98, 102,
  119, 148, 220, 309
Robben Island, 146, 291
Rockman, Police Lieutenant Gregory, 302

Rooigrond, 230
Rooihell prison, Port Elizabeth, 172
Roosevelt, Mrs Franklin D., 'What women can achieve', 242
Runciman, Beverley, x, 230, 232, 263–5, 273, 277–8, 287
Runciman, Dunstan, 264

Saloojee, Suliman, 155
Sash (formerly *Black Sash*) magazine, 42, 45–7, 50, 60–1, 155, 168, 169, 178, 190, 192–4, 195–6, 200, 201, 202, 215, 229, 247–8, 310; seizure of May 1986 issue, 260
Sauer, P., 34
Savage, Andrew, 165, 169, 175
'Save Crossroads Campaign', 88
Schoeman, Ben, 33
Sebe, Chief Lennox, 120, 298
Second Carnegie Inquiry into poverty (1984), 115
Security Forces *see* South African Defence Forces; South African Police
Senate (Upper House), 24, 27, 28, 36, 38, 114; enlargement of, 28–32, 38, 44; *see also* President's Council; tricameral parliament
Senate Act, 28–32, 38–42, 44, 48, 54, 55, 262
Separate Amenities Acts, 51, 274
Separate Representation of Voters Bill 1951), 27–8
Seremane, Joe, ix, 22
shack fires in black townships, 127
Sharpeville education in, 234–5
Sharpeville massacre (1960), 68, 71, 283
Sharpeville Six, 271–4
Sikade, Kleinbooi and Pauline, 71–3
Sinclair, Jean, (President of Black Sash), 28, 29, 39, 41, 44, 48, 55, 59, 73–4
Sisulu, Walter, 290
Skukuza camp protests, 34
Skweyiya, Gille, x, 157–8, 170–1, 178, 183
Slabbert, Dr Frederik van Zyl, 5, 214–15
slums, 78, 124, 125–6, 210n, 321
Slums Act 1988, 100
Small, Janet, x, 283–5; detention of, 281–2, 284–5
Smuts, General Jan Christiaan, 26
Sobukwe, Robert, 161
socialist feminism, 252
Society for the Abolition of the Death Penalty in South Africa (SADPSA), 228, 231, 232
Society of Friends, 63
Somerset East, 170
South Africa Act (1910), 24–5, 27, 41, 43
South Africa (Amendment) Act (1956), 41–2, 48

South African Broadcasting Company (SABC), propaganda of, 73, 266
South African citizenship; and denationalisation, 112–15, 116, 121–3, 127–8, 269; reinstatement of, 269
South African Citizenship Act (1986), 269
South African Communist Party (SACP), 20, 98, 135, 162, 190, 205, 217, 221–2, 241; acts of terrorism by, 136–8, 221; banning of (1950), 138, 139; and Defiance Campaign (1989), 275–6; trial of ringleaders, 138
South African Congress of Trade Unions, 139
South African Council of Churches (SACC), ix, 232–3, 274–5, 280
South African Defence Forces (SADF: Army), 223, 224, 282; and End Conscription campaign, 218–23; movement into townships of, 222, 282–3
South African Institute of Race Relations, ix, 2, 165, 234; link between Black Sash and, 209–10
South African Native National Congress *see* ANC
South African Police (SAP), IX, 12–13, 60, 61, 104, 135, 201, 202, 265, 278–82; alleged abuse of children by, 223, 224–5, 234; and Black Sash, 19–22, 68–9, 162, 278–82, 289–90; black youths allegedly assaulted and killed by, 172–4, 223; control in black townships by, 282–4; court prosecutions against, 302; and Crossroads squatters, 95–6, 97; and Defiance Campaign, 275, 278; detention without trial, 154–60; in Eastern Cape, 162, 168, 169–82; excessive and unjustified use of force by, 301–2; Intelligence Unit, 137; *kitskonstabels* (special constables), 283; Langa 'massacre' (1985), 174–6; municipal police ('greenflies'), 283; and murder of Goniwe and friends, 177–9; in Natal, 304, 305; non-interference with Inkatha, 304; Public Relations Department, 12, 19; recruitment of black policemen, 283; riot squads, 279, 302; security police, 223, 280–1, 284, 289; sentencing against policemen, 152; Sharpeville shootings by (1960), 68, 283; size of, 282; in Soweto, 14; torture used by, 155; 'Trojan Horse' killings (1985), 302
South African Red Cross, 95
South African Tourist Board, 12
South African Transport Services, 314
Soviet Union, 135, 218
Soweto, black township, 13–15, 16–17,

200, 291; education, 234; IPA barbecue held in, 13; police in, 14; riots (1976), 135, 136, 242, 247
Special Branch, 68, 69
Spogter, Johannes 264
squatters, 78, 83, 84–102, 106, 124, 214; access to farmers' land in Nordhoek (1987), 293–4; Crossroads, 86–98; enforced removal of, 82, 83
Squatting Act, 293
Stadler, Major-General Herman, ix, 19–22, 135, 136, 137, 199, 205, 217, 282, 283, 301, 318
Star, 196–7, 269
State of Emergency, 10, 23, 214; 1960: 68, 158; 1985–6: 96–7, 137, 141, 152, 153, 154, 156, 180–1, 182, 185, 222, 248, 257, 264, 265, 266, 278, 282, 283, 286, 299; in Ciskei (1988), 121–2
Status of Transkei Act (1976), 113, 117
Stott, Eulalie, 73
Strauss, J. G. N., 48
Strijdom, Johannes, 27, 28, 35, 41; petition calling for resignation of, 31, 32–3
strikes, illegal, 189; secondary or sympathy, 10n
Supreme Court, 24, 28, 76, 77, 96, 128, 140, 152
Suppression of Communism Act (1950), 49, 138, 139, 167
Surplus Peoples Project (1983), 81, 82
Suzman, Dame Helen, 73, 79, 120, 169, 175, 185, 188, 216, 226, 228, 299, 308–9
SWAPO (South-West African People's Organisation), 218, 221–2, 300, 309–10
Swart, C. R., 34, 35
Sweden, 226, 238, 271

Tabalaza, Lungile, 155
Tambo, Oliver, 136, 161, 290, 300
taxis: 'black' ('Zola Budds'), 2, 18; 'combis', 1–2, 13
telephone tapping, 261
Tembisa, 234
terrorism, 20, 136–8, 153, 218, 221–2, 300, 302–3
Terrorism Act (1967), 154
Thompson, Helen Newton, 28
Thompson, Dr Liz, 172, 174
Thornton, Amy, x, 62
Time magazine, 35
totalitarianism, 190–1
trade unions, 10n, 116, 120, 139, 161, 189, 213, 275, 289
Transkei, homeland, 1, 5, 71, 76, 77, 86, 118, 128, 130, 131, 162, 167, 230, 298; Independence (1976), 113, 117
Transvaal, 25, 105, 113, 130, 153, 188, 234, 238; deproclamation of townships,

82; Eastern, 8, 104; FEDSAW in, 257, 258; language and franchise rights, 25
Transvaal Rural Action Committee (TRAC), 104–5, 107–13, 298–9
treason trials, 138, 139–40
trespass, 78
tri-cameral parliament, 139, 191, 199, 216, 218, 247, 275, 305; and 'own affairs' government, 267, 306, 317
'Trojan Horse' killings (1985), 302
Tshegane, Wilfred, 1–2, 4
Tsotsi, Linda, trial of, 300–1
Tutu, Archbishop Desmond, x, 14, 108, 195, 233
Tyita, James, 155

Uitenhage, 171, 172, 175; police station assaults, 172–4
Umkhonto we Sizwe (ANC military wing), 20, 22, 161, 204, 228, 300, 313
Umtata, capital of Transkei, 167
unemployment, 81, 117, 171, 296, 304, 305
Unemployment Insurance Fund, 303
unfair dismissals, 303
UNITA, Angola, 222, 238
United Democratic Front (UDF), 10, 64, 98, 168, 171, 177, 183, 193–4, 195, 206, 304; arrest of leaders, 139; AZAPO's feud with, 178; Black Sash's relations with, 192, 209, 210–18, 221, 245, 292; coercive strategy of, 195; Delmas Trial (1986), 117, 139–40; and Freedom Charter, 211–12; government restrictions on (1988), 217; internal democracy principle of, 193; inaugural declaration, 212; launching of (1983), 138–9, 210; national convention, 210, 215
United Nations: 'Decade of Women' (1975–85), 246, 247; Declaration on the Rights of the Child, 225; Namibia independence plan, 300; Universal Declaration of Human Rights (1948), 55, 227
United Party, 26, 27, 29, 48, 73, 195
United States of America, 20, 306–7
United Women's Congress, 255
Universal Declaration of Human rights, 57, 227, 314, 315
University of Cape Town, 281, 289; Legal Education and Action Project, 157
University of the Western Cape, 277; 'Forward to the 1990's Conference' (1989), 22
University of Witwatersrand, 234; Academic Staff Association, 237; Centre for Applied Legal Studies, 120; William Cullen Library, ix
Unlawful Organisations Act (1960), 138

Urban Areas Act 89, 94
Urban Foundation, 90, 116
urbanisation, 296, 305; 'orderly', 77–8, 80; *see also* black townships
'An Urbanisation Strategy for the Republic of South Africa' report (1986), 77–8

Vaal Triangle, 139
Van De Merwe, Sue, x, 273
Venda, homeland, 5, 112, 230; Independence (1979), 113
Verwoerd, Dr Hendrik, 34, 81
Vietnam War, 136
vigilante assaults, white, 265–6; *see also witdoeke*
Viljoen, Gerrit, 121
violence, 7, 22, 224, 265, 270, 303–4, 311; Black Sash debate on, 187–208, 209; headhunting, 196–7; reactive/defensive, 188, 194–5, 200, 203; structural, 194, 200, 203; *see also* civil disobedience
Viti, David, x, 97, 134, 145
Vlok, Adriaan, 285
'voluntary removals', 103–28, 132; *see also* influx control; relocation
Voortrekker Monument, Pretoria, 59
Vosloo, Dr, 88
voting rights *see* franchise

Walt, Hennie van der, 94
War Veterans' Torch Commando, 36, 54; protest march of (1951), 29
Weekly Mail, 207, 313
Wellington, 230
Wentzel, Jill, ix, 188, 189–90, 191, 192–3, 194–5, 197, 198, 199–200, 202–3, 214
Wessels, Leon, 298
Western Cape, 103, 141, 146, 149, 252, 273; Black Sash court-monitoring in, 141–2, 152, 153; Coloured Labour Preference Policy in, 62–3, 87; ECC meetings banned in, 222; education, 235; FEDSAW in 252, 255–9
Western Province Council of Churches, 143
Westville prison, Natal, 226
witdoeke vigilantes in Crossroads, 95–6; *see also* vigilantes, white
women, women's rights (feminism), 317; ANC'S view of role of, 253–4; 245–52, 253–4; black women offenders, 130–2, 134; black women's rights, 245–8; Charter for Women, 251; eco-feminism, 317; FEDSAW, 241–2, 244–5; franchise restricted to European women, 26; Kontak, 243; lesbians, 249–50; pass laws for Africans, 52–5, 56, 61–7, 69, 70–1, 130; removal of voting rights from non-white (1930), 26; *see also* Black Sash
'Women for Peace, 237, 242, 243, 255
'Women in Prison' campaign, 258
Women's Day (1987), 252
Women's Defence of the Constitution League, 24, 29–49, 57
Woods, Donald and Wendy, 162
work permits, 52, 70, 90, 115
Workbench Centre, 119
Workman's Compensation Act cases, 303
World Alliance of Reformed Churches, 11

Xhosa speakers, 3, 64, 133, 150, 162, 181

'You and the New Pass Laws', booklet, 114, 116
Young Christian Students, 237

Zihlangu, Mamma, 256
Zille, Helen, x, 6, 279
Zimbabwe, women's rights in, 247
Zwelitsha, 122
Zwide, 181